H O W   T O   C L I M B ™   S E R I E S

Learning to Climb Indoors

Third Edition

Eric J. Hörst

FALCONGUIDES

GUILFORD, CONNECTICUT

To my sons, Cameron and Jonathan—
I cherish our days climbing together.

FALCONGUIDES®

An imprint of The Rowman & Littlefield Publishing Group, Inc.
4501 Forbes Blvd., Ste. 200
Lanham, MD 20706
www.rowman.com
Falcon and FalconGuides are registered trademarks and Make Adventure Your Story is a
trademark of The Rowman & Littlefield Publishing Group, Inc.

Distributed by NATIONAL BOOK NETWORK

British Library Cataloguing in Publication Information available

Library of Congress Cataloging-in-Publication Data available

ISBN 978-1-4930-4310-1 (paperback)
ISBN 978-1-4930-4311-8 (e-book)

♾️™ The paper used in this publication meets the minimum requirements of American
National Standard for Information Sciences—Permanence of Paper for Printed Library
Materials, ANSI/NISO Z39.48-1992.

Printed in the United States of America

Contents

Foreword

Indoor climbing is one of the fastest growing sports in the world, and if you give it a try you'll quickly discover why!

Besides being an excellent physical workout, climbing is also an incredible mental exercise that teaches you how to challenge fear, act with strategy, and focus intensely. Furthermore, one of the greatest beauties—and benefits—of climbing is how it can reset your emotions and clear a mind clouded by the chaotic world we live in. With indoor climbing, you get to challenge yourself against an unbiased climbing wall, and with every ascent you'll gain mental clarity, confidence, and a rich, pure sense of joy and autonomy.

So, what are you waiting for? With one or more commercial gyms now open in every major city, chances are there's a rock wall nearby awaiting you. Whereas the climbing gyms of yesteryear were often dingy and uninspiring, the latest generation is well-lit with clean interiors and colorful, multifaceted walls that will get your heart a-pumping. Not to be glossed over, however, is the fact that indoor climbing does have inherent dangers—but with proper instruction and vigilant use of a few basic safety protocols, climbing is in fact an exceedingly safe activity that's far less risky than driving the freeway.

The book you are holding offers an excellent introduction to the vertical world of indoor climbing. Penned by a true expert, Eric J. Hörst, *Learning to Climb Indoors* delivers outstanding instruction on all the critical aspects of the indoor climbing experience. In addition to coverage of vital climbing gear and safety procedures, Hörst delivers easy-to-understand instruction on how to develop effective climbing technique, build mental skills, and train strength and endurance. There's also authoritative instruction on the emerging specialty of training youth climbers—chapter 10 contains essential information for every parent and coach of an aspiring young crusher. Given the breadth, depth, and quality of this text, USA Climbing endorses *Learning to Climb Indoors* as the go-to guide for individuals beginning their journey as an indoor climber. Of course, no book replaces the invaluable instruction of a knowledgeable climbing coach, so we urge you to use this book as a complement to the personalized instruction and coaching available at your gym.

The rapid growth of climbing, both here in the United States and around the world, makes this an exciting time for all of us here at USA Climbing—as the governing body of competition climbing in America, we are thrilled that you're giving climbing a try! Our climbing competitions—which range from local-level comps for all ages and abilities to professional-level and World Cup events—are growing bigger every year, and we have a participant and spectator group that rabidly supports us. So why don't you join us? No matter if you're a participant or a spectator, our competitions offer an exciting way to socialize with like-minded individuals and, excitingly, the chance to get involved in a sport that is being considered for addition to the Olympic Games!

No matter if you aspire to simply climb for fun and fitness or to become an advanced climber that ventures out onto the many magnificent crags of the world, we wish you the best of times and many safe, wonderful climbs!

—USA CLIMBING
(USACLIMBING.ORG)

Acknowledgments

Writing this book took me on an immensely enjoyable trip down memory lane as I reflected on my formative years as a climber. It was more than thirty years ago that I was a youngster learning to climb, and my brother, Kyle, is the person responsible for starting me on this incredible journey. Thanks, Kyle! Of course, the learning process never ends, so to this day I continue to glean new distinctions and lessons from my experiences as a climber and from all those whom I meet. Consequently, I must begin by thanking my partners past and present for the many wonderful days climbing together. Furthermore, I appreciate the countless friends I've made, climbers I've coached, and everyone else with whom I've talked training throughout my years and travels.

Given the rapid growth of indoor climbing, there's a great need for a book like this, and I thank John Burbidge and everyone at FalconGuides and Globe Pequot Press for seeing this project through. There are many others who contributed along the way, and this book, like all others, was really a team effort. First up, I must credit the photographers whose pictures helped save me many thousands of words! Thanks to Robert Scoverski, Nathan Welton, Wade David, Keith North, Chris Noble, Keith McCallister, Shawn Brünner, Eric McCallister, artist Mike Tea, and Nicros Wall Division for helping bring the pages of this book to life. Equally important are the gym owners who so graciously allowed me to shoot instructional photos at their facilities. Thanks to Vertical World, Philadelphia Rock Gym, Rock'n & Jam'n, Vertical Endeavors, Sport Rock, Movement, Reading Rocks, and the crew at Boulder Rock Club. Finally, I'm grateful for the input and constructive feedback from Jason Noble, Robyn Erbesfeld-Raboutou, Lisa Ann Hörst, and Eric McCallister.

As a veteran climber who still hits the road on climbing trips and for training-for-climbing seminars, I extend sincere thanks to the companies who continue to support my climbing and numerous projects. I must first acknowledge Nate and Pam Postma, Nic, Jason, Sara, Trinh, and everyone else at Nicros, Inc. You guys are such a big part of my various training projects, and I tremendously enjoy working with you all! Likewise, I thank Jonathan and Ian at La Sportiva for keeping me climbing in the best shoes on the planet; ditto to JB and Carolyn at Sterling Ropes for supplying my lifelines; and to Christian Griffith for the great Verve threads. Also, many thanks to Lisa Gnade and Steve Petro of Excalibur/Wild Country for providing top-shelf harnesses and hardware.

Finally, I extend heartfelt thanks to my wife, Lisa Ann, for her unconditional love and support; to my sons, Cameron and Jonathan, for all the joyous times we share; and to my parents. I am truly blessed to have all of you in my life.

Introduction

Welcome to the exhilarating world of indoor climbing! Regardless of your age, background, or level of fitness, indoor climbing will present you with many unique challenges—and rewards—that are far different from other sports. As you will soon discover, the wonder of indoor climbing is the unique way in which it engages both the mind and body. Each climb reveals a novel challenge that offers the opportunity for self-development. Solving a puzzling sequence of hand- and footholds is akin to a vertical chess match requiring a dynamic mix of problem solving, positive thinking, and fear management. Physically, climbing will challenge your flexibility, stamina, body control, and almost every muscle from your legs to your abdominals to your soon-to-be-pumped arms. In aggregate, climbing provides what may be the most complete mind–body workout available. And it's an absolute blast!

Learning to Climb Indoors presents comprehensive instruction on all the vital topics you need to know for your first few days and years in the sport. Chapter 1 begins with an overview of the commercial climbing gym experience. You will gain a sense of the rules of the game and requisite safe-climbing instruction that most gyms mandate. Chapters 2 and 3 will introduce you to the basic gear and safety techniques that make indoor climbing safer than

playing soccer or mowing the grass. Yes, climbing is a remarkably safe activity given proper equipment, expert instruction, and diligent use of the safety techniques you will learn in this book.

Chapter 4 is unique among how-to-climb books as it reveals several not-so-well-known strategies for rapid learning of climbing skills. While the majority of new climbers stumble slowly through the maze of trial-and-error learning, you can take a more direct path to improvement by applying the eight powerful learning strategies outlined in this chapter.

The core technical instruction of *Learning to Climb Indoors* is found in chapters 5 through 7. A wise beginning climber will strive to learn—and make habitual—the optimal use of hand- and footholds, body positioning, and techniques of movement. These chapters will describe all the fundamental techniques and tactics required for beginner-, intermediate-, and advanced-level climbs. You will learn a variety of technique-building drills as well as several proven strategies for solving difficult routes and programming your brain for success.

Supporting this instruction, you will find dozens of photos depicting the fundamental techniques, body positions, and movements. Many of these photos contain an overlay of symbols and labels (annotations) that reveal optimal application

of force to hand- and footholds, as well as proper positioning of the body's center of gravity. It's my hope that these value-added photos will underscore the importance of body awareness and enhance the learning of proper technique.

Next up, in chapter 8, is an in-depth look at mental training and fear management. It's a fact that climbing requires uncommon discipline and mental fortitude compared with other sports. Thus, elevating your mental game is an essential part of improving your overall ability. To this end, you will learn ten proven techniques for controlling tension, challenging fear, and conquering the fright of flight.

The final three chapters of *Learning to Climb Indoors* complete the circle of becoming a solid all-around climber. Chapter 9 provides a plan for physical conditioning, so that you can develop the strength and endurance needed for climbs of increasing difficulty. And since indoor climbing is an increasingly popular youth activity, chapter 10 provides insight on

how to coach and train the next generation of up-and-coming climbers. Chapter 11 then reveals a few of the secrets for climbing your best, including the keys to staying motivated and upwardly mobile for many years to come. Lastly, I'll provide a primer on what it takes to expand your climbing to the great outdoors, including a review of the unique techniques, risks, and rewards of rock climbing.

Throughout the text, climbing terms and lingo are **bolded** on first use. Complete definitions are available in the glossary located in the back of the book. You will also discover an afterword that presents some of the climbing wisdom culled from the pages of this book. I trust you'll discover—as I have—that climbing provides many wonderful lessons for effective living on this third rock from the sun.

As you begin your adventures as a climber, I want to wish you a rich and rewarding journey that lasts a lifetime. Be safe and have fun!

NATHAN WELTON

Technique Photos: A User's Guide

Climbing is a vertical dance requiring precise hand and foot "steps," body positions, and movement. Unfortunately, this dance is sometimes difficult to illustrate on the static pages of a book. In *Learning to Climb Indoors* I've adopted, from college biomechanics texts, a method of labeling instructional photos with words and symbols that depict the application of force on hand- and foot-holds. I hope these enhanced photos will underscore the importance of body awareness and help you learn proper technique. Here are the three classes of symbols to look for:

1. Center of Gravity and Line of Gravity

The earth's gravitational pull is most concentrated at your center of gravity—the theoretical point at which gravity's pull acts on you. Standing with your arms by your sides, the center of gravity for males is about an inch above the navel, while for females it averages an inch or two below the navel. (The changing arm and leg positions of a climber in motion, however, can cause the center of gravity to shift side-to-side and up and down.) Center of gravity is designated here by a bullet or circle, and the earth's gravitational pull, or line of gravity, is indicated by a dashed line and arrow pointing downward.

2. Force Vectors

When you climb, you ascend by contracting your muscles to generate force—a push or pull—that is applied to the rock via the hand and foot points of contact. The direction and amount of force applied at a point of contact is called a force vector. Force vectors are represented in this book diagrammatically by arrows. Each arrow's head depicts the direction you should apply force, while the size of the arrow is scaled to the amount of force—a larger arrow means more force, a smaller one, less. You'll find small, medium, and large arrows here.

3. Finesse and Dynamic Moves

Of course the purpose of climbing is to go up. Still, sometimes the most efficient way to do that is by twisting—or flagging, deadpointing, lunging, or other angular and dynamic movements. Such finesse movements are illustrated with a dotted line and an arrow.

PHOTO SYMBOLS

Closed circle with dashed line—center of gravity and line of gravity

Small vector—light, minimal force

Medium vector—moderate force

Large vector—maximal force or dominant point of contact

Dotted line with arrow—twisting/rotational and dynamic movement

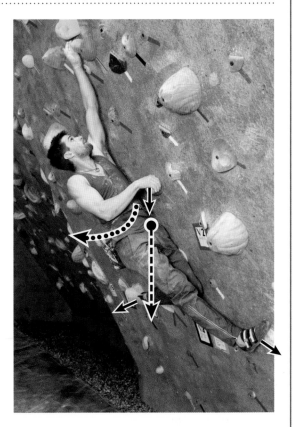

The symbols applied to this photo indicate that the climber uses both of her hands—as well as her right foot—to apply minimal force (note the small arrows, or vectors) to the hold. Meanwhile her left foot carries the bulk of her weight, applying maximal force (indicated by the large arrow, or vector). This positioning is achieved by shifting the center of gravity near—or better yet, over—the left foot.

This climber is using his hands and feet to apply nearly equal force (note the medium vectors). He twists his body (a movement represented by a dotted line) to position his left hip and center of gravity close to the overhanging wall. This shifts the line of gravity closer to his feet, putting more of his body weight onto his feet and extending his left-hand reach.

CHAPTER ONE

Welcome to the Vertical Extreme!

Are you ready to rock your world? Do you dare leave the plane of flatlander sports and engage the challenges (and rewards) of the vertical extreme? Are you prepared for the intense exhilaration and head-to-toe workout that climbing so uniquely provides? Do you aspire to stretch your personal limits and, in doing so, redefine what you view as possible in your life? If so, read on!

Rock climbing is one of the fastest-growing recreational activities of the new millennium, and it's through the doors of climbing gyms that most people get started. Unlike past generations who learned to climb in the more serious environment of outdoor crags, today's aspiring climbers can gain their skills in a safe, controlled indoor setting that affords rapid learning of skills. It is for this new breed of climber that I have crafted the contents of *Learning to Climb Indoors.*

To begin, I'll provide a primer on the challenges, history, and risks of indoor climbing, as well as the must-know issues relating to your initial visits to a climbing facility. Next, I'll describe the subtypes of climbing you will encounter—bouldering, toproping, and lead climbing—and how climbers classify the style of an ascent. The chapter wraps up with a look at the human-made vertical terrain, its shapes and features, and how unique paths up the wall are defined and graded.

The Challenges and Rewards of Climbing

Climbing offers challenges and rewards that are very different from—unlike, and often more intense than—those of other sports. As you will soon discover, climbing is steeped in paradox. Yes, it's child's play—watch a four-year-old at a playground and you'll see that climbing is indeed intuitive—yet solving a climbing sequence while hanging by your fingertips on the side of a rock wall can be perplexing and stressful. Quite often your climbing attempts will end in failure as you hang on the rope pondering the difficulties of the route. It's at these times that you are faced with my favorite climbing paradox: To succeed, you must embrace and learn from failure.

If you are beginning to sense that climbing is also a process of self-exploration, you're right. To me, that's one of this sport's greatest rewards—climbing releases untapped resources, it reveals unknown potentialities, and it provides an endless series of metaphors for effective living. Most people begin climbing for the rush of the new experience, but in time they find it's the motion and emotion—how it makes them feel and grow—that hooks them as climbers for life.

A Brief History of Indoor Climbing

Technical rock climbing was born in the late 1890s as an offshoot of mountaineering; in fact, early climbers practiced roped climbing on short cliffs primarily as a method of training for expeditions to the mountains. Gradually rock climbing became popular in and of itself, and the 1950s and 1960s produced major breakthroughs in equipment and technical ability. This was the Golden Age of American rock climbing, though the first indoor climbing wall had yet to be built!

Portable walls are now commonly featured at fairs, shopping malls, and parks.
COURTESY OF NICROS, INC.

In the 1970s British climbers frustrated by their perpetually damp climate created crude indoor practice climbs up concrete block walls. But it was not until the advent of synthetic climbing handholds in the early 1980s that modern indoor climbing was born. Indoor walls and competition climbing exploded across Europe during the mid-1980s, but the trend was slow to spread across the Atlantic. American climbers, enamored of traditional crag and big-wall styles, viewed climbing on artificial surfaces as contrived and purposeless. Still, in 1987 the first climbing gym in the United States opened in Seattle, Washington. A major paradigm shift soon followed. Many American climbers came to embrace indoor climbing as an efficient method of training for outdoor climbing, as well as a valid activity in its own right.

Twenty-five years later there are more than 1,200 indoor climbing walls scattered across the United States, from Miami to Maine and from Seattle to San Diego. More than 300 facilities are run as full-service commercial climbing gyms with bouldering areas, lead-climbing walls, and a training section. But perhaps the ultimate endorsement of climbing as a unique source of great fun and self-development are the myriad walls recently added to high schools, colleges, churches, and rec centers from the Great Lakes to the Gulf Coast, an area basically void of mountains. Indoor climbing walls bring some of the joys and lessons of rock climbing to our urban flatlands, allowing more than 6 million Americans to try their hand at the sport each year.

The Differences Between Indoor and Outdoor Climbing

Indoor climbing and outdoor climbing are vastly different activities, and competency as an indoor climber does not guarantee safe climbing in the great outdoors. It is vitally important that all indoor climbers recognize that there are wide-ranging complexities and dangers to rock climbing in a natural setting. Not even the most realistic indoor facility provides the experience and training needed to transition your climbing outside.

Yes, outdoor climbing can be a most gratifying progression for a skilled indoor climber, but you must treat the move outdoors as if you are beginning a new sport from scratch. Don't even ponder venturing out to the crags by yourself. More than a few novices have tried this approach and ended up with broken bones, or worse.

Rule number one of outdoor climbing is to bring a pack load of prudence. For the beginner, this means signing up for a weekend class in outdoor climbing or, better yet, obtaining one-on-one instruction from an American Mountain Guides Association (AMGA)–certified climbing guide.

While you can learn the basics of indoor climbing in a day or two, the many nuances of real rock climbing demand several days of quality instruction. If you find the outdoor experience pleasurable, your next step would be to join a local climbing club or find an experienced climbing partner to hook up with for regular outings. In the end, you may find the unique experiences afforded by both indoor and outdoor climbing to be equally enjoyable. I, for one, enjoy training on an indoor wall during the workweek, but I do so with the intention of pulling down on some of Mother Nature's finest on the weekends.

Your First Visit to the Climbing Gym

Your first step through the doors of a climbing gym will be eye opening, energizing, and likely a bit frightening. For an instant you may contemplate a retreat from the facility; resist this urge with the knowledge that indoor climbing is completely safe and that you are up to the challenge. Remind yourself that new experiences and pushing personal boundaries of any kind always result in some degree of anxiety and discomfort. However, you will soon learn one of climbing's great life lessons—pushing through discomfort and harnessing anxiety into productive energy is the strategy for uncommon experience and personal success.

Okay, you accept the challenge, and you are ready to tie in and begin climbing. Well, almost. First, you'll need to fill out some paperwork and pay your dues, literally. You will also need to make a few decisions regarding equipment and instruction, so let me take you step by step through all the key issues.

Types of Gyms and Fees

Climbing gyms come in all shapes and sizes, ranging from a modest 20-foot-high wall installed in the back of a school gymnasium or health club to a multimillion-dollar commercial facility possessing a maze of 40- to 80-foot walls. While walls at schools and community centers may be open to the public free of charge (or included as part of tuition), commercial climbing gyms require a membership or daily access fee. Expect to pay between $10 and $25 for a single day's pass, depending on the size of the gym and cost of doing business in a given city. Annual memberships typically run between $400 and $700, with fees at most full-service gyms in major cities falling near the high end of this range.

Waiver of Liability

In this age of litigation, don't expect to make it past the gym's front desk without signing a waiver of liability. Yes, indoor climbing is safer than crossing the street, but streets don't have employees, investors, and a balance sheet to protect. The waiver shields the gym, its owners, and their insurance company from potential lawsuits brought by climbers injured as a result of their own inexperience or errors. Of course, the waiver does not prevent you from seeking compensation should you get injured due to the gross negligence of the business. Again, this is all "fine print" stuff; the odds are about one in a million that you'll be seriously injured while climbing indoors.

Renting Basic Equipment

As you pay the entry fee and sign the waiver, you'll also be asked if you want to rent any climbing equipment. While I'll provide detailed coverage of climbing gear in chapter 2, I'd like to touch here on your most basic needs—a safety harness and climbing shoes.

Like a seat belt, a climbing harness is the most vital piece of safety equipment. It's the link between your body and the safety rope. Climbing shoes are also important, although the need for these specialized shoes is all about performance, not safety. While some people climb their first day in sneakers or hiking boots, I urge you to rent a pair of sticky-soled climbing shoes. The difference these shoes will make in your climbing experience cannot be oversold—it's like the difference between skiing with shaped skis versus a 2-by-4 board strapped to each foot. Rent the shoes, please!

Expect to pay between $5 and $10 to rent a harness and shoes for the day. If after your first few days of climbing you feel you are hooked, then invest the $125 to $200 needed to purchase your own harness and shoes. By the way, pass on any offers to buy used gear. If you are serious about climbing, treat yourself to a perfectly fitting harness and brand-new shoes.

Climbing Lessons and Belay Tests

Most gyms require first-time climbers to go through an introductory class. Some gyms charge a fee for this basic instruction, while others build the cost into the entry fee. The typical lesson provides a crash course on the fundamentals of climbing movement, as well as vital issues of putting on your harness, tying into the rope, and belaying. **Belaying** is a two-person rope-management technique that allows for safe ascent and descent of the walls. It's a simple process that takes only a few minutes to understand, yet most people require a few days in order to feel completely comfortable as a belayer.

Table 1.1 *What to Expect on Your First Visit to a Climbing Gym*	
On Your First Day Climbing	**Fee, If Any**
Pay entry fee	$10–25
Sign waiver	—
Rent climbing shoes and harness	$5–10
Take introductory climbing lesson	$10–35
Pass belay test	—
Have fun climbing	Priceless!

I'll cover all these subjects in great depth later on, though you must remember that reading is not doing. In climbing, there is no replacement for personal instruction and real-life experience. Most gyms will require you to pass a basic knot-tying and belay test at some point during your initial visits. Don't sweat the test; it's all pretty easy stuff.

An Introduction to the Climbers' Lexicon

Send. Pumped. On-sight. Thrash. Flash. Like many sports, climbing has its own lexicon of terms and slang words, which you'll hear echoing throughout the gym. While I will largely avoid using slang—you can have some fun trying to decipher the lingo you hear at the gym—I will introduce you to the terminology needed to effectively learn, describe, and engage in gym climbing. Remember that key terms are typeset in **boldface** on first use, and you will find each term defined in the glossary.

Types of Climbing

Most commercial gyms offer three very different types of climbing: **bouldering, toproping,** and **leading.** A fourth approach to climbing found at some pay-to-climb facilities involves the use of an **auto belay.** Each of these activities comes with unique challenges, rewards, and safety requirements, which I'll cover below. Should you settle in as a regular gym climber, you'll likely develop a preference for one of these activities, yet from the perspective of optimal learning, it's best to spend time practicing within each subdiscipline. (You'll find more on accelerated learning techniques in chapter 4.)

Bouldering

Bouldering is arguably the purest form of climbing, since all the complexities of gear and ropework are removed. The goal in bouldering is to ascend short sections of wall, each called a **problem,** typically ranging from 7 to 15 feet in height. Most gyms have an area designated specifically for bouldering, and in a few big cities there are entire climbing gyms dedicated to it. In some circles bouldering

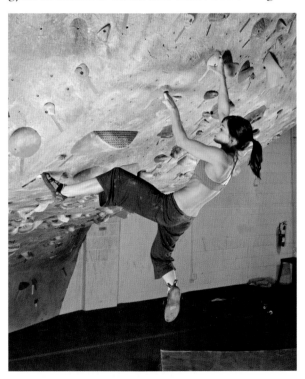

The challenge of bouldering is to ascend a short, difficult section of wall within jumping distance of the ground.

has evolved into a sport of its own, which is understandable given its highly engaging nature and the common tendency to work boulder problems with a group of comrades.

During your initial visits, bouldering offers an easy way to practice footwork, develop balance, and experiment with different ways of moving in your new vertical environment. Since in bouldering you rarely climb more than several feet off the floor, it's easy to step or jump off the wall and try again. In fact, that is the beauty of bouldering: You can pick a problem and focus on solving it, even if it means jumping off and trying the problem over and over. This process of targeting your efforts on solving a specific sequence will challenge you physically, mentally, and technically, all without the distraction of a rope, belayer, or dauntingly long climb.

When bouldering more than 6 or 8 feet off the floor, it's vital that you employ a **spotter,** as well as having a **crash pad** in your landing zone. Jumping off such **highball** problems is hard on the ankles, knees, and lower back. Worse yet, a surprise fall from a steep problem can send you twisting and turning out of control with little time to right yourself for a clean landing.

Most gyms possess cushioned floors and bouldering crash pads intended to soften your impact and reduce the risk of injury. Still, it's best to have a spotter (of the same or greater size than you) help protect you during an attempted ascent of a steep or high boulder problem. As you climb, the spotter stands just behind you—not under you, unless your spotter wants to be pancaked—with hands reaching toward the back of your hips. Should you jump or fall from the problem, the spotter grasps near your hips and helps direct you feetfirst toward the crash pad. In the rare case of a tumbling fall, the spotter may only be able to push on your back in an attempt to prevent your head from hitting the ground first. Spotting, like belaying, is an activity that demands vigilance—your partner's safety is on the line. See chapter 3 for detailed instruction on spotting.

Toproping

Toproping is the most popular activity for beginners, since it allows safe movement up even the highest, most scary-looking walls. The name *toprope* describes the rigging of the safety line that runs from the floor up through an anchor atop the climb, then back down to the bottom. Gyms commonly have a dozen or more topropes hanging in place and ready to go—you just need to tie into one end of the rope and have someone belay you

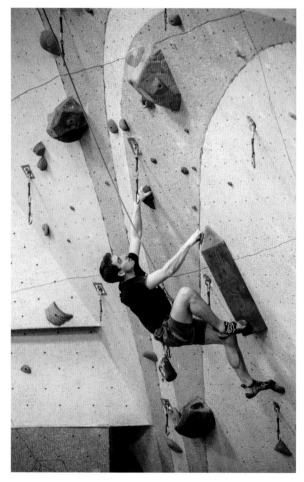

Toproping is the most popular form of climbing for beginners.

from the other end. The specifics of belaying are upcoming in chapter 3.

Like bouldering, toproping is an excellent way to practice your skills, but with a toprope it's the belayer, not a spotter, who's got your back. With a snug toprope belay, you can safely try your hand at any climb and be softly lowered back to the ground at a moment's notice. Some toprope climbs will be easy; you'll breeze up the wall on your first try. Other routes might spit you off onto the rope—called a fall. Fortunately, the toprope will hold you in place at the problem spot so you can hang there and work on the sequence. Sometimes it will only take a few tries to unlock the sequence and continue on to the top; other times you may be stymied, and you'll need to lower off and try the climb another day.

In the earliest stages of learning, it's important to log a lot of mileage on easy climbs and to avoid difficult routes that will frustrate or demoralize you. Toproping is the ideal way to test the waters and see just what level of difficulty you are climbing on a given day (more on the grading scale of routes in a bit). What's more, toproping is highly time efficient—it lets you pack in the most climbing mileage per session. There are also specific practice drills you can perform while toproping. Chapters 5 and 6 will detail nineteen powerful drills for developing good technique and accelerating your progress as a climber.

Auto Belay Climbing

Auto belay climbing is growing in popularity, especially at climbing walls located in sporting goods stores, health clubs, amusement parks, and shopping malls. These mechanical belays do not require a second individual to hold the other end of the climbing rope—in fact, the auto belay is your belayer. The actual belay machine is located atop or behind the climbing wall; the safety cable (not a rope) hangs from the top of the climb, with the end dangling near the base of the route.

Using an auto belay is elementary and completely secure, as long as you properly clip into the belay cable before you start climbing. The auto belay draws in the cable as you move upward; should you fall, it will catch and slowly lower you back to the ground. While auto belays are indeed an efficient way for commercial facilities to process a large number of novice climbers, they do have drawbacks in terms of learning. If you are serious about pursuing climbing long-term, it's beneficial to leverage the partnership that a human belayer provides. An auto belay can't provide encouragement or helpful tips when you struggle on a difficult move, nor can it share the joy of a great ascent. In climbing, your greatest resource is often the human resource—the dynamic give-and-take process among like-minded climbers that accelerates learning and makes for so many wonderful experiences.

Leading

Lead climbing is the bomb! For me, nothing beats the intense game of trying to lead the **sharp end** of the rope from the ground to the top anchors of a climb. Unlike the snug belay afforded by a toprope, the hallmark of lead climbing is the dangling rope that trails from the climber's harness down to the ground. Periodically the lead climber comes upon anchor bolts to which the trailing rope is clipped, while a belayer on the ground pays out rope. The upshot (or more appropriately, "downfall") of this way of climbing is that a slip-up yields a true free fall until the rope draws tight onto the last anchor bolt that was clipped. The permanent anchor bolts for lead climbing are typically spaced so that such free falls are limited to just 5 or 10 feet. However, an inattentive belayer and rope stretch can turn a short fall into a 15- or 20-foot **screamer.**

Make no mistake: Lead climbing is not a beginners' activity. It is, however, a wonderfully powerful experience you should look forward to as you become a more competent and confident climber. When is the right time to get into lead climbing? Depending on your degree of natural ability and how often you climb, you could be ready as quickly as a few months or maybe not for several years or more. Most gyms have an additional competency test you'll need to take before you are lead certified. Talk to instructors about your desire to begin leading, and let them be the judge as to whether you are ready to tie into the sharp end.

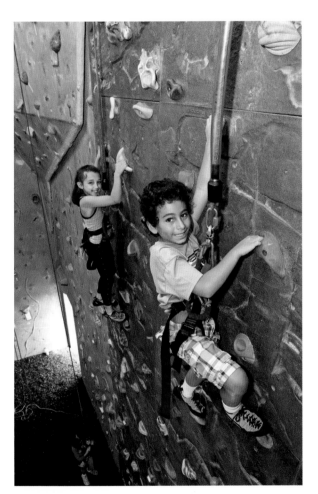

No matter your age, auto belays provide a safe, enjoyable climbing experience.
COURTESY OF NICROS, INC.

Learning About the Climbing Walls

Although most indoor walls have little resemblance to real cliffs, climbing the two kinds of walls can feel remarkably similar. Climbing wall technology, both the wall surface and the handholds, has come a long way over the last twenty-five years. The shape, height, and topography of climbing walls are becoming more dramatic and varied every year, so the realism of a wall tends to be a function of the age of the facility and, of course, budget. The route-creating process of placing and arranging handholds on the wall surface also contributes to the realism of

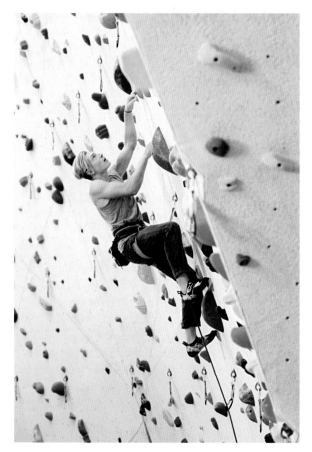

Lead climbing is the most challenging and "heady" style of climbing.
COURTESY OF NICROS, INC.

the climbing movement. It's a fact that good route setting can make an average wall "climb good," while a great wall can be spoiled by poor route setting. Assessing route quality is certainly subjective, but you'll soon come to know a good route when you feel it.

Following is a primer on climbing wall features, the designation of routes, and the popular scales for rating the difficulty of a climb. The section concludes with a look at climbing style and the terms used to describe the quality of an ascent.

Wall Features

The most obvious characteristic or macro feature of a climbing wall is often its steepness. Steepness can be assessed as an angle compared with vertical— say, 10 degrees less than vertical or 30 degrees past vertical—or as the angle the wall is offset from the ground as it would be measured with a protractor. For example, the 10-degrees-less-than-vertical wall mentioned above would be called an 80-degree wall, whereas the 30-degrees-past-vertical wall would be classified as a 120-degree wall. The final, simplest method of describing wall angle is simply to refer to a less-than-vertical wall as a **slab,** a vertical wall as **vert**, and a wall angle past vertical as **overhanging.**

Three other features of steepness are **overhangs, roofs,** and **ledges.** An overhang is a section of wall that juts out horizontally, parallel to the floor; it's a common **crux** feature on indoor climbs. A ledge is the opposite of an overhang, in that the wall briefly cuts back in horizontally so that you can stand up on a perch as if you were standing on the floor. While ledges are a common feature on natural cliffs, they are a rarity on indoor walls. A roof is a large overhang that juts out horizontally more than a body length. For example, some indoor lead climbs conclude with a dramatic 10- or 20-foot sequence out the actual underside of the building's roof (hence the name).

Well-designed indoor walls possess a wide variety of other topographic features that add to the complexity and enjoyment of climbing. An inside corner or **dihedral** is a common feature consisting of two walls that intersect at a 90-degree angle, as in the squared corner of any room. In some cases the inside corner forms a more obtuse angle (greater than 90 degrees) called an **open book.**

Another variant that's a favorite of wall designers is the outside corner or **arête.** These prominent features possess a sharp edge formed by two intersecting walls, as in the outside corner of a building. When the walls meet to form a clean 90-degree angle, the feature is usually called an outside corner. More commonly the angle is skewed away from 90 degrees, making a more visually and technically interesting arête.

A final wall feature to recognize is a fissure or crack. Ubiquitous among Mother Nature's rock walls, cracks are a rarity on human-made walls since they are difficult to create using the typical plywood substrate of indoor walls. Some high-end gyms, however, possess a more realistic concrete-based wall system that does allow the creation of cracks. These fractures are usually oriented vertically, and they can vary from about ½ inch up to a few feet in width. Climbers typically refer to smaller cracks by how much of their hand fits into one. Thus, from small to large, cracks are classified as fingertip, full finger, shallow hands, full hands, and fist. Cracks large enough to fit an arm are called **offwidths,** while a body-size fracture is known as a **chimney.**

Route Setting and Naming of Climbs

Since the macro features of a wall are fixed, it's the placements of modular hand- and footholds that ultimately dictate the movement and difficulty of a route. Climbing gyms employ a route setter or **forerunner** to reposition the holds and set new routes every few weeks. With thousands of different types of holds possessing nearly an infinite range of texture and relief, a skilled forerunner can create routes of amazing realism for climbers of all abilities.

In order to maximize the climbing possibilities

A typical gym route nameplate with grade, tape or hold color designation, the route setter's name, and the date the route was set.

at an indoor facility, a forerunner typically sets three or four different routes up a given section of wall. Each route is identified by the color of the holds or the color of a tape swatch placed below each hand- and foothold. At first glance a section of wall may look like a random array of rainbow-colored holds (or tape swatches), but you will quickly learn to distinguish the various routes by focusing on a single color. For instance, in climbing a route marked with red tape (or red holds), only the holds marked with red tape are considered on route, whereas holds of all other colors are off route. While it would be just fine to climb the wall using holds of any color, it's not the way the climb was designed, nor the way the indoor climbing game is played.

Upon setting a route and marking all the holds with a single color of holds (or tape), the forerunner climbs the line and then assigns a name and grade to the creation. This identifying information is usually written on a piece of tape at the base of the route. Naming routes is a carryover from outdoor climbing; the names enable cataloging of routes in a guidebook. While not all indoor climbs are named,

Open Book

Roof

Overhanging Wall

Arête

"Vert" Wall

Dihedral

it's a fun practice that enables you to talk about a specific route with your friends, an instructor, or the gym staff.

Difficulty Rating Scales

Grading the severity of a climb is highly subjective and sometimes controversial. Consider that how difficult a climb feels may be affected by issues other than absolute skill—height, arm length, flexibility, endurance, and so on. A route may feel harder than its grade should you not be able to reach a critical hold. Fortunately, a highly skilled forerunner is able to set routes that do not penalize climbers of non-average build. Still, it's not uncommon for a grade to change slightly as a consensus develops based on repeat ascents by many other climbers.

The primary rating scales used in the United States are the **Yosemite Decimal System** (YDS) for roped climbs and the **V-Scale** for boulder problems. The YDS is a pseudo-decimal running from 5.0 (easiest) to 5.9, then continuing in the sequence 5.10, 5.11, 5.12, 5.13, 5.14, and 5.15 (hardest). The 5 refers to fifth-class climbing, which is the general classification for steep climbing that requires a safety rope and belay. Some gyms truncate the fifth-class designation and decimal point, and simply list the grade as, say, a 9 (instead of 5.9) or 12 (instead of 5.12). Two subdivisions of the YDS are also commonly used to help indicate subtle differences in difficulty within a given grade. Routes rated between 5.7 and 5.9 sometimes carry a minus sign (-) or a plus sign (+), indicating easy or hard for the grade, respectively. Ratings of 5.10 and harder often carry a nuance subgrade of a, b, c, or d. For instance, 5.10a is considered an easy 5.10, while 5.10d is a hard 5.10.

Common indoor climbing wall features.
COURTESY OF NICROS, INC.

Table 1.2 *Comparison of the YDS Scale and the V-Scale*

YDS	V-SCALE
5.5	
5.6	V0-
5.7	
5.8	
5.9	V0
5.10a	
5.10b	V0+
5.10c	
5.10d	V1
5.11a	
5.11b	V2
5.11c	
5.11d	V3
5.12a	V4
5.12b	V5
5.12c	V6
5.12d	
5.13a	V7
5.13b	V8
5.13c	
5.13d	V9
5.14a	V10
5.14b	V11
5.14c	V12
5.14d	V13
5.15a	V14
5.15b	V15
5.15c	V16

The V-Scale has become the most popular rating system for boulder problems. Still, a few gyms prefer to use fifth-class grades or, possibly, a mix of the two scales to rate boulder problems. The V-Scale is open ended, beginning at V0 and currently extending up to V16. Plus (+) and minus (-) signs are commonly appended to the grade to provide further grade distinction. Since boulder problems are short and intense in nature, the V-Scale begins at a harder absolute difficulty level than the YDS. Knowing roughly how the two scales relate will help you determine boulder problems appropriately rated for your roped climbing ability (see table 1.2, "Comparison of the YDS Scale and the V-Scale"). Given the brief nature of boulder problems, however, you may discover that you can boulder at least one to two V-grades above your corresponding maximum YDS roped ascent.

Classifying the Style of Ascent

Climbing is a sport in which style matters. No, I'm not talking about fashion style, but instead climbing style—the manner in which you ascend a boulder problem or route.

Climbing style has both subjective and objective elements. First, your style of movement on a climb is a quality assessment based on subjective factors such as smoothness of movement, poise, and execution of fundamental techniques. More clearcut is the style in which you work on and come to succeed on a climb. The purest style of climbing is **on-sight,** which means you climbed the route on your first try and, literally, first sight of the route. The next best style of ascent, called **flash,** refers to climbing a route first try, but with prior knowledge of the climb. Flash ascents are common in a gym setting where you might watch another person climb the route or gain verbal **beta,** or tips, from someone as you climb.

Upon hanging on the toprope or falling on lead, you lose the chance to ever on-sight or flash the route. Still, you can make an ascent in good style by working for a **redpoint**—climbing the route from bottom to top without hanging or falling. Sometimes you can redpoint a climb on your second attempt, whereas a difficult route may require repeated attempts over the course of several days before you achieve the redpoint.

In bouldering, style of ascent also matters, and on-sight or flash is the ultimate goal. However, boulder problems of a steep and intense character (common) are often tough to flash despite their short length. It's not uncommon to try a given boulder problem over and over, or to take turns working the problem with a group of friends. Such an approach is a good way to learn climbing moves, and it's great fun. As for style of ascent when working problems in this manner, most people simply count the number of attempts it takes to succeed on the problem. Thus you might say, "I sent the problem second try," or "It took me twelve attempts to do the problem." Of course, the modus operandi of some people is to work boulder problems beyond their ability, which means they'll likely lose count of the number of attempts or just not care how long it takes to succeed. This approach is completely valid, too. One of the beauties of climbing is that you can make up the rules if you choose.

While it's great to strive for the highest style of ascent, it's vital that you not obsess on having to on-sight or flash every route. In chapter 8 you will learn that the best mental approach for effective climbing is to focus on the process and let the outcome (on-sight, flash, or fall) just happen. Recognize that even if you're failing, you're still learning and getting a good workout. Enjoy the process of climbing regardless of the result, and you'll naturally become a climber of great style.

CHAPTER TWO

Equipment and Safety Gear

Clubs, bats, sticks, balls, and rackets—this is the equipment of most mainstream sports.

Fingers, toes, muscle, and the mind—these are the only mandatory tools for climbing.

In its essence, climbing is simply a vertical dance. The wall is the medium on which you perform; the selected route up the wall is your challenge, or partner, if you will. The need for gear arises only as you ascend to a height from which you cannot safely jump down. Even so, the necessary safety equipment will go hardly noticed as you safely rise above terra firma.

Compared with climbing outdoors, indoor climbing requires minimal equipment and only a small financial investment. Climbing shoes, harness, and a belay device are the only absolutely necessary pieces of gear, although there are a few other items you'll likely want to acquire, such as a chalk bag and a rope. During your first few visits, it's often best to simply rent this gear from the gym. Should you begin to climb on a regular basis, however, you will want to purchase a perfectly fitted harness and pair of shoes.

Following are descriptions of the mandatory equipment for indoor climbing, as well as some not-necessary yet common items you may see in use around the gym. While you can use this chapter as a sort of buyer's guide, I encourage you to do further research on manufacturers' websites and by visiting your local climbing store or gym pro shop.

Shoes

No one will ever mistake a climbing shoe for a street shoe—they are worlds apart in look, feel, and function. Sure, you can get away with wearing a tightly laced pair of sneakers during your initial foray at indoor climbing, but after your first day you should upgrade to wearing climbing shoes. Try out a rental pair, and I guarantee you'll be sold on the value of these sticky-soled shoes. However, exercise due diligence before purchasing a pair, because there are a wide variety of brands and designs to consider. Pull up a chair, and let's try on some shoes.

Finding the Right Shoe

The right climbing shoe for you depends on several factors, including the shape and width of your foot, as well as your body weight, ability, and budget. With more than fifteen different brands of shoes on the market and over one hundred different styles, picking out your first pair can be daunting.

Let's begin with cost. Technical climbing shoes—not to be confused with hiking boots or approach shoes—run anywhere from $80 to $170 a pair. The most expensive models may be a bit overkill for an entry-level climber; the lowest-priced shoes are often of low quality and are best avoided. There are many excellent models in the $100 to $150 range, so make this the price point at which to begin your search.

Within this price range you will find many models and a variety of design features. The most obvious feature is whether the shoe is a lace-up or slipper design. Lace-up models maintain a tighter

fit throughout the life of the shoe and tend to have better support than slipper styles. As an indoor climber, however, you'll be switching in and out of your shoes several times over the course of a session, and the slipper designs simplify this process. Some manufacturers make a hybrid slipper that incorporates a Velcro strap–closure system. This unique design provides a snug fit similar to a lace-up, but with the ease of exit of a slipper. Give serious consideration to this style of shoe.

If the Shoe Fits ...

Fit is everything when it comes to buying the right climbing shoe, so don't be overly swayed by what a friend or the local rock star wears. Ideally you want to visit a large outdoor store or well-stocked gym pro shop that carries six or more styles of shoes. Evaluate the quality of fit for each shoe based on three criteria: last shape, stiffness, and comfort.

LAST SHAPE

The last is the general mold around which a climbing shoe is designed and constructed. Most brands of shoes feature styles built on several different lasts—hopefully one of them will be similar to the shape of your foot.

Observe how the shape and width of the shoe compare with those of your foot. Is your foot narrow, wide, or about average? Is your foot asymmetric (longest at the big toe) or more symmetric (longest near the second or third toe)? It's these aspects that you are trying to match.

STIFFNESS

Consider the stiffness of different models and, in particular, test the flexibility of the shoe around the forefoot. Midsole thickness and whether the shoe is

Three styles of shoes by La Sportiva: the Python slipper; the easy-on, easy-off Miura with Velcro closure; the high-performance, lace-up Testarossa.

slip-lasted or board-lasted determine how stiff and supportive a shoe feels. The stiffness produced by board-lasted designs facilitates the use of small footholds, yet this benefit comes at the price of reduced sensitivity and feel—important for optimizing your foot placement on small holds. The heavy-duty support of a stiff-soled shoe is most important for a climber with a larger-than-normal build (in terms of weight), while an individual of average or slight build tends to perform best with a less stiff, slip-lasted shoe.

Lightweight, super-sensitive slipper models possess the least stiffness and are quite popular among indoor climbers. However, these minimalist shoes require significant foot strength and precise footwork, making them a poor choice for a novice. More appropriate as a first pair of shoes would be a slip-lasted model possessing a modest amount of stiffness and the snug fit provided by Velcro closures.

Finally, consider size and comfort. Unfortunately, picking the right size climbing shoe is far more difficult than sizing a street shoe. Complicating matters are the stretch inherent to climbing shoes, size variations among manufacturers and styles, and the fact that some brands use European units of shoe size while others use the American scale. Ultimately, finding the right size shoe comes down to trial and error and a bit of luck. Also, be sure to try on shoes without socks, since that's the way you'll be wearing them to climb.

As a guideline, the right size shoe will be snug from heel to toe with no air pockets or dead space anywhere around the front half of the shoe. In fact, it's best to select a size small enough to induce some toe curl. A rough rule of thumb is to size unlined shoes about two full sizes smaller than your street shoes; lined shoes need only be one size smaller, since they will stretch much less. You can easily determine whether a shoe is lined or unlined by looking inside the shoe toward the toe box—the shoe is lined if you see a smooth white material and unlined if you see only brushed leather.

Some stores and gyms allow you to test the shoe out on a climbing wall. If that's not an option, take a walk around the store to determine whether you can wear the shoe for ten to fifteen minutes without severe pain. The shoe should be tight and somewhat uncomfortable to walk in—they are climbing shoes, not hiking boots!—yet you should not be wincing in pain with every step you take. Bottom line: It's best to err on the side of half a size too small rather than half a size too big, since most shoes tend to stretch more than you would expect.

Harness

The harness is the link between your body and the climbing rope. The fit should be snug and secure, yet the harness should not inhibit movement or feel bulky. As in selecting a pair of climbing shoes, it's

A standard adult harness by Wild Country.

A youth harness, shown here by Wild Country, is ideal for most kids between ages seven and thirteen.

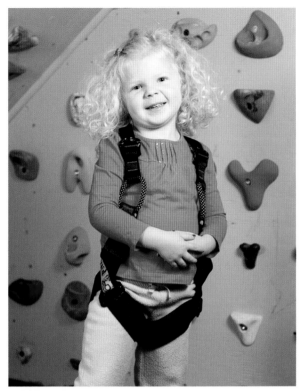

Kids younger than seven or eight should use a full-body harness.

ERIC MCCALLISTER

best to try on several different midpriced harnesses ($45 to $75). Here are the three criteria to consider.

1. Is the harness a full-feature model or a minimalist, bare-bones design? Avoid purchasing one of the overdesigned, highly padded models, which are primarily designed for the rigors of climbing outdoors. For indoor climbing, a sleek, lightly padded harness is the ideal choice—you definitely do not need all the bells and whistles found on high-priced harnesses.

2. Does the harness feature adjustable leg loops and waist belt, or just an adjustable waist belt? The rental fleets of most gyms are filled with fully adjustable harnesses with buckles on both legs and waist, but such designs can be bulky

and bothersome. In purchasing a model, look for a harness with leg loops sewn to the proper size and possessing only a single buckle to adjust the fit around the waist. Most designs incorporate small elastic straps to keep the leg loops comfortably snug to your body—a nice feature to look for.

3. Many manufacturers now make women's harnesses that are uniquely proportioned around the legs, hips, and waist. While some women can find a good-fitting unisex harness, others swear by the perfect fit afforded by the women's styles.

As a final note, kids under the age of seven (or less than sixty pounds) should wear a specially designed full-body harness. Even the smallest adult-style harness will not properly fit around the legs, hips, and waist of a child. However, a full-body harness with its legs, waist, chest, and shoulder straps is supremely secure and will allow parent and child to climb with peace of mind. A few companies make a "youth harness" that's specially designed to fit most youngsters ages seven to thirteen; beyond this age a small adult harness will work fine.

Belay Devices

After buying shoes and a harness, a belay device is your next likely investment. There are two basic types of belay devices—a belay plate and a self-locking device such as a Grigri—and it should be your goal to become proficient in using both pieces of equipment. Interestingly, gyms tend to have an affinity for one device or the other, so inquire about this before you make a purchase.

A belay plate, and the more modern Air Traffic Controller (ATC) and Reverso, are the belay devices traditionally used for both indoor and outdoor climbing. These basic belay devices are available at any climbing store and most gyms for between $17 and $35.

Increasingly popular among indoor climbers are self-actuating belay devices such as the Petzl Grigri.

Popular belay devices: ATC guide (left) and Grigri 2.

Wild Country carabiner quickdraw (left) and a DMM locking carabiner.

As you will learn in chapter 3, these self-locking devices are more foolproof than the traditional belay plate. As the Cadillac of belay devices, however, they come at a higher price: $80 to $95.

Carabiners and Quickdraws

In addition to a belay device, you will also need a large safety-pin-like climbing link called a **carabiner.** Carabiners are made of an extremely light and incredibly strong aluminum alloy. Climbers use them in a number of different ways, but none is more important than as the link between their belay device and harness. While a closed carabiner will never fail, there is always the remote chance that the carabiner's gate could open and come unhooked from the rope or harness. As a safeguard, most manufacturers make a specialized locking carabiner, which possesses a twist-lock gate that secures the closed position. Purchase one locking carabiner ($8 to $17) for use with your belay device. Never use a nonlocking carabiner to belay.

Initially you will need only a single locking carabiner to engage in toprope climbing and belaying. If you someday delve into lead climbing, you may need to purchase some additional biners. As

discussed in chapter 1, lead climbing involves leading the rope up the wall and clipping into anchor bolts with **quickdraws** as protection against large falls. A quickdraw is a couplet of carabiners connected with a short sling of nylon webbing. Most gyms affix permanent quickdraws to all anchor bolts on lead climbs. However, some facilities may have a few routes without them so that you can practice clipping into the bolts as you would when climbing outdoors. This is actually a good thing to practice if you plan to venture onto real rock, but you will need to invest in a dozen quickdraws ($15 to $24 each).

Chalk

Just the thought of climbing likely makes your palms sweat, so imagine how your sweat glands will react when you are actually up on the wall hanging by your fingertips! To combat sweat and improve grip, climbers use magnesium carbonate, better known as gymnastics chalk. The chalk is carried in a small pouch or chalk bag ($20 to $35) attached to the back of your harness so that you can easily dip the fingers of either hand into the chalk in the midst of a climb. It won't be long before you

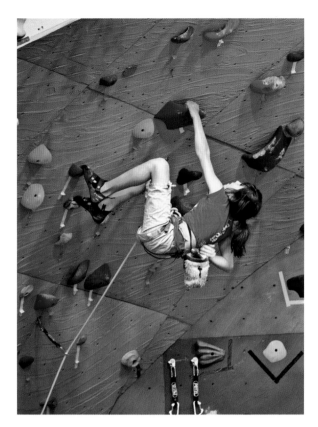

Most climbers agree that a chalk bag is an indispensable piece of equipment. Here a climber pauses briefly on a steep route to chalk up.

discover that chalk is almost as important to effective climbing as sticky-soled shoes.

One downside of chalk use at indoor facilities is the dust it creates. In poorly ventilated gyms you can often see a haze in the air during peak hours. Furthermore, the dust eventually settles out, producing a fine accumulation of chalk on all flat surfaces. In an attempt to control this problem, many gyms disallow use of loose chalk. Instead, the chalk in your bag must be contained inside a panty-hose-like nylon sleeve that yields a slow release of chalk but no spillage. Many gyms sell premade chalk balls ($3 to $5) that provide a controlled release of chalk onto your hands.

Rope and Rope Bag

A climbing rope is unlikely to be an investment you'll make anytime soon, since climbing gyms supply and pre-rig topropes on most of their walls. Still, it's good to know about the equipment to which you trust your life, so let's cover the basics.

Climbing ropes are made of extremely strong and durable nylon, so straight up we can dispel any fears that a climbing rope might ever break. That said, a mistreated rope will wear out prematurely, and a rope that is drawn tight across a sharp edge may be damaged or cut. Consequently, there are four critical rules of rope care:

1. Keep the rope clean.
2. Avoid stepping on it.
3. Prevent the rope from touching anything sharp—whether it's a sharp edge on a climbing wall or a sharp object in the trunk of your car.
4. When storing your rope, keep it in a dark, clean location away from batteries, solvents, or any other products containing harsh chemicals (which can weaken a rope without visible damage).

There are two basic types of climbing ropes: dynamic and static. A rope is dynamic if it stretches under the load of body weight or the force of a fall. In catching a falling lead climber, the rope's stretch absorbs energy, making for a soft catch and reducing peak forces on the climbing anchors, belay device, and belayer. Consequently, a dynamic rope is mandatory for all lead climbing.

Conversely, static ropes stretch very little. Their use for indoor climbing is limited to toprope routes, where there's little force generated by the very short falls. Some gyms use static ropes on all their toprope routes, since static line wears better and lasts longer than dynamic rope. Other gyms only use dynamic rope as a safeguard in case the rope somehow finds its way onto a lead climb. The bottom line: There's no reason for an indoor climber to ever purchase a static rope.

When you begin lead climbing, however, you will likely need to purchase a dynamic rope. Most climbing gyms do not supply dynamic ropes for lead climbing, but even if they did, I'd prefer to use my own versus a heavily used communal rope. Dynamic ropes are available in a variety of thicknesses ranging from 8.9 to 11 millimeters (with 9.4 to 10.5 millimeters being the most common) and lengths of 60 and 70 meters. Given that most indoor walls are less than 25 meters (80 feet) in height, a 60-meter rope is plenty long to lead and then lower off almost any indoor wall. However, if you plan to climb outdoors, it would be wise to buy a 70-meter rope. Upon determining length and thickness, most people select a rope based on color preference and price. Expect to pay between $195 and $300 for your lifeline.

You should also consider purchasing a rope bag ($35 to $50) to protect your investment and extend its effective life. Most rope bags are designed to open up into a small tarp at the base of a climb. The opened rope bag makes a more visible no-step zone, and it also serves as a barrier between the rope and any foreign matter native to the floor of the facility.

Belay Gloves

While I climbed for more than twenty years without ever using belay gloves, I'm now a huge advocate and hate to belay without them! Simply put: Belay gloves improve your grip on the rope and keep your hands clean. Certainly you can belay just fine without gloves, but they are the cheapest piece of climbing equipment covered here and, as you will soon find out, they are extremely practical. There are some overpriced specially made climber's gloves on the market, but I've found that a pair of generic work gloves from Home Depot or Lowe's work just fine.

Helmet

Helmets are not required equipment at most gyms, although some instructors and facilities recommend their use. While head protection is extremely important when climbing outdoors (where rockfall is a very real danger), the risk of a head injury indoors is minuscule. The only imaginable risks are a swinging fall into an adjacent wall or the remote chance that you might invert while falling and hit a surface headfirst. Ultimately it's a personal choice, and for many climbers the comfort and freedom of climbing hat-free predominate. I suggest discussing the matter with a few instructors and then making an educated decision as to whether a helmet is right for you. Don't make cost the determining factor—a good brain bucket only costs between $50 and $100.

Clothing

Unlike most traditional sports, there is no uniform or dress code for climbing. All that really matters is that you don comfortable clothes that won't inhibit your movement. Well-fitting athletic sweatpants or shorts along with a T-shirt or tank top will serve you just fine. Lightweight, cotton-based fabrics with a small amount of Lycra usually provide the best combination of fit, function, and comfort. Most important, avoid anything that's overly baggy or oversize—a loose shirt can get stuck in your belay device, and excessively baggy pants will get in the way of your view of footholds.

If cost is not an issue—and if you like a trendy, fashion-conscious look—you might want to shop for a few pieces of climbing-specific togs. There are several excellent apparel lines designed by climbers for climbers, such as Verve, prAna, Vertical Girl, The North Face, Kuhl, and Mountain Hardwear. While a single shirt-and-pants outfit can run upward of $100, in most cases you do get what you pay for from these companies. The designs are thoughtful, tested, and generally quite attractive. And you certainly can't blame a lackluster day of climbing on your clothing!

Table 2.1 An Equipment Checklist

Indoor Climbing Gear	(approximate cost)	Bouldering	Toproping	Leading
Technical climbing shoes	($100–150)	x	x	x
Harness	($45–75)		x	x
Locking carabiner	($8–17)		x	x
Belay device	($20–95)		x	x
Chalk bag	($20–35)	x	x	x
Belay gloves	($10–25)		optional	optional
Rope and rope bag	($195–300)			x
Quickdraws	($15–24 each)			x
Helmet	($50–100)	optional	optional	optional

A final consideration in dressing for indoor climbing is that some facilities are not well climate controlled. In winter the gym may be a little colder than you'd like, while in summer it can be rather hot, especially as you near the top of the climbing wall (remember, warm air rises). If conditions are uncomfortably warm, wear a light-weight shirt, drink lots of water, and consider just bouldering for the day so as to stay close to the floor where the coolest air resides. In cold conditions, however, dress in layers that can be removed as your core temperature rises.

CHAPTER THREE

Learning the Safety Systems

Climbing gyms offer an awesome setting for an amazing workout. A multitude of routes blazed up sheer walls are the apparatus, and your mind and body are the only tools for performing the exercise. One of the beauties of indoor climbing is the simplicity of engaging the rock wall with just your fingertips, toes, and mind, while all the complexities of life are left behind on the ground. Still, to engage in safe climbing requires use of the safety system called belaying, which will guarantee you live to climb another day.

While you will spend many months learning all the subtleties of climbing technique and movement, the must-know safety information is something you'll pick up during your first few visits to the gym. This chapter presents an overview of the most fundamental safety techniques for bouldering and roped climbing. You must recognize, however, that reading about belaying is not a replacement for personal instruction. The bottom line: Use this section as a primer on these safety techniques, but vow to participate in a formal belay class to learn—and then perfect—the system.

Putting on Your Harness

Putting on your harness isn't much more difficult than pulling up and buckling a pair of pants. Of course, the consequences of not properly securing your climbing harness are much greater!

Although the dozens of different harnesses on the market vary slightly in design, the one common feature is a master buckle on the waist belt. Upon stepping into the leg loops, pull the waist belt up over your hips and wrap it around the narrowest part of your waist. Be sure to tuck in your shirt so it lies smoothly underneath the waist belt. Thread the loose end of the waist belt through the buckle and pull until it's comfortably snug. Now the most vital step—take the loose end of the waist belt and double it back through the master buckle. Although the harness may feel secure with just a single pass through the buckle, it is nowhere near full strength without this second pass. Thus it's critical to double-check the master buckle every time you tie into the rope.

Tying into the Rope

The vital link between your harness and the end of the rope can be established in a couple of different ways. The most popular method is the simple retraced figure-eight knot in which the rope ties directly to your harness. Consult the instruction booklet that accompanied your harness to determine the exact place through which to tie the rope. With most designs, the rope passes under the piece of webbing connecting the leg loops and then up under the waist belt. You do not want to tie into the belay loop that connects the waist belt and leg loops.

Retraced Figure-Eight Knot

Strong and secure, the retraced figure eight is the best knot for tying into a harness. Some gyms recommend completing the eight knot with a "Yosemite finish" (not shown).

Gyms with auto belays have a different setup that's mechanically foolproof. A locking carabiner is affixed to the end of the belay cable, so you need only clip the carabiner to your harness and then begin climbing. Sounds simple, right? Alarmingly, I've heard of climbers starting up the wall only to realize halfway up that they had forgotten to clip into the auto belay cable! Most gyms have an employee working as a wall monitor to check knots and keep an eye on the auto belays, but it's ultimately you, the climber, who's responsible for your own safety.

While these tie-in techniques are indeed simple and quick to perfect, there is obviously zero room for error. Accidents have occurred due to a botched knot or an unbuckled or misclipped harness. Make it a habit to inspect your connection to the rope before starting up every climb. Make *Double-check everything* your preclimb mantra.

Learning How to Belay

Roped climbing requires two people—a climber and a belayer—working in concert. As the climber ascends the wall, the belayer takes in or pays out the rope according to the climber's movement. And should the climber slip from the wall, it is the belayer who arrests the fall and lowers the climber back to the ground. Fortunately, there are specialized belay devices and techniques that make catching a fall a relatively easy endeavor.

Who Should Belay?

Belaying is a solemn duty of highest importance. It is not an activity for an immature or flighty person of any age, nor should kids under about the age of thirteen be permitted to belay. Each gym has its own rules as to who is allowed to belay and what is required to be "belay certified."

Ultimately, a climber must have complete faith in the belayer and the system—any doubts make it difficult to climb effectively or have much fun.

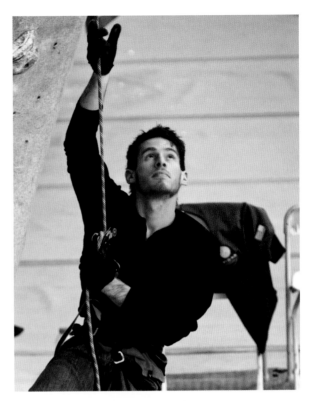

Belayer using a Grigri.
WADE DAVID

Select a belayer whom you can trust and forget about while climbing. Similarly, you should strive to be a focused, world-class belayer when it's your turn to hold the rope.

Belay Techniques

Proper belay technique is dependent on the type of belay equipment you use and whether the climber is ascending via top rope or leading. While there are several assisted-braking belay devices on the market (e.g., Petzl Grigri, Trango Vergo), most climbing gyms require you learn to belay with a passive device such as the ATC (Black Diamond Equipment) or the Reverso (Petzl). There's a strong consensus in the climbing gym industry that it's best for new climbers to learn proper belay technique

Belaying with a Passive Device

Ready Position. Brake hand grasping the rope just below the belay device. Upper hand ready to take in rope as the top rope climber moves upward.

Step 1. Pull. Your top hand pulls rope downward while your lower (brake) hand forcefully pulls rope through the belay device as the climber makes a move upward.

Step 2. Brake. Your bottom (brake) hand pulls strongly downward to lock the rope in the belay device. This is the position you must instantaneously assume when you see the climber slip or fall, and in situations when the climber requests a "take" in order to allow them to hang in place.

Step 3. Under. With the rope locked off by the brake hand, you now move your upper hand to firmly grip the rope just below the brake hand. (This is also the position you will utilize to lower the climber to the floor by regulating a slow, control release of the rope.)

Step 4. Slide. While maintaining a firm grip on the rope with the lower hand, you can now slide the brake hand up the rope to a position just below the belay device.

Return to the "Ready Position". Once the brake hand is firmly engaged you can return the other hand to climber's side of the rope to repeat this four-step process cycle.

with a passive belay device, and so I will limit my instruction to belaying with a passive device. (Note: Many intermediate to advanced sport climbers transition to using one of the assisted-braking belay devices—seek proper instruction if you consider making this transition.)

The photo sequence on pages 26 and 27 depicts the four action steps of top rope belaying—*pull, brake, under,* and *slide*—a process cycle that's repeated many times as the climber ascends the wall. Notice that the "brake hand" (the hand always gripping the rope below the belay device) never leaves the rope throughout this four-step belay process. Letting go with the brake hand for even an instant could have dire consequences—therefore, expect to be scolded or even lose your belay credentials if a gym employee observes you releasing the brake hand for even an instant!

When the climber completes the top rope ascent, you will assume the *brake* position (Step 2 photo) so that the climber can "take"—that is, be held in place atop the route. Next, bring your top

hand down to also grasp the rope in the under position (Step 3 photo). Keeping both hands engaged below the belay device, you can begin to slowly lower the climber by letting rope slide through your hands or by shuffling your hands below the belay device to direct a controlled release of the rope. Strive for a slow, steady descent rather than a jerky

Fundamental Rules of Belaying

1. Always keep your brake hand on the rope.

2. Only slide your hands when the rope is in the brake position.

3. Give your complete attention to the climber! Leave your phone in your backpack and politely dismiss anyone who tries to engage you with conversation.

or fast descent which can be scary and tempts losing control of the rope.

Make it your goal to become the best belayer in the climbing gym. You can achieve this by keeping your eyes fixed on the climber and anticipating their next move (or a potential fall). Conversely, you can quickly become one of the worst belayers in the gym by looking at your phone, having a conversation with a passerby, or, worst of all, taking your brake hand off the rope.

Not covered here is the belay technique and compounding factors of belaying a lead climber—this is a more challenging endeavor that you may not advance to for a year or more. Seek personal instruction from a qualified gym employee or AMGA certified guide. A good educational resource on the various belaying techniques is The American Alpine Club's YouTube Channel (search "AAC Universal Belay Standard").

Belay Commands

There is a unique "belay-speak" that facilitates unambiguous communication between the climber and her belayer. This is a universal language that you can use at any climbing gym in America to ensure a

Right—A toprope belay provided off the belayer's harness. Some gyms require the belayer or belay device to be anchored to the floor.
COURTESY OF NICROS, INC.

Table 3.1 *Common Belay Commands*

Speaker	Command	Meaning
Climber:	"Am I on belay?"	(Are you ready to belay me on this climb?)
Belayer:	"Belay on, climb when ready."	(Yes, the belay is ready; you may begin climbing.)
Climber:	"Climbing."	(I'm going to begin climbing now.)
Climber:	"Up rope."	(The toprope is hanging too loose, so please take some in.)
Climber:	"Slack."	(The rope system is too tight; please loosen it a little.)
Climber:	"Tension" or "Take!"	(Pull the rope tight and hold me here.)
Belayer:	"I've got you."	(I have the rope locked off—you are safe to hang on the rope.)
Climber:	"Watch me."	(I'm in a tenuous position, so please keep an alert belay.)
Climber:	"Clipping."	(I'm pulling the rope upward to clip an anchor bolt.)
Climber:	"Falling!"	(I'm coming off the wall—prepare to arrest the fall!)
Climber:	"Lower" or "Dirt me."	(I'm done climbing, so you can lower me to the ground.)
Climber:	"Off belay."	(I'm on the ground and done climbing, so you can take me off belay.)
Belayer:	"Belay off."	(I have taken you off belay.)

safe climbing experience. Here's a sample exchange between a climber and belayer.

Upon tying into the rope, the climber asks the belayer, "Am I on belay?" If the belayer has the rope threaded through his belay device and is ready to go, he responds, "Belay on; climb when ready." The climber then responds, "Okay, I'm climbing." As the climber moves up the wall, she will occasionally instruct the belayer regarding her rope-management needs. For instance, a "take" command tells the belayer to pull the rope tight, whereas "slack" asks for the rope to be loosened. The dialogue continues as needed until the climber returns to the ground and unties from the rope. To conclude, she instructs, "Take me off belay"; the belayer responds "Off belay" upon removing the rope from his belay device. See table 3.1 for a complete list of belay commands.

Catching Toprope Versus Lead Falls

Catching a falling lead climber and catching a falling climber on toprope are significantly different experiences. While the way in which the rope locks in your belay device is the same, the force generated in the two cases is vastly different. A toprope fall onto a snug rope induces very little force onto the belayer, whereas a 10-foot lead fall can pass on hundreds of pounds of force.

In the belay system, the belayer serves as a counterweight while catching a falling climber. Should the force generated by the falling climber exceed the weight of the belayer, then the belayer will be pulled off the ground. This rarely happens when toproping (unless the belayer's body weight is much lighter than the climber's), but it's the norm when catching a falling lead climber. Short lead falls may just pull you a step or two forward, while a larger lead fall may jerk you sharply forward or even lift you off the ground. This is only a concern should you collide with the falling climber or the climbing surface itself. In rare instances, belayers have been hurt in this way. Becoming a

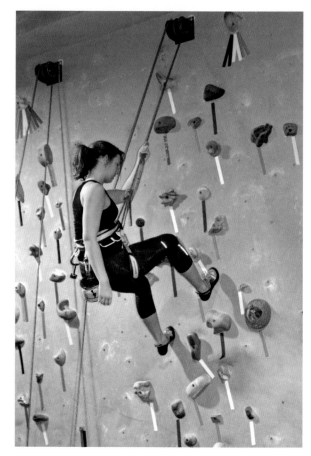

Lowering from a climb. Steady yourself by grabbing the rope (just above the knot) with one or two hands, sit back, and bend at the hips to form an L-position. Relax and walk down the wall while keeping your feet roughly level with your hips.

top-notch belayer of lead climbers—and providing a soft "catch" when the leader falls—is a skill that takes time to develop. With experience you'll develop a keen sense of when to take in and pay out rope; you'll also learn in which situations you can safely soften the leader's fall by stepping forward (or even making a small upward jump) when catching the fall.

Lowering Off a Route

Quite often you will climb a route to the top without falling onto the safety rope. Still, you will need the service of the rope to gain a ride back to the ground floor. For some beginners, lowering down a route is actually scarier than falling off the climb. This difference in fear factor is a function of the time you have to ponder the prospect of having to trust the rope—a fall happens in an instant, so there's little time to worry. Of course, any fears about the trustworthiness of the rope are unwarranted, given that the entire system is indeed bombproof.

In any case, upon topping the route you simply need to command the belayer to "take," at which time he will draw the rope snug. With your feet on good holds, ask the belayer to begin lowering you. As the rope initially begins to loosen, keep your feet on the holds and allow your rear end to drop down until your torso and legs form an L-position (with legs nearly straight and hips about level with your feet). As the rope continues to pay out, simply walk down the wall with your feet about shoulder-width apart and your body maintaining the L-position throughout. Soon enough your feet will be back on firm ground.

Safe Bouldering and Spotting

Spotting is to bouldering as belaying is to roped climbing. Both types of climbing have inherent risks, and it's the spotter's or belayer's job to help mitigate these risks for his partner.

In recent years bouldering has become exceedingly popular among indoor climbers. Bouldering

How to Become a World-Class Spotter

If you've ever participated in gymnastics, you're already familiar with the core demands on a spotter. If not, here are the solemn duties of a spotter and the techniques you need to learn to fulfill your duties!

1. **Fix your eyes on the boulderer's hips throughout the duration of the climb.** You can only provide an excellent spot if you can react quickly and apply force near the climber's center of gravity. It's a common mistake to watch the climber's hands or feet, instead of the hips—being a good spotter demands acute attention and resistance to distractions that may surround you.

2. **Keep the boulderer upright to prevent his head from hitting the floor.** This is paramount, and it is quite possibly the only thing you will be able to do in the rare case of a tumbling fall from a steep boulder problem. In this situation, you need to push forcefully on the boulderer's upper back near the shoulder blades or, possibly, grab under his armpits. Either way, you want to use the palm of your hands and not be shy about being forceful in your application of the spot. Executed properly, this technique slows downward movement of the head and shoulders just enough so that the feet reach the ground first.

3. **Help break the fall by absorbing some of the energy with your arms and legs.** Most often the boulderer will fall from a route feetfirst and in a relatively controlled manner. In these cases your primary duty is to serve as a shock absorber. The technique is simple: As the climber begins to drop, simply grab him at the hips and help slow his fall to the floor. Two important subtleties of this technique are to maintain a slight bend in your arms and legs (which allows your muscles to absorb more energy) and to keep your thumbs folded against the side of your hands (to prevent your thumb from getting hooked and bent backward).

is an excellent way to warm up and train for roped climbing, not to mention a terrific activity in and of itself. Hanging out in the gym's bouldering area and working some problems with friends can be great fun. But to participate in the good times, it's vital that you become a competent spotter.

There are two steps to effective spotting: determining and preparing the landing zone for a given problem, and the actual act of providing a trustworthy spot. Let's look at each.

Landing Zone and Crash Pads

Compared with the highly variable landing zones common to outdoor bouldering, the level base inherent to indoor climbing provides an excellent landing surface. Furthermore, most gyms have shock-absorbing flooring and copious crash pads in the bouldering area; this alone makes indoor bouldering vastly safer than doing it outdoors. Still, an unexpected fall onto a padded floor can be injurious. Thus it's best to boulder with a partner and take turns playing the roles of spotter and climber.

Working as a team, examine each boulder problem to determine the landing zone and best location for the spotter. Every problem is different, so visualize the fall line from different points on it. In the case of an overhanging problem, the landing zone will change as the climber ascends the wall. Make your best guess as to the footprint of the landing zone and position a couple of crash pads along this line. Of course, sometimes a best guess may be wrong, and a falling climber will surprisingly land off the edge of the pad. For this reason, it's vital to proceed with caution on the initial attempt on a problem. You might even consider climbing partway up and then cautiously jumping off to determine the exact landing spot.

In any case, it's your goal to position the crash pads so that the falling boulderer will land as near the center of a pad as possible. Many climbers have injured their ankles and knees because they landed on the edge of a crash pad or in the gap between pads. Another possible risk is landing on a foreign object lying in the landing zone. Common objects to watch out for are water bottles, street shoes, and backpacks—make sure the area is cleared of such objects.

A spotter is a boulderer's "belayer," so he must dedicate complete attention until the climber tops out or achieves a safe landing.

The Keys to Rapid Learning of Skills

What could be simpler than climbing? Watch kids swarming over playground equipment, and you will quickly recognize that climbing is as intuitive and natural as walking and running. In fact, it may be an inborn, primal need to climb that draws adults to a different sort of playground—the cliffs and climbing gyms of the world!

You will soon discover, however, that these adult playgrounds yield a remarkably complex and demanding activity. Consider that the climbing gyms and crags of the world offer a playing field of infinite variation, along with endless potential to discover and learn. Compound this with the adrenaline-releasing risks and perplexing challenges of ascending a steep wall, and you'll come to realize that climbing is indeed one of the most complex—and rewarding—forms of recreation.

Thus the goal of this chapter is to provide guidelines and expert tips for accelerating your learning of climbing skills. While the majority of new climbers stumble slowly through the maze of trial-and-error learning, you can take a more direct path to improvement by leveraging known strategies for improving climbing performance most rapidly. Following are nine powerful strategies that you can put to work beginning today.

Hire a Climbing Coach

The basic instruction you receive on your initial visit to a gym is but a first step in your long journey of learning to climb. The wealth of remaining knowledge is something you can try to discover on your own little by little—or you can hire a coach to tutor you on the critical skills and techniques. Sure, playing around on boulder problems and on a toprope is a fun and invaluable way to test skills and develop feel, but targeted, interactive instruction shifts learning into high gear.

Begin by taking a few of the optional classes your gym offers. Most gyms have several tiers of instruction, with each one- to two-hour class typically costing $20 to $50. In these sessions you'll learn much more about the subtleties of movement, mental preparation, and refining your skills as a belayer. Group classes are also a great way to meet other climbers of similar ability—you just might find a good training partner and climbing companion!

After a few months of climbing, your skills will advance beyond the level of typical "climbing 101" classes, so a personal coach is your new ticket to higher learning. Unlike the basic instruction provided in the group classes, a climbing coach will shape his lessons around your current skills and performance goals. For instance, he could help you learn very specific moves and tactics, or prepare you to test the waters of lead climbing. A good climbing coach can also develop an appropriate strength-training program to enhance your capabilities.

Given the pricey nature of hiring a climbing coach ($30 to $60 per hour), you might consider a modest commitment of one lesson per month. This way, the coach can observe your development on a more macro scale that makes it easier to spot the development of bad habits or poor technique. Such objective evaluation and a proactive approach to correcting weaknesses is part of the prescription for steady improvement and, ultimately, climbing excellence.

Warm Up Properly Before Every Climbing Session

Climbing is a rigorous activity that places unique strains on your body. For example, consider the way you lock onto small handholds and pull a large portion of your body weight on only a few fingertips. The acute strain placed on the tendons in your fingers and arms is unlike anything your body has likely experienced before. To compound matters, over the weeks and months ahead your muscles will grow stronger at a faster rate than will the tendons that connect them to the bones. This simple fact of human physiology is a primary reason so many climbers experience tendinitis in the fingers and elbows.

A thorough warm-up is a good first step in preventing such injuries. The resultant increase in blood flow and core temperature enhances muscular function and flexibility, and it may help make tendons and other connective tissues more resistant to strain. Furthermore, you will climb and feel noticeably better after a brief warm-up than you would just jumping on the wall stone cold. The bottom line: Warm up before you go vertical.

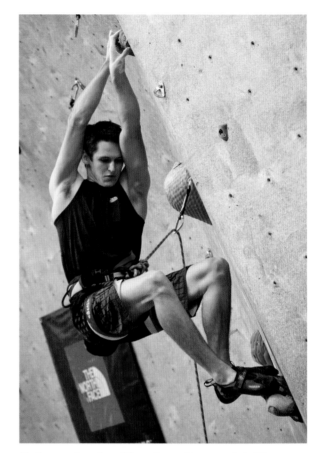

Strive to develop "foot focus" . . . and deliberately set your foot on the best part of each hold.
WADE DAVID

The perfect warm-up would begin with a few minutes of light aerobic activity. The goal is to do just enough to produce a light sweat, but not so much that it tires you out. A few possibilities would be going for a short jog, riding a stationary bike (found in some gyms), or at the least doing fifty jumping jacks. Next, perform some gentle stretching of the forearms, shoulders, torso, and legs (see chapter 9 for details). Complete your warm-up with a nonmaximal single set of push-ups, pull-ups, and abdominal crunches. This will bring your muscles to a simmer, and you'll be ready to rock!

Focus on Developing Technique and Mental Skills over Muscular Strength

Struggling on a climb almost always produces a muscular pump, so the seemingly obvious conclusion is that you were not strong enough to do the route. In climbing, however, things are not always what they seem.

The fact is that pumped muscles (and failure) most commonly result from improper sequences of moves, poor technique, and mental anxiety. Inefficiencies in these subtle areas multiply physical exertion and accelerate energy use in a way that induces premature failure of the muscles, most commonly in the arms. Thus it's important to view deficiencies in the areas of technique and mental control as a deadweight you are hauling up the climbing wall. Given this paradigm, do you think it would be best to engage in strength training (so you can continue to haul this extra weight around)—or to improve your mental and technical skills so as to permanently eliminate this weighty baggage? Hopefully, you agree that the latter approach is more intelligent, especially given that you can improve technique faster than you can strengthen your muscles.

Make refining technique and mental control the hallmark of your climbing gym workouts. When you fail on a climb, ask yourself, *How can I climb this route more efficiently?* not *How can I get stronger?* During your initial months your upper-body muscles will naturally adapt to the stresses of climbing and grow stronger simply by climbing a few days per week. There's really no need for a large commitment of time to strength-training exercises. Instead, invest your gym time on learning new moves, conquering your fears, and developing smooth, fluid technique. Strive to climb like a fuel-efficient Honda, not a gas-hogging Hummer, and you'll soon be tearing up the walls!

Model Advanced Climbers to Learn New Techniques and Tactics

An excellent way to learn new skills is to mimic the movements and tactics of more advanced climbers. This learning strategy, known as modeling, is highly effective for opening your eyes to new body positions and techniques that you might not discover on your own. One caveat to modeling, however, is that you must always practice the new move on a route of your ability, not on the route the advanced climber was on.

Here are some specific things to model from a more advanced climber: How did she prepare for her ascent? What did she do to warm up and how did she scope the route before beginning to climb? How fast did she move on the route, and how did her pace vary with the steepness of the climb or size of the holds? What unusual body positions did she use? How often did she stop to chalk up, shake out, or catch a rest? If she hit a sticking point on the route, how did she work the problem moves and how long did she spend on this crux before calling it quits (if, by chance, she couldn't solve the move)? All of these are actions you can test out on a climb of your own ability. Use what works, and modify or discard what doesn't.

It's important to point out a few things you should not model from advanced climbers. First and foremost, do not try to mimic their training routines. Experienced climbers possess muscle and tendon strength that takes years to develop, so attempting to copy their training program may get you hurt. Similarly, don't attempt the severe routes or sheer volume of climbing performed by these elites—this would hamper learning and might even lead to poor technique and bad habits of movement.

One thing you will quickly come to appreciate is beta, a verbal explanation of a specific move or crux sequence. In the sometimes festive gym environment, it's not uncommon to have one or more people providing (maybe even yelling) beta as you are in the midst of a climb. In the earliest stages of learning, beta can indeed be quite helpful, because it helps you see critical holds and unlock complex sequences that you might never figure out on your own. It's best, however, if you have just a single person—your belayer or climbing coach—providing beta; overlapping or conflicting beta will only confuse you. Of course, it's also important to experiment with moves that differ from the beta you receive—you just might find a better way.

As your technical ability improves, you must shift to a more autonomous approach to working routes. While beta might help you solve a crux more quickly, it does shortcut the learning process. Remind yourself that learning to problem solve on the fly is a big part of becoming a better climber. Therefore, you will gradually need to begin saying no to beta. Make your intentions known to your belayer and others around you; if you don't want beta, express this in no uncertain terms before you leave the ground.

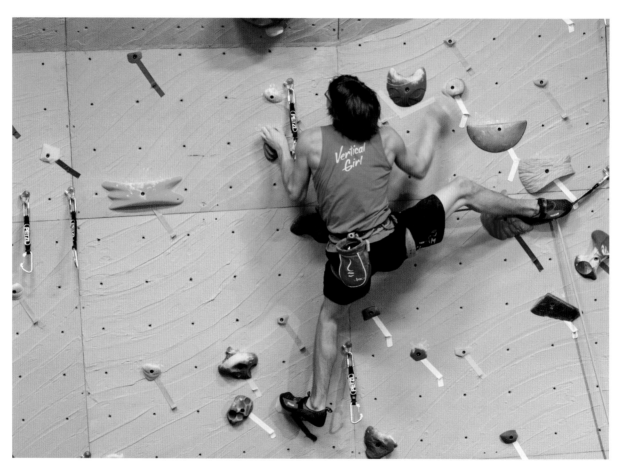

Modeling the techniques and tactics of advanced climbers, such as the use of the heels on steeper routes, is a powerful learning method.
ROBERT SCOVERSKI

Embrace a Practice Perspective and Resolve to Always Have Fun

We get into climbing because it's an enjoyable activity that diverts attention from the serious or stressful aspects of daily life. Ironically, some climbers gradually come to take climbing too seriously. They create a self-imposed pressure to perform that generates stress and anxiety—and ultimately ruins the fun of climbing.

As a wide-eyed beginning climber excited at the prospect of simply playing around on the walls, you may find it hard to believe that climbing could ever not be fun. Well, just look around the gym and you'll likely observe a couple of climbers (or more) losing their cool when they fall from a boulder problem or climb. Sure, it's natural to be disappointed and frustrated when you fail on a route, but to throw a tantrum or spew expletives as some climbers do is a sure sign they are taking the activity too seriously. Interestingly, the more pressure you place on yourself to climb well, the more difficult it becomes to think and climb proficiently. Another great paradox of climbing is that it's easier to climb harder by not needing to!

The same goes for the process of learning to climb. Optimal learning of skills comes when you embrace a carefree practice perspective, as opposed to a more serious performance perspective. The neuromuscular system is most effective at coding new motor programs when you are in a fresh, relaxed state. As fatigue and tension grow, it's harder to either learn new skills or perform up to your current ability.

Another vital distinction for effective learning is that you must strive to perfect technical movements, not just get by with them. This is true regardless of the difficulty of the climb you are on, but it's most important when climbing near your limit. The common approach is to call an ascent successful when you solve the crux and successfully ascend the route from bottom to top without falling. In doing this redpoint ascent, you might struggle and fight through the hardest moves—a good mental success—but with less-than-perfect technique. Becoming an outstanding technical climber, however, comes only by means of a constant resolve to master every sequence with perfect economy. This goal may take a few more attempts or even a few more days to achieve, but in striving to meet this high technical standard, you will develop true climbing excellence.

Finally, make it a goal to foster a constant self-awareness of your changing mental and physical state throughout your climbing gym workout. Strive to break new ground—technically and mentally—during the first part of your session when you are feeling fresh. When you sense a growing level of fatigue or frustration, it's time to redirect your efforts to another climb more within your capabilities. The bottom line: Resolve to always have fun, regardless of the quality of your climbing on a given day, and you'll maintain the requisite disposition for developing uncommon ability.

Strive to Become a Self-Aware Climber with an Acute Proprioceptive Sense

One of the most overlooked keys (some might even call it a "secret") to rapid improvement is to make it a kind of personal obsession to develop a high level of self-awareness while climbing. No matter if you are ascending a 10-foot boulder problem or a 50-foot lead wall, one of your most important tasks—one ignored by many climbers—is to monitor your climbing technique and efficiency of movement. This is critical because it's the aggregate of minor inefficiencies and slight flaws in technique that prevents you from doing climbs beyond your current limit. The evidence is played out at gyms and crags across the country, and I'm sure you can observe it at your gym's bouldering area right now! It'll look something like this.

Tune into your body's proprioceptive feedback and learn to really "feel" each move. Strive to gain an acute sense of the location of your center of gravity and the various levels of tension or relaxation in your muscles during difficult moves.

A group of climbers are working a route whose crux sequence has one best solution. Each climber attempts the same sequence, but only one person succeeds. Why does the sequence work for one person but not the others? In many cases the answer lies in a number of minor technical flaws that are unknowingly sabotaging performances. These flaws may include climbing too slowly, undue tension in antagonistic muscles, sloppy foot placements, less-than-optimal body positioning, overgripping holds,

and the mental weight of doubt and fear. The key to nixing these problems is self-awareness—never-ending checks and rechecks of the goings-on in your mind and body, followed by tiny adjustments. More advanced climbers do this many times throughout an ascent, whereas beginners may never do it because they are overwhelmed by fearful thoughts or an obsession to pull through to the next hold.

Make a conscious effort to foster high self-awareness now (rather than later), and it will empower you to identify and eliminate many bad habits of movement, making way for steady long-term improvement. Remember, just as climbing skills become hardwired into the brain after a few repetitions, so do bad habits such as overgripping handholds, excessive body tension, imprecise and sloppy footwork, and so forth.

A more subtle, yet vitally important, type of self-awareness is the physical awareness of your body's "feel" and movement in space, called **proprioception.** No matter what you do physically, proprioceptive data from the sensory receptors in your muscles, tendons, joints, and inner ear is available for you to use to determine your effectiveness and quality of movement. This vast amount of sensory feedback from the limbs and inner ear is processed unconsciously in doing simple tasks such as walking, cranking pull-ups, or dancing up an easy climb that requires little thought. More complex tasks (like climbing), however, require conscious attention to proprioception.

Awareness of specific aspects of proprioception, or what I call proprioceptive cues, varies on a continuum from extremely coarse and general on one end to exquisitely subtle and well defined on the other. As a beginning climber you will initially possess a coarse, limited sense of internal feeling as you climb. For example, you may sense the basic quality of a foot placement, whether you are in balance, and, most obvious, how pumped you are getting. This most basic proprioception is important, but it represents just a tiny fraction of the broad bandwidth of proprioceptive cues that you can learn to perceive and leverage. With more experience and a determination to grow your awareness of proprioceptive cues, you will be able to recognize a steady stream of valuable movement cues from your body's internal sense organs.

Becoming an intermediate or advanced climber, therefore, will correlate to your deepening sense of proprioception in a wide variety of climbing situations. Each wall angle, type of climbing, body position, and type of move provides unique proprioceptive feedback that you must learn to interpret in order to move with fluidity and high efficiency. Much of this proprioception (and the subsequent physical adjustments) occurs subconsciously when you are climbing submaximal sequences. Crux movements and many novel moves, however, demand full attention to proprioception, thus leaving little remaining cognitive focus for other purposes. Many falls off crux moves that you have rehearsed and know well—or off easier moves when on-sighting—are the result of poor attention to proprioceptive cues.

Ultimately, the more subtle the level of proprioception that you can perceive, the better you will be able to climb given your current skill level and physical abilities. Becoming a smooth, efficient climber of advanced ability, therefore, demands that you develop your self-awareness and use of proprioceptive cues. You can best do this by regularly directing your focus inward to tune into the "feel" of doing a move or sequence rather than letting your attention be consumed by a constant outwardly directed where's-the-next-hold focus (a common affliction among "average" climbers).

Regularly Experiment with New Techniques and on New Terrain

Most climbing gyms possess a wide range of wall terrain, and the person serious about learning to climb should commit to exploring every square foot of this climbing surface. In the earliest stage of learning, you'll obviously need to practice on the lower-graded, nonimposing sections of wall until you develop some of the basic skills. As your confidence and ability increase, however, you must gradually progress to the more novel, daunting features such as arêtes, overhangs, cracks, and steep faces. Continued technical growth comes only when you consciously push yourself onto foreign and uncomfortable-feeling sections of wall.

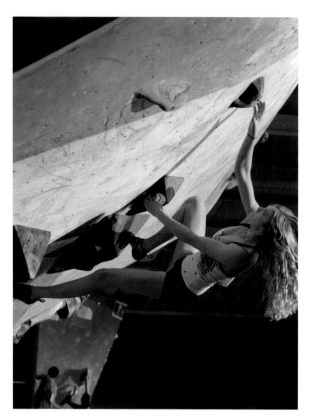

Regularly test yourself on new terrain to expand your abilities.

TAYLOR CLARKIN COLLECTION

Consider that climbing is a highly complex sport with an infinite variety of moves and crux situations. Mastery comes only to those who pursue the long-term goal of doing it all. That means gradually exposing yourself to every wall feature a gym has to offer, and eventually traveling to different gyms and maybe outdoor crags to expand your learning even further. In a technical sense, climbing is similar to golf—both sports require many years to develop a high level of competence, because both have playing fields of infinite variety. Thus becoming excellent at either sport is not something that just happens—it's something that happens by way of intelligent, disciplined practice in a wide range of settings.

Push Yourself, But Know When to Call It a Day

Just as it's important to explore new terrain, it's also fundamental to regularly push the boundaries of what you feel is possible. Given the YDS and V-Scale grading used at most gyms, this is a strategy that's fairly easy to execute. Here are some guidelines to testing the waters of more difficult climbing.

During your first few weeks of climbing, you'll come to understand the YDS scale as well as gain a sense of your current level of climbing. While your first day at the gym may be spent learning the basics on a beginners' section of wall (which may not have YDS grades), you'll no doubt venture onto other routes during subsequent visits. Most beginners quickly gain comfort in ascending routes graded between 5.5 and 5.9. Let's assume, for example, that 5.9-rated routes are the highest level you can successfully climb bottom-to-top without falling. My rule is that you should spend 70 percent of your climbing time on routes between your limit and two grades below your limit. In this case you'd spend most of your time practicing on routes rated between 5.7 and 5.9. The other 30 percent of your session should be spent on routes up to one full grade above your maximum ability; in this case you'd want to work on one or two 5.10 routes.

Climbing a route more than two grades below your limit is useful as a warm-up, but not for advancing your technical abilities. Similarly, flogging yourself on a climb more than a number grade beyond your limit is generally not productive. It might also be demoralizing and tempt injury.

The best plan is to break a climbing session into three parts. Begin by warming up on several routes that are two or more number grades below your limit. Strive to develop rhythm and smooth movement. Next, get on a couple of routes that are at or just above your limit. The goal here isn't necessarily to succeed on the routes—though it would be great

The Keys to Rapid Learning of Skills

1. **Hire a climbing coach.** Obtain the objective evaluation and sage guidance of a climbing coach to get on the fast track to climbing excellence. Even just one session per month will be extremely beneficial.

2. **Warm up properly before every climbing session.** Perform a progressive warm-up to reduce injury risk and modulate your neuromuscular system for optimal learning and performance. Spend twenty to thirty minutes on easy climbs and doing various warm-up activities.

3. **Focus on developing technique and mental skills over muscular strength.** Refining movement and mental skills is the shortest pathway to climbing stronger. Invest most of your gym time on climbing, not strength training.

4. **Model advanced climbers to learn new techniques and tactics.** Stretch your imagination for climbing movement and strategy by observing and mimicking the techniques and tactics of top climbers.

5. **Embrace a practice perspective and resolve to always have fun.** Optimize learning of new skills by maintaining a curious, carefree disposition and having fun regardless of climbing outcomes.

6. **Make it your mission to develop a high level of self-awareness.** Tune into your body's proprioceptive feedback and learn to really "feel" each move, including the quality of your contact with the holds, the location of your center of gravity, and the various levels of tension or relaxation in your muscles. Use this information to discover the most efficient way to do each sequence.

7. **Regularly experiment with new techniques and on new terrain.** Challenge yourself on a wide range of wall features to expand your skill set and develop confidence. Avoid the rut of always climbing known routes and training in the same familiar ways.

8. **Push yourself, but know when to call it a day.** Spend about one-third of your climbing time on routes just beyond your limit to effectively stretch your boundaries. However, focus the majority of your practice on routes just below your limit to fortify skills and confidence.

9. **Get on a regular climbing schedule.** Climb two to four days per week (never more) to maximize learning and improvement. Only disciplined, regular practice over the long term will yield consistent improvement and climbing excellence.

if you did!—but instead to stretch your boundaries and gain exposure to new moves and situations. Finally, spend the last third of your session on routes that are roughly a number grade below your limit. Your goal is to reinforce control and poise while elevating confidence with a few solid, no-falls ascents.

Follow this plan long-term and you will obtain uncommonly good results. Many climbers do not operate in accordance to this training principle, as they spend most of their time climbing—or, more correctly, flailing—on routes way over their head. While they may occasionally beat a route into submission, there's little learning going on. In fact, I've seen climbers behave this way for years, and many end up getting injured or simply burned out on climbing. The best approach is to gain a high win-to-loss ratio: Spend most of your time winning on routes close to your maximum ability, with only limited exposure to testing the waters of the next higher grade.

Get on a Regular Climbing Schedule

As in learning any skill sport, you need to engage in a regular schedule of climbing in order to realize gains in ability. Consider climbing once or twice per week the minimum commitment if you want to improve. Climbing less frequently can still be great fun, although you will see little improvement.

If you are serious about improving, you can maximize learning by practicing your climbing three or four days per week. Enthusiastic individuals may ponder going to the gym more than four days per week—this is not wise! While you can play golf or, say, practice the piano seven days per week, it's a flawed and dangerous practice strategy to apply to climbing. Climbing is an uncommonly rigorous activity that requires copious rest for the neuromuscular system to recover and **supercompensate** to greater capability. The bottom line: Climbing too frequently is the ultimate bad investment in terms of developing skill, since you will eventually succumb to overtraining syndrome, a plateau in performance, and quite possibly injury.

A good two-day-per-week practice schedule is to climb once during the midweek (say, Wednesday) and then one day over the weekend. The most popular routine among gym climbers may be the three-day-per-week schedule of climbing on Tuesday, Thursday, and Saturday. This can be upgraded to a four-day-per-week program by adding a Sunday session as well. However, you do not want to climb on more than two consecutive days—another common pathway to **overtraining** and injury.

How long should you climb on a given day? Your goal for actual time on the wall should be thirty to sixty minutes. Obviously you'll take many breaks between climbs (resting, socializing, and belaying), so you may only log about fifteen to twenty minutes of climbing per hour in the gym. Given this ratio, you need to plan on two to three hours at the gym in order to accomplish an effective workout.

Basic Skills and Drills

This is where the rubber meets the road—or, more correctly, where your shoe rubber and fingertips meet the rock.

Almost all climbing movement results via the four points of contact that your hands and feet afford, and thus nothing is more fundamental for effective climbing technique than the ways in which you engage the rock with your fingers and toes. A wise beginning climber will learn and make habits of optimal hand and foot contact early on, or risk developing poor techniques that could stunt improvement for years to come. Same goes for your body positions and methods of movement, the quality of which directly affects your energy consumption and apparent strength on the rock. Therefore, the following pages of instruction on basic skills and drills are as important and powerful as any other portion of this book. Don't skip over this material because of its seemingly basic content.

Four Points of Contact

There are countless ways in which your hands and feet can make contact with our infinitely varying playing field. However, the majority of finger grips and foot placements you execute will be but slight variations on a more finite number of basic methods of contact.

Detailed below are the six most common finger-grip techniques and the five basic arm positions you will utilize in leveraging off a handhold.

Following this you will learn the four most common methods for securely positioning your feet on holds of any shape or size.

It's important to recognize that the hand and foot positions covered in this chapter are the staple techniques of face climbing. There's a completely separate class of hand and foot placements used for climbing crack; these involve inserting and **jamming** your appendages into a vertical fissure in the wall. Given that crack climbs are a rarity at climbing gyms, it's not essential that you learn the jamming techniques at this time. Chapter 11 does provide a primer on crack climbing since you will eventually want to expand your skill base to cover all novel types of climbing.

Finger Grips

The basic finger-grip positions are full crimp, half crimp, open hand, pocket, pinch, and palm. You will find some of these grips to be more intuitive and comfortable to use than others. Many climbers simply use the comfortable grip positions and ignore the rest—do not fall into this trap! As you execute the drills presented later in the chapter, strive to regularly practice each grip position. In doing so, neuromuscular adaptations will gradually make you stronger and more comfortable in using all the grips. It's this kind of attention to the subtle details of effective practice that will pay huge dividends in ability in the months and years to come.

ROBERT SCOVERSKI

Basic Finger Grips

Full-crimp grip

Half-crimp grip

Open-hand grip

Pocket grip

Pinch grip

Palm or friction grip

FULL CRIMP

The full crimp is favored by many climbers since it provides what feels like the most secure lock onto small handholds. The hallmark of the full crimp is the hyperextension of the first joint of each finger and the sharp flexion of the second finger joint. The full-crimp grip is then secured by locking your thumb over the end of the index finger.

Unfortunately, this grip position places the highest force load on the joints and tendons, and overuse can result in nagging finger injuries. While it is absolutely necessary to use and train the crimp grip, the best approach would be to limit it to holds that cannot effectively be gripped any other way. The full-crimp grip excels on small, square-cut edges, shallow flakes, and any hold that possesses a small incut or recessed edge.

HALF CRIMP

The half-crimp grip is just a variation on the full crimp in which you do not thumb-lock over the index finger. This reduces slightly the aggressive angles on the first and second joints of the finger, thus making the grip a bit more ergonomic. The trade-off is that the half crimp often feels less secure than the full crimp, although you can develop strength and comfort in the half crimp through regular use.

Once again, it's important to use the practice drills to experiment with the half-crimp grip. Initially it's a good practice to compare the full- and half-crimp grips on a given hold. Which feels more secure? Can you use the half crimp even though it might feel less secure than the full crimp? If so, use the half crimp, and save the full crimp only for holds that absolutely demand its use.

OPEN HAND

The open-hand grip, also known as the extended grip, has distinct advantages over the crimp grip. First, the open-hand position is kinder to the finger tendons and joints since it softens the joint angles and may allow the rock to provide some tendon support (as your fingers wrap naturally over a curved hold). Furthermore, despite its frequently less secure feel, the open-hand position can be trained to become your strongest grip position on all but small, incut holds (which require a crimp grip). Use this knowledge to fuel diligent practice, and you will gradually develop amazing open-hand grip strength. Make the open-hand position your first choice on all medium to large handholds with smooth, rounded features.

POCKET

Pocket holds are exceedingly common on indoor climbs, and they are quite often part of the recipe for a frustrating crux sequence. Pockets can range in size from a small dimple barely big enough to fit a single fingertip to a large hole in which you can stuff all four fingers. Of course, it's the little pockets that fit only one or two fingertips that are most disconcerting. Fortunately, regular practice will increase your strength and confidence in being able to hang on to even the smallest pocket hold.

A subtle but important difference in how you grip pocket holds relates to whether the fingers used are clinging to the pocket via an open-hand (extended-finger) position or with more finger flexion, as in the half-crimp grip discussed earlier. As a rule, the depth and sharpness of the pocket will be the determining factors. For instance, if a pocket is shallow and possesses a sharp edge, you'll almost always want to grip it with your fingers in a half-crimp position. A deeper, more rounded pocket will generally feel better with your fingers in the open-hand position.

Finally, there's the matter of which fingers to insert into pockets too small to fit all four. Pockets that only fit two fingers, commonly called two-finger pockets, are most securely gripped with the index and middle fingers or the middle and ring fingers. The ever-scary one-finger pocket is best avoided—but if you must, the middle finger tends to work best. Comparatively, the pinkie is a wimp in terms of strength; however, it is useful when it can be stuffed into a small three-finger pocket along with the middle and ring fingers. A large three-finger pocket can best be gripped with the index, middle, and ring fingers working as a powerful team.

PINCH

The pinch grip is vital for grasping protruding holds such as pebbles, ribs, "bread-loaf" holds, or opposing edges. Due to the protruding nature of indoor climbing holds, use of the pinch grip is far more common indoors than on natural rock faces.

The good news is that our hands were designed to excel at pinching motions. Difficulties in using this grip tend to relate more to the smoothness or shallowness of the gripping surface—as always, there are many possible shapes, ranging from a small, shallow pencil-size rib to a giant bread-loaf blob. Like all the other grips, strength at pinching holds is specific and requires regular practice. You can best increase strength in this slippery grip by seeking out and working on boulder problems possessing a variety of pinch holds.

PALM/FRICTION

This final grip is hardly a grip at all, since your point of contact is simply the friction created by pressing or wrapping your palm over the rock surface. Although the palming technique isn't needed for the typical beginner-level climb, it is extremely valuable when attempting more complex routes that feature corners, arêtes, or large featureless holds. The bottom line: While the positive grip provided by all the other grips will almost always exceed that of the palm grip, you still need to have the palm grip in your bag of tricks as you advance to more difficult climbs.

Arm Positions

Regardless of how you grip the rock, it's the arms that utilize this point of contact to create torque, leverage, and upward movement. Therefore, it's vital to distinguish between grip position—the point of contact—and arm position, which connects this point of contact to your torso. You will soon discover that you'll be using your arms in countless different ways and directions, yet every arm position is but a slight variant on one of five basic positions: the down pull, the **mantle,** the **undercling,** the side pull, and the reverse side pull or **Gaston.**

It's important to recognize that each arm position places your hand in a different orientation with respect to your center of gravity. In viewing the photos, note how the different arm positions place the palm—and therefore the application of force—facing either downward, upward, inward, or outward. Which arm position you choose for any given move will be determined by whether the role of the arms is to provide balance, locomotion, or both. Initially, you'll need to make this determination through sometimes clumsy experimentation. With practice, however, you will rapidly develop the ability to intuit the proper arm position for almost any novel move.

DOWN PULL

The down pull is by far the most common arm position used in climbing, as it's the arm position you would use in climbing hand-over-hand up a ladder. With each grip on the rock, the arm begins in a position above your head with the palm facing the rock. From this starting position you can either hang straight-armed in a static rest position or you can pull downward to aid in upward movement. When used to aid in locomotion, the down-pulling arm often concludes its work in the lock-off position typified by the arm bent at an acute angle with the elbow pointing downward and your hand pulled in tight against the side of your chest. This

Basic Arm Positions

Down pull

Mantle (left hand)

Undercling (right hand)

Side pull

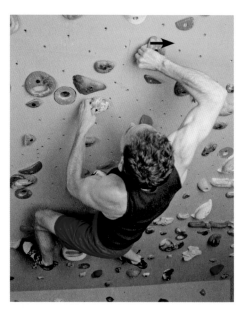

Gaston (right hand)

range of motion from the above-the-head, straight-armed position to hand-against-chest lock-off is the single most fundamental arm movement in climbing. Consequently, your strength and endurance at this pulling motion will increase simply by climbing a few days per week.

MANTLE

The mantle, or press-down, position is essentially the opposite of the down-pull position in that your arm begins in a bent position near your torso and then pushes palm-downward. An ordinary-life use of mantling is the simple act of pushing yourself out of the water at the edge of a swimming pool—both hands contact the edge of the pool palms-downward as they push down from near your chest to below your waist. In climbing, the mantle move is significantly more difficult, since there's no water to provide the lightening effect of buoyancy. Furthermore, in climbing it is rare to come upon a large, flat surface on which to mantle (except when you arrive at a ledge or the top of a boulder problem). Instead, you will often need to mantle on the top of a large handhold, a shallow edge, a pocket, or in extreme cases even press down with only your thumb resting on the top edge of a hold.

UNDERCLING

An inverted, downward-facing handhold demands gripping the usable surface palm-up while contracting the arm muscles with the arm bent in an elbow-down or elbow-back position. Your palm-up contact with the handhold is usually a half-crimp, open-hand, or pinch grip. Underclinging a hold above your head is a difficult feat that provides little more than balance; leverage increases exponentially, however, as the handhold nears your center of gravity. Therefore, the most common use of this arm position is to utilize a downward-facing handhold located somewhere near your torso. What's more, combining this undercling with an opposing foot placement makes for a winning combination that's both stable and powerful.

SIDE PULL

The more difficult a climb, the more likely it becomes that you'll need to use side-pull arm positions. As the name implies, this position involves grabbing a hold that faces sideways and away from your body, not upward or downward. As in the down-pull and undercling arm positions, you can execute a side pull by grasping a handhold using just about any grip position. The primary difference is the lack of locomotion that you can create by simply pulling with your arm in a side-pull position. Consequently, the side-pull arm position is less intuitive and more technical to use effectively.

Although you will come to use side pulls in a wide range of body positions, the most common is to grab an outward-facing hold somewhere off to the side of your body and then pull inward to gain leverage and balance. A side pull can also be used in pairs, with both the right and left arms pulling inward toward the torso. This is a method of attaining balance when the rock is void of upward- or downward-facing edges, but you'll need your feet to provide locomotion from this body position. This leads us to the important idea that the hands and feet must work together in unison—this is, in fact, a fundamental concept, and it's something we'll look at later in the chapter.

REVERSE SIDE PULL OR GASTON

The reverse side pull, also known as a Gaston, is a more difficult arm position used on inward-facing holds located near your body. The Gaston position is typified by a bent-armed, elbow-out position with the hand gripping the hold thumb-down. Force is applied in a sideways pull away from your body—the arm position is similar to that of grabbing the edge of a sliding door (in front of your face) that you intend to fling open. Of course, it's also possible to use opposing Gaston holds such that both hands are positioned thumbs-down in front of your face as if getting ready to separate two window curtains.

Most people are naturally stronger and more comfortable using a standard side pull, where you grab a hold off to the left or right and pull inward toward your body. However, the more difficult reverse side pull must be used on many side-facing edges that are located in front of your body. For instance, imagine a left-facing vertical edge in front of your face. The best use of this hold would often be to grab it with your right hand (thumb-down) and pull outward to the right. This is the classic Gaston technique.

As with the side-pull arm position described earlier, it's next to impossible to glean upward movement exclusively from the Gaston. Gaston arm positions are most commonly used for balance or to help maintain a static body position as you advance a foot placement, although they can also be used for upward motion when combined with pressing of the opposite foot.

Foot Positions

You have four points of contact while climbing, and it is vital that you make the most of each. The hand contact points just discussed will be easy to learn and experiment with, especially given the close proximity of the handholds to your eyes. You can inspect each handhold close-up and determine exactly the best way to grab it. This, unfortunately, is not the case with foot placements. Trying to optimally stick the edge of your shoe to a small nubbin several feet from your eyes can be surprisingly difficult. And to make matters worse, "feel" with your feet is greatly diminished due the layer of rubber and leather that separates your feet from the holds.

Consequently, developing solid footwork demands pinpoint focus and lots of deliberate practice. The goal is to place each foot in a way that maximizes the area of contact between the shoe rubber and rock, while also placing your foot in a stable position that doesn't shift as you stand up on it. Ultimately, lots of real-life experience on the walls is the only way to develop such feel skills. You

will want to experiment with the four basic foot positions described below and assess how the security of each varies with the shape and size of different footholds. You will find that certain footholds demand use of a specific foot position, whereas other times it will be your body position or direction of movement that determines how to best place your foot on the hold.

TOE-IN (AKA FRONT-POINTING)

The toe-in foot placement is the same one you'd use to position your foot in climbing a stepladder. The front part of your shoe is contacting the foothold while your heel extends straight out from the wall. This style of foot placement is indeed most natural to the novice climber, but it is rarely the optimal method when climbing. In standing toe-in on a hold, your foot becomes a long lever; this requires significant calf muscle strength to maintain. Below you'll learn how using the inside or outside edge of your shoe reduces the lever length of your foot, and also brings the best part of the climbing shoe—and more rubber—into play.

Pockets and other recessed holds are the one situation where the toe-in foot position excels. You can gain the best purchase inside a pocket if you simply stick the tip of your shoe straight into the hole. Some asymmetric-style climbing shoes possess a more notable point at the big toe and thus provide an even more secure placement on pockets.

EDGING

The most secure foot placements usually come from positioning the inside or outside edge of your shoe on the top edge of a foothold. Although every foothold—and therefore foot placement—will be different, the goal is to maximize the area of contact between the edge of your climbing shoe and the hold. With the more common inside-edging, you'll want to utilize the sharp rubber edge that runs from the ball of your foot to the end of the big toe. Climbing shoes are designed to provide tremendous

Basic Foot Positions

Toe-in or pocket

Inside edging

Outside edging

Smearing

Rest step

Foot-stack rest step

support and feel through this area, and you'll soon learn to use this portion of your shoe like a finely tuned instrument.

Outside-edging is a less instinctive yet still vital foot technique, especially on tricky moves with the holds spaced far apart. In these situations you can increase reach and stability by turning your foot inward and placing the outside edge of your shoe on the foothold. There is a definite sweet spot on the outside edge of your shoe—usually near the side edge of your little toe—that can provide excellent purchase in some difficult situations. Experimentation and practice will eventually yield an instant sense of how to best use your outside edge on any given climbing hold.

Two rules of effective edging relate to the stability and angle of foot placement. First, keep your foot steady on the foothold throughout its use. Readjusting or shifting your foot in the slightest way may cause the shoe to pop off the edge. This underscores the importance of precise foot placement from the get-go. Paste the shoe rubber on the edge, then stand on it with no doubts or foot wobble. Second, since not all footholds possess horizontal surfaces to stand on, you need to try to match the angle of your shoe edge to the angle of the hold in order to maximize contact area. For example, an edge that angles downward toward the centerline of your body is best used by lowering your heel and trying to match the inside edge of the shoe to the angle of the hold.

As a final tip, strive to develop a sense of foot feel with every step you take. As a true novice, you may have no idea what I'm talking about; you will, however, gradually develop a heightened awareness of foot-placement quality. You can develop this important sense most rapidly with focused practice of footwork, either on toprope or while bouldering. Try to feel each hold as you engage it—is your foot seated on the best part of the hold?—and then apply weight to the hold by shifting your center of gravity toward the foothold. Strive to maintain a steady foot position as you shift weight onto the foot—movement of the ankle joint, or repositioning the foot while under weight, may cause it to slip off the hold.

SMEARING

Many climbing holds lack crisp, distinct edges on which to place your feet, and thus present you with the challenge of standing on a rounded, sloping surface. Use of the smearing technique will usually provide a secure point of contact, although the act of smearing is more subtle and heady than edging.

The name *smearing* describes the process of using the shoe sole to smear onto the surface of the foothold. Smearing is all about maximizing friction between the sole of the shoe and the hold. Depending on the angle of the climbing wall and the size of the hold, you may need to smear with your foot turned inward, outward, or in the toe-in position. No matter which orientation you use, it's vital to bend at the ankle in order to place as much of the shoe sole on the hold as possible. More rubber contact means more friction and less chance of slippage.

As in edging, effective smearing comes only with an acute sense of feel and attention to each placement. View each foothold as unique, and determine the ideal place to smear for maximum security. Some footholds possess a few different surfaces on which to smear, so you'll need to make a quick assessment of which spot looks most promising. Consider the texture of the surface and whether there is an irregularity or rugosity that might dig into the shoe rubber and provide more grip. As you step onto the smear, do so with confidence and a firm pressing feeling. Many climbers do the exact opposite—and their doubt in the smear and tentative placement often result in slipping or skidding feet.

The climbing shoes you choose to wear also play a role in how well you can smear on a hold. Flexible slipper-style shoes tend to smear better since they will conform to the surface of sloping holds as well as provide superior feel. Smearing with stiff-soled shoes is far more challenging and will likely lead to a higher frequency of foot slips.

REST STEP

In learning to climb you will surely be surprised by how much foot and calf-muscle strength is required to stand on small footholds. You will discover first-hand that standing on a particular foothold too long will pump out the calf muscles of your lower leg and possibly lead to shaky leg (aka sewing-machine or Elvis leg). To help prevent the pump, it is important to regularly utilize the rest step.

The rest step can be performed on most any medium to large hold on a slab or vertical route (although it's of little use on overhanging walls). Just place your heel on the foothold and stand with a straight leg so that your weight is supported by the bones, not muscular contraction. In some cases you may be able to place the heels of both feet onto holds and cop a super rest! You can further speed recovery by wiggling your toes and deliberately trying to relax the calf muscle.

While relatively easy climbs will feature lots of opportunities for the rest step, the smaller holds found on more difficult climbs make getting a rest step more difficult. One trick for making a rest-step hold is to stand toe-in on a hold with one foot, then place the heel of the other foot on top of the laces part of the supporting shoe. This foot-stack rest step is just one example of the many clever moves you will learn—or discover—to excel on more difficult routes.

Fundamental Techniques

The essence of climbing is a dance up the wall using the four points of contact as your dance steps. Since each climb possesses a novel configuration of hand- and footholds, your challenge is to unlock the perfect sequence of moves and leverage your points of contact into this dynamic dance.

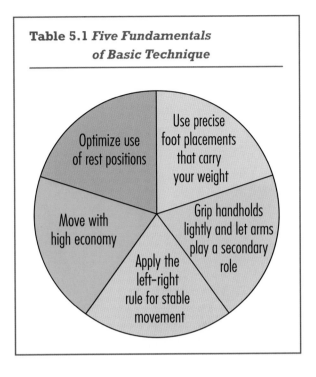

Table 5.1 *Five Fundamentals of Basic Technique*

- Use precise foot placements that carry your weight
- Grip handholds lightly and let arms play a secondary role
- Apply the left-right rule for stable movement
- Move with high economy
- Optimize use of rest positions

In executing any physical skill—whether it's shooting a basketball or simply running—there are fundamental techniques that represent optimal use of body position, leverage, and physical energy. While the specific techniques may be hard to observe with an untrained eye, just about any novice can spot an athlete steeped in the fundamentals: Her movements are smooth, crisp, and confident, and her demeanor reveals a poise and ease of execution, despite inherent difficulties of the situation. The bottom line: Fundamentally sound movement affords perfect economy and looks easy.

In climbing, achieving near-perfect economy of movement is the Holy Grail that few individuals ever realize. You can become the exception, however, by means of a constant focus on climbing in accordance with the fundamentals of this sport. Please recognize that becoming a well-skilled climber is a conscious decision that takes a plan and disciplined long-term follow-through.

Precise Foot Placement

Climbing with precise placement is critical. Aim to shift your center of gravity over the leg you've just advanced higher up the wall.

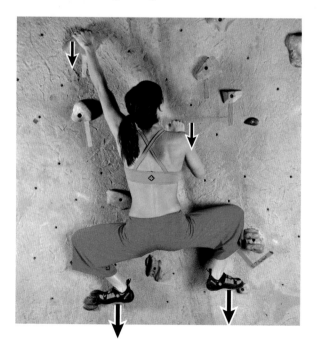

Let's consider the two basic modi operandi of climbers at a gym. Most individuals tie into the rope and just climb. They move in ways that feel easiest based on their experience. However, beginners' lack of experience will often lead them down a road of clumsy movement and poor technique that can solidify into bad habits.

The more effective, but less common, second mode is to climb with the intent of doing each move and every route in accordance with the fundamentals. It's this attention to detail that imparts technically sound skills and leads to rapid gains in ability. These

Pushing with both feet, with your center of gravity in close to the wall, is a highly efficient technique on near-vertical walls.

results are indeed remarkable, and they are achieved only by an individual who is uncommonly effective in his practice and training. Okay, it's time to learn the first of five fundamentals for effective climbing.

Precise Foot Placements That Carry Your Weight

Given that your legs are stronger than your arms, the first fundamental of climbing is that the legs should do the majority of the work. The exceptions to this rule are overhanging routes, which demand greater use of the arms. Coming up in chapter 6, you will learn six additional fundamentals for climbing difficult overhanging routes.

The process of effectively using your feet begins with spotting the footholds and positioning your feet on the best part of each hold. Directing your foot placement demands attention to detail beyond that given to hand placements. Whereas handholds are easy to inspect, the greater eye-to-foot distance commonly leads to less-than-ideal foot placements. Furthermore, your feet don't provide the same degree of feel as the hands, making the quality of each foot placement more difficult to assess.

Positioning Your Center of Gravity

  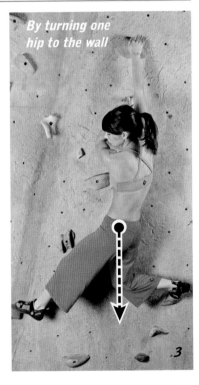

Balance, stability, and application of force are optimized when your center of gravity is positioned directly over your feet, forming a line perpendicular to level ground. Depending on the wall angle and position of the hold, there are several ways to accomplish this. 1. By climbing straight-on. 2. With hip turnout. 3. By turning one hip to the wall.

For these reasons, developing good footwork isn't something that just happens—it's an attribute you make happen via constant foot focus and practice.

Upon spotting a foothold and positioning your foot for optimal purchase, you want to shift some body weight over the hold before standing up on it. It's this downward pressure that helps the shoe rubber stick to the hold, so not properly weighting a hold often leads to the foot slipping off it. Of course, the location of your other three points of contact will dictate a unique balance point and weighting for every new foothold.

In many cases you will be able to advance both feet so they can push in unison. However, it's more intuitive to climb with one foot pushing at a time (as in climbing a ladder), so you'll need to make a conscious effort to develop this important foot skill. To this end, use the practice drills at the end of this chapter to step up your performance.

The final aspect of fundamentally sound footwork is proper alignment of your center of gravity directly over a foothold. Balance, stability, and application of force are optimized when your center of gravity is positioned directly over your feet, forming a line perpendicular to level ground. On a less-than-vertical wall or slab, this requires a hip position out from the wall and over the foothold. On a near-vertical climbing surface, you simply need to keep your body position straight and over the feet as much as possible. When the climbing wall overhangs, it becomes impossible to position your center of gravity directly over your feet, so new fundamentals take over (to be discussed in chapter 6).

Grip Handholds Lightly and Let Arms Play a Secondary Role

In a sport where anxiety and fear often rule, it's understandable that many climbers hang on with their hands for dear life. This tendency manifests itself with overgripping of the handholds and unnecessary muscling of moves with the arms. The end result is rapid fatigue, pumped forearms, and an eventual need to hang on the rope in order to rest and recover. You will no doubt experience this scenario during your initial days learning to climb.

You can avoid this outcome by practicing—and making habitual—the fundamentals of proper hand and arm use. These critical skills include gripping each handhold with the minimum force required, using the arms mainly for balance and not as a primary source of locomotion, and pushing with the feet in unison with modest arm pull.

Begin by making each hand contact a conscious process. Whereas many climbers just grab a hold with little thought and continue with the process of climbing, you must make each hand placement a thoughtful act. First, consider where the best place is to grab the hold. It's not always on the top of the hold, and it often relates to the location of your last foot placement. Now, as you grab the hold, focus on using a light touch that yields soft forearms. Sure, certain holds will demand that you bear down hard on them, but many don't. Your goal must be to try to use each hold with a light touch, and then increase the gripping force only as much as is required for the move at hand. This process of minimally gripping each handhold takes but a split second, yet it's a master skill that separates the best from the rest. Commit to targeted practice of this important skill (use the drills detailed on page 68), and in time it will actually become an unconscious act as you cruise up hard routes with high efficiency!

Beyond gripping the rock, you need to decide just how much you need to pull down on a given handhold. As discussed earlier, it is imperative that you push with your feet and let the leg muscles carry the load. In climbing a slab or near-vertical wall, think of your arms as points of contact that simply prevent you from falling backward off the wall. In climbing a ladder, for example, your legs do all the work while the arms mainly provide balance. While rock climbing is far more complex, hold this model in your mind as the ultimate goal—the arms maintain balance while the legs drive movement.

Gripping Handholds

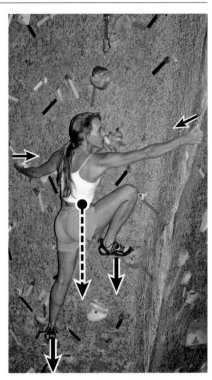

Grip each handhold with the minimum force required, using the arms mainly for balance and not as a primary source of locomotion.

Still, there will be occasions in which your arms will need to briefly carry much of your weight. In these situations it's imperative that you pull quickly through the strenuous move in order to get back onto good footholds that can carry your weight. A final tip for strenuous situations is to maintain straight arms as much as possible—this way, much your weight is supported by the skeletal system of your upper body and not by your muscles.

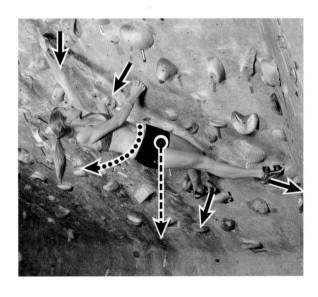

In situations where the arms must briefly carry much of your weight, it's imperative to maintain straight arms.

The Left–Right Rule for Stable Movement

The magic of efficient climbing movement comes from the synergistic interaction of the arms and legs and a constant transfer of force and torque through your body. To this end, the Left–Right Rule states that maximum stability and ease of movement come from the pairing of a left hand and right foot (or a left foot and right hand) into harmonious action.

Let's again use climbing a ladder as our model.

Ascending a ladder with opposing hand–foot combinations (say, the left hand pulling and right foot pushing at the same time) is so intuitive that it's almost impossible to climb a ladder any other way. Suppose you tried to climb a ladder with non-opposing hand–foot combinations, such as a right hand and right foot working together; you'd immediately begin to **barndoor,** or rotate sideways off the ladder. Thus, the Left–Right Rule is a fundamental for balanced, stable movement.

The Left–Right Rule

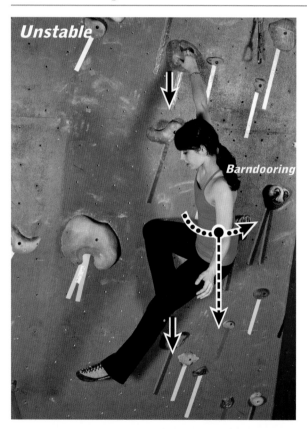

Use of just a right hand and right foot (or left hand and left foot) creates instability and can result in an uncontrolled swing away from the wall, known as barndooring.

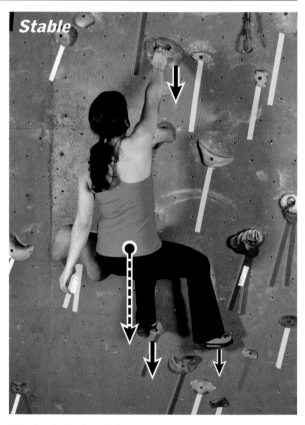

A left–right hand–foot combination maximizes stability and allows for better center-of-gravity positioning over the feet.

While you don't need to even consider the Left–Right Rule in ascending a ladder, formulating movement up a climbing wall is much more complex since the position and shape of the hand- and footholds sometimes wreak havoc with your intuitive sense of movement. Thus, in seeking to reposition your hands and feet on the wall, it's helpful to ponder which holds will provide the best opportunity for a left–right combination. Easy climbs will often provide a pulling right hand that can combine with a pushing left foot (or vice versa). More difficult climbs tend to be more devious, because the holds are smaller, farther apart, or displaced off to the side of the route line. Later in the chapter you will find several toprope drills to develop skill in using left–right combinations.

Move with High Economy

The technical paramount is to climb with high economy. Make these two words—*high economy*—your mantra every time you touch the rock.

High economy means discovering the way to do each move, and an entire route for that matter, with minimal energy expenditure. If you have a cat, you can observe highly economical movement firsthand. Most of the time a cat moves in a slow, smooth, deliberate way; however, sometimes a situation demands a powerful, dynamic leap to maintain high economy. Catlike movement should be your technical model for efficient climbing: smooth, quiet, leg-driven movements, but with an unhesitating shift to an arm-pulling, dynamic movement when it is required to most efficiently execute a difficult move. Here are five attributes of economical movement that you should aspire to acquire.

QUIET FEET

Quiet foot movements are one of the hallmarks of a climber with great technique. Conversely, feet that regularly pop off footholds or skid on the wall surface are typical of an individual possessing lackluster footwork and poor economy.

For many climbers, noisy footwork is just the way they climb—it's a habit that developed over a long period of time, as well as a flaw in their technique that will prevent them from ever reaching their true potential. Your goal, of course, is to learn to climb with good foot technique from the start. This means concentrating on each foot placement, holding the foot steady and firm to the hold, and standing up on the foot with confidence as you proceed smoothly to the next hand- or foothold.

RHYTHM AND MOMENTUM

Like any dance, climbing should have a natural rhythm that utilizes momentum and inertia. Climbing in a ladderlike motion yields the rhythm *step, reach, step, reach*. However, a better rhythm for effective movement is often *step, step, reach, reach*, since it allows the legs to direct and drive the movement. There are obviously many other rhythms, such as *step, reach, step, step, reach, reach* and *step, step, reach, step, reach, reach*. Consider that every unique sequence possesses a best rhythm of movement, and you'll eventually learn to intuit this on the fly. As a beginner climber, however, it takes a conscious effort to avoid leading with the hands in a strenuous and inefficient *reach, reach, step, step* rhythm. Strive to tap into the rhythm of each route, and climb accordingly.

Similarly, you want to utilize momentum in a way that helps propel successive moves. This is especially important on difficult climbs with large spacing between holds. Think of how you would move hand-over-hand across monkey bars at a playground, each movement blending with the next in a perfect continuity of motion. This style of smooth, continuous motion is critical when climbing through crux sequences. Interestingly, many folks do just the opposite, engaging the crux sequence with measure and caution. In doing so, they not only lose upward movement but also have the inertia of stillness to overcome. Hopefully you can avoid this tendency by consciously directing a steady rhythm that maintains forward momentum through the most difficult parts of a climb.

SMOOTH MOVES AND RELAXED BODY

Smooth, fluid movement is another sign of high economy. A climber appears to flow up a route when only the muscles necessary for stability and upward motion are contracting and all other opposing, or antagonist, muscles remain relaxed and relatively passive.

Unfortunately, many climbers, wrought with anxiety, fear, or the need to perform, find themselves contracting almost all their muscles from head to toe in an attempt to hang on or fight through a crux. Such tension in the antagonist muscles forces the prime movers to work harder than needed and leads to inefficient movements and rapid energy expenditure. You can spot climbers suffering from this affliction by their stiff, rigid, and forced movements, which will likely soon have them hanging on the rope in frustration. And if they somehow succeed in fighting up the route, it will be at the expense of a great amount of energy and further ingraining of bad habits of technique.

The key to smooth, efficient movement is to maintain a high level of relaxation throughout the climb. You can best achieve this with a two-pronged approach. First, think about contracting only the muscles necessary for engaging the rock, maintaining stability, and directing movement; usually these will be the muscles of your forearms, shoulders, core, thighs, and calves. Next, switch your focus to the antagonist muscles and scan for unnecessary tension that might be developing in your upper arms, hips and legs, neck, and face. While taking deep, slow breaths, visualize this tension escaping like air from a balloon—such mental imagery really helps the process. Now return your focus to executing the next climbing movement, but continue alternating your focus back and forth between directing movement and directing relaxation.

Developing a habit of relaxed, fluid movement is something that takes time and heightened awareness (review the section on proprioception on page 41). This is largely a mental endeavor, because anxious thinking rapidly manifests itself in muscular tension. To help you on this journey, chapter 8 presents several effective strategies for preventing or mitigating mental tension.

PACE

Pace is another aspect of climbing economy that becomes increasingly important as a route gains in steepness and difficulty. While an easy climb with large holds allows you to ascend at a leisurely pace, a crux sequence or overhanging terrain will demand that you kick into high gear and surmount the difficulty in short order. When climbing near your limit, make it your goal to move as briskly as possible without any drop-off in technique (skidding feet, botched sequences, and such). Reduce the pace at the first sign that your technique is suffering. It helps to identify obvious rest positions ahead of time, and then make it a goal to move from one to the next as fast as possible. Ultimately, knowing just the right pace on a given route is a sense you will develop with experience. Practice climbing at different speeds and on different types of routes, and you'll quickly foster the subtle skill of proper pace.

STEADY BREATHING

Breathing is the essence of life. Steady breathing is essential to sustain the life in your climbing. Conversely, restricted breathing is akin to tightening your muscles, constraining your thinking, and fostering failure.

Obviously, a steady flow of oxygen to the muscles is important for energy production and recovery, and it's the slow, deep, steady belly breaths that best get the job done. Many climbers, however, have

Smooth, fluid movements that look relaxed and easy are a sign of optimal technique and high economy.
ROBERT SCOVERSKI

a tendency to shift into shallow, rapid breathing as fatigue and mental anxiety grow. Worse yet, some climbers unknowingly hold their breath at times of high stress. These are two tendencies that you must be aware of and proactively counteract if you are to climb your best.

Before every climb, take a moment to close your eyes and take several slow, deep breaths. Feel your belly expand outward as you slowly inhale, and then allow the air to escape sparingly through pursed lips in a slow ten-second count (count in your mind). Visualize a wave of relaxation washing across your body—this sets the stage for optimal performance. As you commence climbing, strive to maintain the same slow, steady breathing that you initiated on the ground. This is, of course, often difficult since a dicey sequence or strenuous move can trigger irregular breathing patterns. Consequently, it is critical that you use every rest position as an opportunity to reset your breathing cycle with a few slow, deep belly breaths. Such proactive breath control is like topping off your gas tank—do it frequently, and you'll rarely hit empty.

Optimize Use of Rest Positions

Finding efficient rest positions is as important as finding the best way to do a crux sequence. If you miss a good rest stance, you miss an opportunity to physically recover as well as mentally "read" and prepare for the next section of the climb. Consequently, locating rest positions on a climb should be viewed with the same sense of importance as locating all the key holds.

This process begins with on-ground visualization of the route (to be discussed in depth in chapter 7) in an attempt to estimate the location and body position of rest stops. Upon reaching a rest step, assume a body position that will allow the most fatigued muscles to rest (usually the forearms, biceps, and calves). An optimal rest position would consist of your feet in the rest-step position, legs straight, and hips over the legs or in a position

midway between the feet (should they be on holds more than shoulder-width apart). If the climb is less than vertical, your upper body can relax completely, and in some cases you might even be able to assume a no-hands rest position. Such a casual stance places no time limits on how long you can remain parked there—although this luxury is rare on more difficult routes.

Rest positions on vertical to overhanging climbs make complete weighting of the feet more difficult and often impossible. While you still want to place as much weight as possible on the footholds, a significant amount of weight will remain on your arms. In this case it's absolutely vital that you hang with straight arms, so that the bones are providing the support, not the muscles of the upper arm. It is also advantageous if you can obtain a heel hook above your center of gravity from which you can hang a high percentage of body weight. Still, your forearm muscles will need to contract in order to maintain a grip on the handhold. The best strategy, then, is to attain a stable stance and shake out alternate arms every five to ten seconds. This way, both arms take turns resting. At some point, however, hanging out at the rest begins to cost more energy than you can recover. It's at this time that you need to begin climbing toward the next rest spot.

Fortunately, there's a recovery technique that I popularized called the **G-Tox,** which can markedly accelerate recovery of finger strength while at a marginal rest position. Instead of simply hanging the resting arm by your side, alternate the arm position every five seconds between the normal dangling position and an above-your-head raised-hand position. This simple technique has been shown by a British researcher to increase recovery by 50 percent or more over the standard dangling-arm shakeout. This should be evidence enough to make the G-Tox a regular part of your climbing stratagem.

A big part of becoming a fundamentally sound climber is learning to gain brief rests in the midst of even the most difficult routes. Practice and

Four Rest Positions

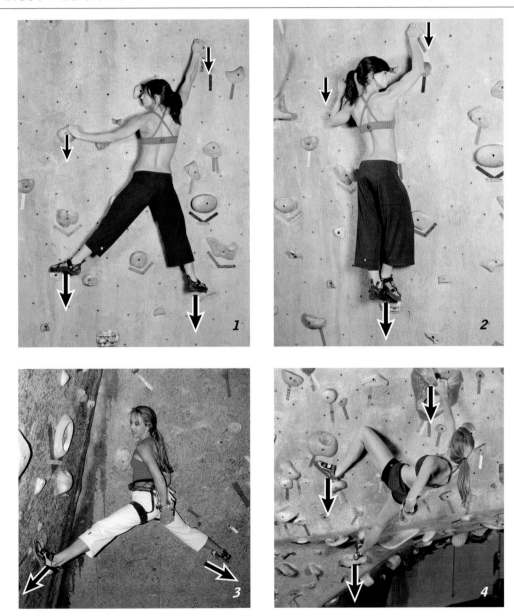

Ideal rest positions consist of a straight-legged stance that largely unweights the arms and positions the center of gravity over the feet. 1. Here's the stem rest with center of gravity positioned evenly over both feet. 2. This position is known as the foot-stack rest step with straight arms and legs. 3. A corner stem yields a classic no-hands rest. 4. On overhanging walls, heel hooks are often the key to attaining a good shake-out position. Notice the straight (right) arm position and hip turn that shifts the climber's center of gravity closer to the wall.

unbridled creativity are the only two requisites for solving difficult sequences and finding vital rest positions. Remember that the best climbers are not always the strongest; their prowess instead comes from uncommon mastery of climbing economy and effective resting.

Seven Basic Drills

Practice drills are the backbone of training for increased performance in sports. Consider that in practicing soccer, golf, or almost any other traditional sport, execution of certain drills helps develop fundamental skills, techniques, and mental control. Strangely, however, most climbers just climb for practice. In doing so, they miss out on many powerful methods of developing the critical climbing skills.

Following are seven skill-building drills to make a staple of your climbing gym workouts. Use these drills as warm-up exercises, or integrate them throughout your climbing session as a reminder of proper technique and the good habits of effective climbing. The long-term aggregate effect of performing these drills will be exceptional technique grounded in the fundamentals, as well as a level of performance that's above and beyond the average climber (who just climbs).

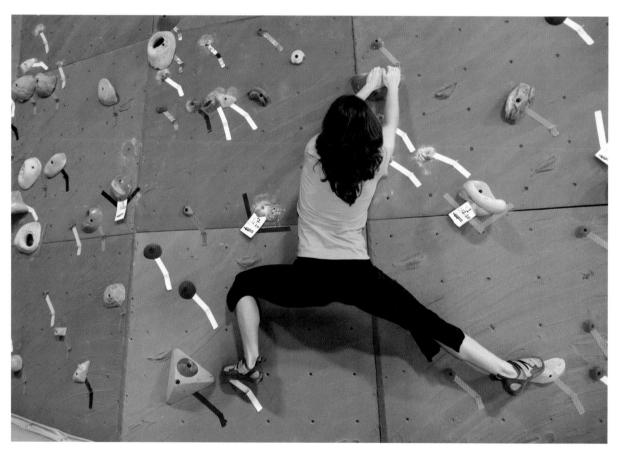

Long, moderate-intensity traverses are a good way to work on technique and build forearm endurance.

The "piano move," in which the fingers of one hand are lifted off one by one to allow the fingers of the other hand to latch on to the hold one by one, is a useful technique for matching hands on a narrow hold.

Traverse Training Drills

Perform these drills in the designated bouldering area or along the base of a roped climbing wall that is not in use. Traverse drills are ideal for experimenting with techniques, refining your movement skills, and developing higher awareness of valuable proprioceptive cues. But it is vital that you hold yourself to a high standard of quality—as the saying goes: Practice doesn't make perfect; it's perfect practice that makes perfect. To this end, make it your goal to foster these six subtle yet fundamental skills:

1. Pinpoint focus on each foot placement.
2. A sense of feel as you weight each foothold.
3. Maximally weighting each foothold by shifting your center of gravity over the leading foot placement. Strive for awareness of

proprioceptive feedback from your arms and legs, so you can discover the most economical way to move across the rock wall.

4. A relaxed grip that uses the minimum amount of force required to stick each handhold.
5. Quick, smooth movement through thin sequences.
6. Anticipation of rest position locations and a commitment to stop and rest only at these spots.

 SHUFFLE DRILL

In this most basic drill, you simply shuffle your hands and feet sideways as you move horizontally across the wall. The key lesson to be learned is the importance of leading with your feet and letting your legs do the bulk of the work. In traversing to the right, for example, you should initiate each horizontal move with the right foot stepping ahead onto a hold, and then shifting your hips over the right foot. In doing this, your hands play a subordinate role in providing only stability and balance. Let your feet run the show—this should always be the goal in striving to climb with perfect economy. Continue traversing for ten to fifty total foot moves.

MATCHING DRILL

This practice drill zeroes in on the important technique of hand–foot matching or sharing. Traverse across the wall with your feet in the lead, as above—but now your hands and feet must match on every new hold. For example, in traversing to the right, your left foot will always come to share a hold with your right foot before the right foot advances to the next hold. In the case of a very small foothold, you will need to do a "hop switch" in which you switch feet in a single small "jump." The hands will similarly match left onto right before the right hand advances to the next hold. Matching onto a narrow handhold is difficult and may require use of the piano move (see photo) in which the fingers of the right hand are lifted off one by one, allowing the fingers of the left hand to latch on to the hold one by one. Continue for ten to fifty moves.

ISOLATION DRILL

Use this drill to isolate and strengthen a specific grip or arm position. For example, if you find the open-hand grip insecure and unnatural to use (common for beginners), practice doing an entire traverse using only the open-hand position. Similarly, you could do traverses exclusively using the side-pull arm or undercling arm position, or using only two fingers of each hand! Be inventive and have fun contriving all kinds of restrictions in the "rules" for traversing. Such constraints will demand optimal footwork, and ultimately make you a more complete climber.

Toprope Drills

The two modi operandi in roped climbing are climbing for performance and climbing for practice. Performance climbing is all about attempting routes at your limit, in the hope of breaking new ground and learning new skills. Climbing for practice, however, is the important act of climbing less difficult routes with the intention of fortifying fundamental skills and techniques. Use the following drills when climbing in the practice mode. Select a near-vertical route (not overhanging) that is two or more number grades below your limit.

FROG-FOOT DRILL

This drill teaches the important technique of pushing with both feet simultaneously, much the way a frog would extend its legs in jumping. Beginning with both hands and feet on the wall, step up with one foot and then the other until you are in a sort of squatting position with your knees out to the side and crouching into the wall. Now press down with both feet and in a continuous motion advance one hand, then the other. The hands should be used

primarily for balance, not pulling—let the legs do most of the work. Repeat this process while sub-vocalizing the mantra *Step, step, push, reach, reach.* Continue up the route, striving for smooth movement and a steady rhythm in advancing the hands and feet.

HIGH-STEP DRILL

On more difficult routes you will often need to step high onto a hold near your thigh or hip level. Initially this will feel awkward and difficult, especially if you lack flexibility and hip-flexor strength. You can improve in these areas, however, by regularly performing the high-step drill. On a relatively easy route (one that would surely not require the use of a high step), force yourself to ascend using only high steps. With hands and feet on the wall, begin by high-stepping with one foot onto a hold near hip level. Now rock over this foot—think about moving your crotch over the hold—and then drive downward with that foot and advance your hands until you reach a straight-legged position. Continue the process, but this time high-step with the opposite foot. The rhythm of movement for this drill is *high-step, rock, push, reach, reach* and repeat.

TENNIS BALL DRILL

A common technical flaw that kills climbing performance is overuse of the arms and overgripping of handholds. You won't be able to do this if you climb with a tennis ball in the palm of both hands! Consequently, this is a great drill to develop the vital skill of optimizing use of the feet. Rope up on an easy route with lots of large holds, and then begin climbing by using the tennis balls to hook on to the handholds. Clearly, your hands will only be useful for maintaining balance, so relax and allow your legs to do all the work. Concentrate on shifting your weight from one foot to the other while attempting to keep your upper body relaxed and tension-free. Don't get frustrated if you frequently need to hang on the rope. Persevere and try to make it to the top of the route—this drill will make you a better climber.

STRAIGHT-ARMED DRILL

Use of straight-armed positions is critical for conserving upper-body energy. Thus the goal of this drill is to climb a route while trying to maintain straight arms at least 90 percent of the time. Strive to use straight-armed positions anytime you aren't moving, such as when resting or scanning the wall above you. Practice maintaining straight arms when stepping up or adjusting your feet. In the case of a foot placement out to the side, you may even be able to leverage off a straight arm that's clinging to a side-pull hold. For certain moves, however, you will necessarily be forced to bend your arms in order to pull through a move—proceed through this sequence quickly and regain a straight-armed position as soon as you can. Then continue upward using mainly straight-armed positions, despite the fact that it will feel contrived at times. In forcing this overuse of straight arms, you will discover new ways of moving—and resting—that will heighten your climbing economy.

Advanced Techniques and Drills

Steeper, blanker walls are your destiny as an indoor climber. Such terrain will tap into the very core of your being—physically, mentally, and emotionally—and demand an entirely new set of techniques and tactics.

As you progress onto routes rated 5.10 and above, you'll notice a decrease in the frequency of large holds and a likely increase in wall steepness. Succeeding on these more challenging climbs requires a modified approach from that used on entry-level climbs. Not only are these difficult climbs more strenuous, but they also demand technical and mental acumen that can take many months or years to develop. Thus it's important to assume a long-haul mind-set and not to expect mastery of these skills and success at the lofty grades to come easily. If you are a true novice, then you should probably hold off on testing these techniques for a few months. Upon gaining competence and confidence in climbing 5.9 (or bouldering V1), however, you should begin using some of the practice drills detailed in this chapter.

In the previous chapter you learned five fundamentals of basic climbing movement. While these rules are valid in just about every type of climbing situation, they must be appended with several fundamentals for climbing more severe terrain. For instance, as hold sizes diminish and hold spacing increases, you'll need to leverage a new set of skills in order to surmount these difficulties. Furthermore, steeper climbs accelerate energy drain, so learning to move with high efficiency is tantamount to being a successful steep-wall climber. Let's take a look at six fundamentals of advanced-level climbing.

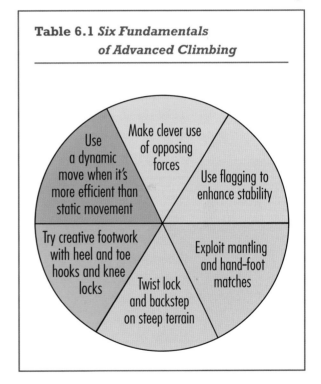

Table 6.1 *Six Fundamentals of Advanced Climbing*

- Use a dynamic move when it's more efficient than static movement
- Make clever use of opposing forces
- Use flagging to enhance stability
- Exploit mantling and hand-foot matches
- Twist lock and backstep on steep terrain
- Try creative footwork with heel and toe hooks and knee locks

Clever Use of Opposing Forces

You have already learned the importance of the Left–Right Rule for enabling stable movement. On easy climbs this left–right combination is usually a pulling right hand along with a pushing left foot (or vice versa). More difficult climbs tend to be more devious, however, so you'll need to consider all the other possible arm positions—side pull, undercling, and Gaston—and figure out how to match one of these with an opposing foot placement.

Detailed below are a few of the most common left–right combinations called into use on difficult climbs. You should practice each of these on the bouldering wall in order to develop its unique motor skills. Vary your hand and foot placements as much as possible to acquire a broad range of use for each hand–foot combination.

Side-Pull Arm and Outside Edge of Opposite Foot

Side-pulling hands are a staple move on almost every moderate to advanced climb. While this move is a bit less intuitive than down pulling, you will quickly gain comfort in its use. Most important is the foot position you select to oppose the side-pulling hand. In many cases it's best to use the outside edge of the opposing foot, not the inside edge. Doing this may feel awkward at first, but you'll find a natural sense of stability once you learn to

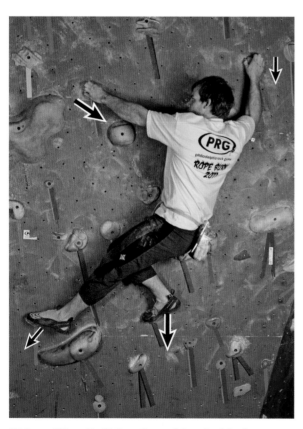

Side-pulling (left) hand combined with the outside edge of the opposite foot.

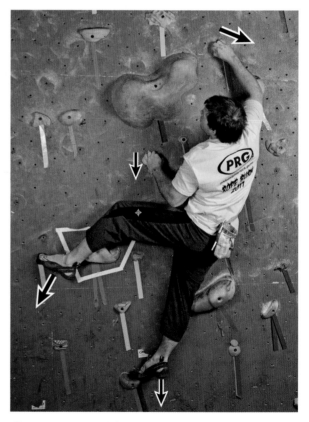

Gaston arm position (right) in tandem with an inside-edging opposite foot.

appropriately set your hips over the outside-edging foot. The key is to concentrate on rotating your hips so that the hip opposite the pulling hand is turned into the wall—that is, your face and chest will rotate toward the side-pulling hand. This very stable position will allow you to step up your free (non-opposing) leg and quite possibly your free (non-opposing) hand as well.

Occasionally a move will dictate that a side-pulling hand must be combined with use of the inside edge of the opposing foot. While this, too, is a fairly stable body position, it provides less reach upward with the free hand. Therefore, anytime you are struggling to reach a handhold, try using the outside edge of your shoe to maximize reach.

Gaston and Inside Edge of Opposite Foot

The Gaston (aka reverse side pull) is the most unnatural and weak arm position for beginners, yet it's a fairly common move needed to unlock many crux sequences. Use of the Gaston is best opposed by the inside edge of the opposite foot. Combining a Gaston with an outside-edging foot is strenuous but doable if absolutely needed. Practice this move in a variety of ways to gain comfort and strength in its use. As with all these advanced moves, the bouldering area is the ideal proving ground to experiment with and learn the skills.

Undercling and Inside or Outside Edge of Opposite Foot

Often overlooked by beginner-level climbers, undercling hand positions are actually quite easy to perform. What's more, an underclinging hand helps maximize your reach with the free hand, and it positions your arm and body in a naturally strong position. Therefore, the undercling is a move you want to practice and put to frequent use.

Typically you will undercling a hold somewhere near your torso while you press with an opposing foot. This foot can edge with either the inside, outside, or toe portion of the shoe, although use of

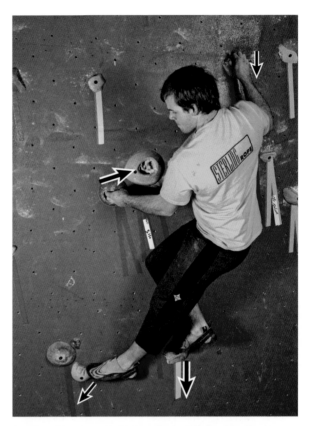

Underclinging (left) hand working effectively with the outside edge of the opposite foot.

the outside edge is best for maximizing your reach. Remember that in edging with the outside of your foot, it's best to turn the hip opposite the pulling hand to the wall. In extreme situations you may even need to use a foot smear to oppose the underclinging hand. This is a very powerful and important move that you can practice on the bouldering wall.

Side-Pulling Left and Right Hands

Use of opposing handholds is a key move for unlocking a sequence that lacks any usable down-pull or underclinging handholds. Most common are two opposing side pulls that you'll draw inward to create tension through your arms, shoulders, and

Using Opposing Holds

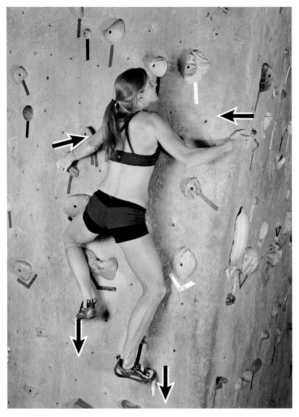

Use of opposing handholds is often necessary to unlock a sequence that lacks a good down-pull or undercling hold. This photo shows opposing side pulls.

This photo illustrates opposing Gastons, an advanced move that requires a great deal of base strength.

upper body. While you will be unable to create much upward movement, this opposition will allow you to upgrade one or both feet. Ideally, you'll want to upgrade the foot that opposes the better of the two side pulls, so that it sets up a stable left–right combination. This will enable you to release the other side-pulling hand so as to upgrade it to the next hold.

Another possibility is opposing Gaston holds.

Though strenuous, you may occasionally need to grab two Gastons at or just above head height and pull outward in order to support your weight while upgrading a foot position. This is a most advanced move that requires a high level of base strength. A word of caution, however: Using a Gaston hold on an overhanging wall places great force on the shoulder joint and in rare cases can cause injury. Proceed carefully.

Flagging

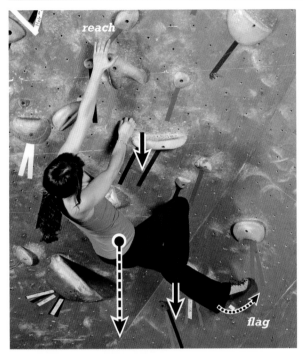

Foot flagging is an important technique for maintaining optimal balance and center-of-gravity positioning when a left–right hand–foot combination is not possible. Here you see outside cross flagging.

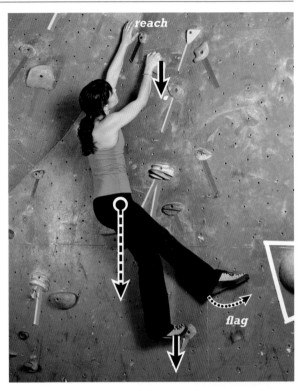

Inside cross flagging. This requires an aggressive hip turn and moderate body tension. Flag the inside leg until you find the balance point.

Use Flagging to Enhance Stability

Flagging is the alternative technique for maintaining stability when a left–right hand–foot combination is not possible. Suppose you are attempting to use a right hand and right foot combination to propel upward movement. Upon releasing your left hand to make a reach upward, you will immediately begin to barndoor (see the photo on page 66). This sideways rotation is hard to fight, and often results in a fall. However, a simple flagging of the free leg (in this case the left) significantly improves stability and balance by shifting your center of gravity more directly over the supporting (right) foot and under the supporting (right) hand.

Let's take a look at the two methods of flagging. Consider a move in which you are edging on the inside of your right foot and pulling with your right hand. In order to avoid barndooring, you would flag the left leg across the right leg. Depending on the wall angle, your body position, and the positioning of the holds you are using, you will want to do either an outside cross flag or an inside cross flag (see photos above). Both flags shift your center of gravity nearer the supporting leg, the only difference is location of your flagging leg (inside or outside supporting leg).

Fingertip press down with foot match.

Palm mantle with foot match.

Exploit Mantling and Hand–Foot Matches

As described in chapter 5, mantling is the act of pressing downward on a handhold. The mantle move is often called upon to overcome a long reach between holds. In such a situation, first consider the possibility of using an undercling handhold; if none is available, you may have no choice but to mantle with one or both hands.

Let's consider the most common scenario of needing to mantle with one hand while the other hand is pulling. The pulling hand will usually be positioned above your head while the mantling hand will contact a hold somewhere near your torso. Depending on the size of the hold to be mantled, you may be able to press your entire palm onto the hold or, possibly, just your fingertips. The left–right combination of pushing and pulling hands provides great stability, so you will be able to upgrade one or, possibly, both feet. Quite often you'll need to match a foot to the handhold on which you are mantling. Regardless, the mantle is complete when you are able to weight your feet, gain balance, and upgrade your hand from the mantle.

Twist Lock and Backstep on Steep Terrain

The twist lock and backstep are the bread-and-butter moves of a steep-wall connoisseur. As a climbing wall tilts back past vertical, it becomes increasingly difficult to place a high percentage of weight on your legs. Consequently, a greater portion of body weight must be supported by the arms—which, of course, possess less absolute strength than the legs. Use of the twist lock and backstep together helps draw your body in toward the surface of the overhanging wall. This changes the force vector on the handholds, making them feel more positive and secure. More important, this drawing-in of the body places more weight onto the footholds. However, proper execution of these moves requires practice and a significant amount of strength through the core muscles of the torso. See chapter 9 to learn exercises for strengthening these core muscles.

The twist lock is typically used to ease the upgrading of a hand on an overhanging section of wall. For example, consider the situation in which your left hand is on a good hold and you'd like to reach up high with the right hand. While you could attempt this move straight-on—chest facing toward the wall in a neutral position—it's far less strenuous to turn your right hip to the wall before making the reach upward. Proper positioning of the feet is critical for making this move work. Since the right hip is turning to the wall, you'll need to use the outside portion of your right foot on a hold somewhere below or in back of your body (hence the term *backstep*). Usually you'll find a complementary left foothold to help maintain the twist-lock body position. The feet then press in unison

Twist Lock on Steep Walls

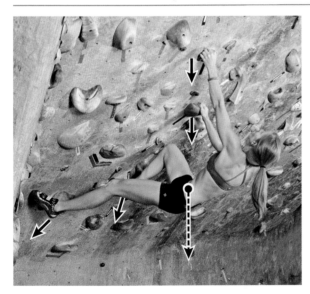

Difficult: Without the twist lock the climber's neutral, straight-on body position places the center of gravity well out from the wall. This makes for strenuous, inefficient movement.

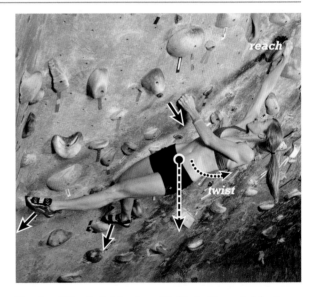

Easier: The twist lock, with its hallmark hip turn, draws the center of gravity into the wall, thus improving weighting of the feet, increasing reach, and enhancing grip on handholds (thanks to improved force vector of the arm pull).

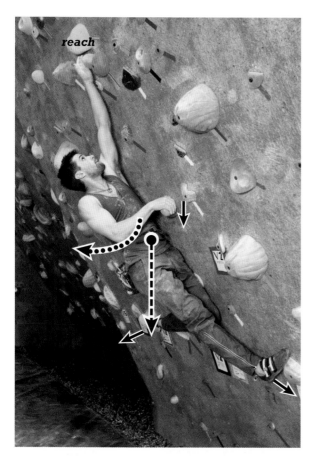
reach

The twist lock is a vital go-to move when a route gets reachy and/or steep. Notice how the climber twists and locks his body with an aggressive hip turn and side-pulling hand drawn in to the torso. This shifts the center of gravity very close to the wall and nearly over his inside foot.

while the left arm pulls down and in toward your torso, creating the twist lock. Finding just the right body position is the key to providing a secure twist lock; when you do, you'll notice that a surprising lack of effort is needed to reach up and acquire the next handhold. This amazingly efficient locomotion over steep terrain is the magic of the twist-lock technique.

Granted, superlative use of the twist lock and backstep is something that will take many hours of practice. In fact, during your initial attempts at using these moves, you might swear that they require more energy than basic straight-on moves. Trust that with practice you will develop the necessary motor skills to make these moves feel quite easy. Initially limit your practice of the twist lock and backstep to boulder problems that overhang about 20 degrees past vertical. As you acquire skill, expand their use onto even steeper boulder problems as well as overhanging toprope climbs.

Use Creative Footwork with Heel Hooks, Toe Hooks, and Knee Locks

So what do you do when you run out of handholds? Consider using one of your feet as a hand! Heel hooks, toe hooks, and knee locks are real difference makers when it comes to surmounting overhangs. Given the strength of the leg muscles, a good heel hook is often better than a handhold in helping turn the lip of a difficult overhang. Similarly, toe hooks and knee locks provide terrific support when attempting a series of inverted moves out a steep wal or large roof. Let's kick into the details of these critical moves.

Heel Hooking

Your primary use of heel hooks will come when turning the lip of a roof, powering yourself up a steep boulder problem, or copping a quick shake-out while on steep terrain. In these cases you'll likely have your hands on holds at or above face level and intend to place one of your heels on a hold off to the side between hip and shoulder level. Which heel you choose to hook with depends on two factors: the availability of a decent-size hold on which to place your heel, and the location of the next handhold that you hope to acquire. This next reach up is best made with the hand on the same side as the heel hook. So if it looks like the next attainable hold is set up for the right hand, it would

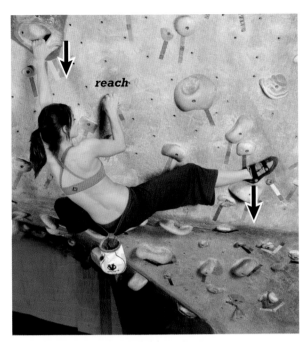

reach

Heel hooks are remarkably effective as a "third arm" on steep walls and overhangs. Here the right heel is pulling in unison with the left hand (Left–Right Rule), enabling the climber to easily upgrade her right hand.

Toe Hooking

Toe hooks are another example of creating a "third arm." This solid toe hook, along with the opposing arm, provides a powerful opposition that holds the climber's body to this roof.
SIERRA BLAIR-COYLE COLLECTION

Combining a toe hook and a pressing foot creates excellent support and stability on a severely overhanging wall.

be best to use a right heel hook. Once set, pull with the heel hook as if it were a third arm and, of course, pull with both arms as well. Often it helps to think about pulling your heel downward and inward toward your rear end; this will maximize use of the leg muscles and help shift your center of gravity toward the heel hook. Meanwhile, the other foot should inside-edge or smear on the wall to help contribute to the upward motion. As you gain elevation, make a quick reach to the next handhold and then switch your heel hook into a standard step-down foot placement.

Toe Hooking

Toe hooking is a foot move used mostly in pulling overhangs or in navigating roofs. This technique involves simply hooking as much of the top (laces) part of your shoe as possible on a large protruding hold. Sometimes you will toe hook onto a hold with a bent leg, and then straighten that leg as your hands move out the roof. Ideally you'll have one foot toe hooking while the other foot pushes off a nearby hold. This opposing push–pull combination enhances the foot purchase on the holds and lowers the chance your feet will come swinging off the roof (a common problem). Strive to keep your arms and legs in the straight position as much as possible so that your body weight is being supported more by bone than by muscles. Done properly, you can navigate a surprisingly large roof, with the limiting factor being forearm endurance. Experiment with this foot technique in the bouldering area, and you'll gradually gain skill and confidence in climbing with your back to the ground!

Knee Locks

Knee locks are a boon on overhanging walls and roofs with large protruding holds—that is, if you know the technique and can find a position to exploit this "thank-God" move. Consider a severely overhanging climb with no obvious rest positions. Chances are the forerunner has positioned two holds in just the right way so that you can place your toe on one hold and then lock your knee against a larger opposing hold. Such a knee lock provides surprising purchase; it will allow you to drop one hand at a time to shake out and chalk up. Occasionally you will come upon a knee lock that's so solid, you'll be able to cop a rare, no-hands inverted rest! Of course, miss the knee lock and you have no choice but to sprint up the climb in the hope of reaching the anchors before the pump clock runs out.

It's unlikely that you'll ever run across a knee lock on a route much below 5.10 or V2. On high-end climbs and boulder problems, however, look for knee locks and toe and heel hooks with the same resolve you'd give to searching for handholds. Practice knee locks on a steep bouldering wall, and you'll soon learn to leverage this technique like the pros.

With his toes on a small foothold, the climber is able to lock his knee onto a large protruding hold. This provides great support on a steep wall . . . and perhaps even a much-needed rest stop.
WADE DAVID

Seven Advanced Drills

Regularly performing these drills is like taking skill-building steroids. Each drill focuses on a specific technique or move that will be repeated for the full length of a climb. Such repetitive practice of a specific technique enhances motor learning and fortifies skills faster than random climbing. Incorporate a few of these drills into every gym session, striving for smooth, controlled execution. Perform each drill on a toprope climb of moderate difficulty—two or three number grades below your maximum ability. While you might think that some of these drills feel contrived and difficult, keep in mind that doing them is about training technique, not performance (getting to the top without a fall). It's not necessary to complete the route you are drilling on—just go as far as you can, then hang and lower off.

INSIDE/OUTSIDE FOOT EDGE DRILL

Turning a hip to the wall and edging with the outside edge of your inside foot is a simple move. The goal of this drill is to climb an entire route in this hip-turned position. For example, beginning with your left hip to the wall, the outside edge of the left foot and the inside edge of the right foot will do all the work. Your hands can use down-pull or side-pull holds for balance and stability. Repeat this drill with your body turned in the opposite direction—in this example, with your right hip to the wall.

FINGER-PRESS DRILL

Climbers typically consider their hands as tools for pulling. Ironically, it's often a hand pushing downward that helps unlock a crux. While you will rarely need to mantle or finger press on beginners' routes, it is an important skill to have in your arsenal for your advance up the grading scale. Use this drill to foster confidence and intuitive execution of the finger press. Attempt to climb an entire route by using a pulling hand and pushing hand in unison. Begin with both feet on the wall and one hand grabbing a hold above your head, while the other hand grips a hold somewhere between your chest and waist. Now step up with one or both feet and then focus on pulling with the high hand and pressing down with the lower hand as you extend with your legs. Ideally all four points of contact will contribute to the upward movement. Try to achieve a balanced, relaxed stance, and reposition your hands with one above your head and one again near your waist. Alternate the pushing and pulling hand as you repeat this process in ascending the wall.

UNDERCLING DRILL

Undercling holds are often the secret to unlocking impossible-feeling moves. Perform this drill to gain competence and confidence in using underclings in just about any situation. Try to climb an entire route with nothing but undercling handholds. Granted, this may be impossible on a route lacking enough downward-facing edges or large holds, so select a climb that appears to possess a large number of high-profile, well-featured holds (probably in the 5.7 to 5.10 range). In climbing, you'll find that your hands are mostly underclinging holds between your face and waist. Progress and energy conservation will depend on your ability to find and use footholds in ways that oppose the underclings. Let the feet do most of the work, and remain open to all possible body positions: hip-turn right, hip-turn left, or neutral. This drill can be performed on vertical to slightly overhanging walls, but not on slabs.

FOOT-FLAGGING DRILL

This drill emphasizes the flagging technique, which provides stability when a left–right hand–foot combination is not possible. Your goal is to climb an entire route by alternating the flagging leg with every move upward. For example, begin with the right hand pulling and right foot pushing, in which case you will need to flag the left leg to maintain stability. Upon finding a balance position, upgrade the left hand, upgrade the left foot, and then begin upward movement on these new points of contact. Notice that you will begin barndooring the other direction; you now need to flag the right leg to oppose this effect. Continue the dance as far up the climb as possible. Yes, it may look strange and feel contrived, but trust that in doing this drill you are coding important motor skills. Select a vertical route with medium-size holds—the goal is not to get pumped, but instead to practice flagging on relatively nonstressful terrain.

 ### TRACKING DRILL

Tracking is a challenging elimination-type drill where the feet are restricted to using only the exact holds used by the hands. Performing this drill will develop a variety of important skills, including high-stepping, finger presses and mantles, hand–foot matches, and balanced stand-ups. Begin with your hands staggered—say, the left arm fully extended to grip a hold above your head while the right hand grips a hold near shoulder level—and work your feet up so that you can high-step your right foot onto your right handhold. Such matching of hand and foot (see page 76, for example) takes practice, but you'll eventually learn to make a smooth transition or hand–foot switch. Now upgrade the right hand and use three points of contact (right foot, and left and right hands) to enable a step up with the left foot onto your current left handhold or the hold your hand previously used. Repeat this process for the full length of the climb, with your feet tracking behind your hands using the exact same holds. This is a challenging drill that will yield a big payoff in ability!

 ### DOWNCLIMBING DRILL

When leading or toproping indoors, it's rare that I climb a route to the top and lower off without trying to downclimb as much of the route as possible. There are benefits to this practice drill beyond the obvious one of doubling the pump. First, in knowing that you plan to downclimb a route, you become a more observant and focused climber on the way up. Furthermore, since poor footwork is a leading handicap for many climbers, there's much to be gained from practice that demands intense concentration on footwork. Initially you'll find downclimbing to be difficult, awkward, and very pumpy. As your hold recognition and fluidity improve, however, you may discover that downclimbing actually feels easier than ascending. Make it a practice to downclimb all warm-up routes as well as any other route that's one or more number grades below your maximum ability. Occasionally test yourself by attempting to downclimb a route at your limit. While you will likely get a vicious pump, you'll also be forced into making the most of your footwork in order to conserve upper-body energy.

 ### FAST-PACED CLIMBING DRILL

When the rock gets steep and the moves hard, it becomes crucial that you increase your pace of ascent. Climbing quickly is primarily a function of skill, not strength or power (we're not talking about lunging wildly up a speed-climbing route). In fact, the less strength and endurance you possess, the more important it is that you can climb swiftly and efficiently. Practice fast-paced climbing on routes you already have wired or climbs two or more number grades below your maximum ability. Begin by climbing the route at your normal pace. If available, use a stopwatch to time your ascent. Rest for a few minutes until you feel recovered, then climb the route again but at a slightly faster pace (say, about 10 percent faster). Repeat the climb one or two more times, with each successive lap about 10 percent faster than the last. Ease off the accelerator at the first sign of degrading technique or botched moves. Perform this drill once or twice per week for several months, and you'll find yourself naturally moving faster when bouldering, toproping, and even climbing on-sight. This new fast-paced style of climbing may very well elevate your ability by a full number grade.

Dynamic Moves

In chapter 5 you learned the importance of climbing with economy—the goal being to climb a move, a sequence, and an entire route in a way that requires minimal energy. In most cases the hallmark of economical climbing is smooth, relaxed movement that utilizes the feet and legs over the muscles of the upper body. Such controlled, fluid movement is referred to as static climbing.

The opposite of static style is dynamic or explosive movement. As a beginner, you will naturally find yourself grabbing quickly or lunging for handholds in a dynamic way that is not very economical. As you gain skill, however, you will naturally come to move in a more static, economical way. Still, there are certain moves and sequences that demand dynamic movement. In particular, vertical routes with tiny handholds and overhanging routes with long reaches often require dynamic movements in order to maintain high economy.

The key is to know which moves are best performed dynamically versus statically, and this is a recognition skill that will take years to fully develop. Often you will need to attempt a crux in both a static and dynamic way in order to determine which style yields the most economical passage. The strategy of trying a move or sequence both ways is vital—if you are satisfied to simply struggle through the crux once, you'll never know if there was a more effective method, and you'll miss out on an important learning opportunity.

The two primary forms of dynamic movement are deadpoints and lunges (or jumps). Although it's a rarity to need either move on a beginner-level climb, you will eventually need to call these moves into action as you progress onto more difficult terrain. As in learning all advanced skills, you can best practice and experiment with these dynamic moves in the bouldering area. Employ some of the bouldering drills described later in this chapter to help accelerate your learning.

Deadpoints

Consider a situation where both hands cling to poor holds and you would fall off the wall if either hand let go for more than an instant. It's in just such a predicament that the deadpoint move will save the day, because it allows you to make a rapid hand upgrade despite the fact that you can't hang on to the wall statically with a single-hand contact point. How's this possible? It's the magic of the deadpoint!

Envision a basketball player making a jump shot. He jumps straight up and shoots the ball at the peak of his flight, a moment of apparent weightlessness before gravity returns him to the floor. This instant of weightlessness and stillness is the deadpoint. Climbers can similarly exploit the apparent weightlessness of the deadpoint to upgrade a hand position as in the desperate situation described above. But instead of jumping as in the basketball example, the climber needs to use a smaller, more controlled motion to facilitate the delicate upgrading of a hand from one small hold to another.

For example, imagine a tenuous move on a vertical or slightly overhanging wall in which you want to upgrade your right hand, but you can't make a static reach for the hold. Initiate the deadpoint movement with a small droop downward (or a release outward in the case of an overhanging wall) immediately followed by a firm drawing inward of the handholds toward your torso. This drawing-in of your body is akin to—but less dramatic than—the basketball player's jump, and there will be an instant when the motion peaks and you'll be able to flash your hand up to snag the next hold. A well-executed deadpoint is calculated and controlled in a way that flows naturally in perfect economy. In extreme cases you may need to execute several deadpoint moves in a row in order to climb through a series of small handholds that you could never hang on to for a static movement.

Practice the deadpoint move at the base of a vertical climbing wall and initially by using large holds

Deadpointing

Begin with a slight flex in your arms from which you can droop down to initiate the deadpoint.

From the bottom of the droop-down, pull with your arms and fire your hips while pressing only lightly with the feet. Reach quickly to the next hold at the peak or deadpoint of the motion.

Catch the hold firmly and immediately tense through your body to establish a solid hand–foot connection.

that you can easily stick. You will rapidly develop a feel for the deadpoint motion, at which time you should begin to practice the move on smaller holds and slightly overhanging walls. Upon gaining a high rate of success and a sense of confidence, you can begin utilizing this move on roped climbs.

Lunges

Unlike the careful, controlled movement of a deadpoint, the lunge (or **dyno,** as it's often called) is a full-on jump for an out-of-reach hold. In lunging, the arms and legs explode in unison to propel your body upward toward the next good hold. Lunges typically end in one of two ways: Ideally you latch

on to a hold and regain control of your body; however, it's also possible that you will fail to catch the target hold and end up falling on the rope or the bouldering crash pad.

Lunging is like any other skill in that it takes practice and a high level of confidence before you will be able to exploit the move in severe situations. It's also a strenuous and stressful move that has led to many shoulder injuries. Consequently, it's best to view lunging as a last-resort move that you only pull out of the bag when nothing else appears possible. In the heat of a crux sequence, though, it often comes down to a gut feeling as to whether you should try to throw a lunge or attempt

Lunging/Jumping

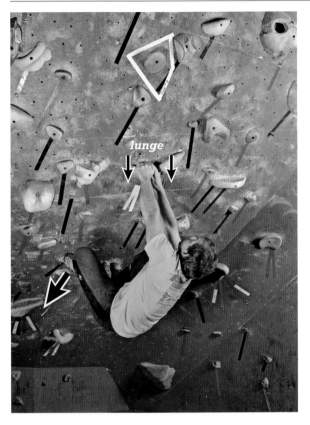

Droop downward to "cock" the lunge; one or two bounces may help generate beneficial momentum that will extend your jump.

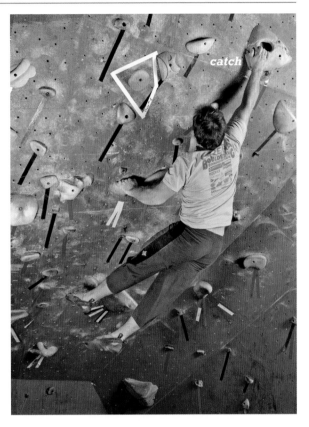

Explode upward, concentrate on driving off the footholds, and then lunge your hand for the target hold. You must believe in the lunge in order to stick it!

a static sequence. Ideally it would be best to lunge only when climbing statically would require more energy. In fact, a perfectly executed lunge in just the right situation is a classic example of climbing with high economy, despite the apparent burly nature of the move.

Executing a lunge is very physical, but also requires good timing and a belief that you can reach the next hold. Much like a gymnast attempting her hardest move, throwing and sticking the perfect

lunge requires laserlike focus and an intense belief in a successful outcome. Begin by locking your eyes on the target hold and visualizing exactly how your hand will hit—and stick!—that hold. Next, look down and concentrate on maximizing an explosive launch off the footholds. In some cases it may help to "cock" your lunge by drooping or bouncing before you jump upward. As you go airborne, your eyes will naturally return to a pinpoint focus on the target hold. Now stick it!

Bouldering Drills and Games

A bouldering wall is the ideal platform for practicing all the advanced skills covered in this chapter—by challenging yourself in focused drills or challenging partners in bouldering games.

Steep-Rock Bouldering Drills

Bouldering on steep walls provides an excellent physical workout in addition to effective practice of technical skills. It's this one–two punch of training strength and technique that makes bouldering such an effective all-around training strategy. Select a section of wall with many large holds for your initial practice sessions, but graduate to boulder problems with fewer and smaller holds as you gain confidence in each new technique.

TWIST-LOCK BOULDERING DRILL

Your goal is to execute a sequence of four to ten consecutive twist-lock moves. Locate a section of overhanging bouldering wall (20 to 45 degrees past vertical) that's littered with large holds. Forget working a set boulder problem; your mission here is to use any hold needed to pull or leverage on in order to gain a solid twist-lock position (see pages 77 and 78, for example). As described earlier, the most secure twist-lock position is with one hip turned to the wall and the opposite hand pulled in tight near your torso, creating the lock. After reaching up with your inside free hand, try to upgrade your feet and rotate your body 180 degrees so as to gain a new twist lock with the other hip against the wall. With practice, you will be able to gracefully ascend a steep wall with consecutive twist-lock moves—at a surprisingly small energy cost.

DEADPOINT DRILL

Perform this drill on a section of wall that overhangs between 5 and 25 degrees. The ideal setup would consist of two small footholds to stand on (just a foot or so off the ground) and four non-tweaky medium-size handholds, two in front of your face and the other two about 2 feet above that. While standing on the small footholds, pull in with both hands to draw your body inward and quickly reach up to the high hold at the moment of the deadpoint. After latching on to the high hold, immediately drop that hand back down to the starting hold. Now perform a deadpoint with the opposite hand to complete the cycle. All the while your feet remain fixed as you continue this drill for a total of four to six cycles.

ONE-ARM DEADPOINT TRAVERSING

This exercise requires a vertical or slightly overhanging wall with enough room available to traverse 10 to 20 feet using medium- to large-size holds. The goal here is to traverse the wall using quick but controlled sideways deadpoint moves with your leading hand. In the case of traversing to the right, it's the right hand that deadpoints from hold to hold while the left hand dangles by your side (or is held behind your back). Use your arm and torso to initiate the movement—this drawing-in of the body produces a brief deadpoint during which you make a quick grab at the next hold. Attempt to traverse for a total of ten to twenty deadpoint moves, with each move traveling between 6 and 18 inches to catch the next hold. Rest for a few minutes, and repeat this drill using the other hand to traverse back across the wall.

Bouldering Games

Who needs a rope to get a good workout? An hour or two of playing in the bouldering area can provide a superb technical and physical workout. While some climbers prefer to simply send boulder problems, engaging in some of these bouldering games adds competitive strategy and challenge to the workout.

ADD-ON

Like a wild mix of chess and gymnastics, Add-On blends skill and strategy with power and strength. Select a challenger of similar ability and agree on a section of bouldering wall to play on—most people prefer a steep section. Determine who will go first. If it's you, step up to the wall and create a two-move sequence. (Play with "open feet," meaning you can place your feet on any holds you like.) Now step off the wall and allow your challenger to climb this exact sequence; however, he must add on one more move to the sequence before jumping off the wall. Now it's your turn to climb the three-move sequence but with the task of adding on a fourth move. Continue in this add-on fashion until one person fails to climb the complete sequence. The strategy of this game centers on your ability to add on moves that are too difficult for your challenger, but still doable for you. You can also add on moves that focus on a known weakness of your challenger—two-finger pockets, long lock-off moves, or whatever. Have fun!

SEND ME

Send Me is a fun game in which your training partner directs you through an impromptu bouldering sequence. Using a laser pointer, your partner will point out a six- to ten-hand-move boulder problem on a steep wall (if it's a complex problem, have your partner use the laser pointer to light up the holds as you're climbing). Like the previous bouldering game, play Send Me with "open feet." You get one attempt to climb the exact sequence, then your partner gets an attempt. Whoever sends the problem first gets a point. Now switch roles and attempt a new problem. You will soon discover that playing Send Me for an hour is an excellent workout in and of itself.

CHAPTER SEVEN

Lead Climbing and Success Strategies

Life with the nerve endings hanging out—that's how it sometimes feels when lead climbing. Given the relatively safe setting of a climbing gym, however, the acute sensations of lead climbing are something that you should aspire to, not avoid. It is on the sharp end of the rope that you fully experience what recreating in the vertical extreme is all about.

Without the snug security of a toprope, you will tap into a whole new level of experience on lead. All aspects of climbing are magnified: the challenge, the fear, the risk, and the reward. Clearly the step up to becoming a leader is a big one that shouldn't be rushed. With the toprope gone you can—and will—catch some air time. Fortunately, lead climbing indoors can be an extremely safe activity given proper training and an intermediate skill level. In this chapter you will learn the crucial techniques and mental skills needed for beginning your adventures on the sharp end.

Climbing strategy is another skill set you need to develop as you advance in ability. Regardless of whether you are leading, toproping, or bouldering, formulating a unique success strategy for every climb is tantamount to performing your best on an on-sight attempt or when working to redpoint a project. To this end, you'll learn proven strategies for reading a route, solving perplexing crux sequences, and programming your mind for success.

Learning to Lead Climb

Learning to lead climb will definitely add some spice to your life as a climber. Clinging to tiny holds with pumped muscles, you will look downward and see a seemingly pencil-thin rope dangling from your harness and running through only a few scrawny carabiners. This adrenaline-releasing sight—and any thoughts of falling—will either refocus you into continuing upward or freeze you in place with fearful thoughts of how you got into this predicament. Of course, learning to lead is a roller-coaster-like process that will surely have you operating in both modes from day to day or even climb to climb. With experience and knowledge of lead-climbing strategies, however, you will gain confidence and comfort in being a lead climber.

Just when you are ready to begin lead climbing is a matter you should discuss with an instructor or a few of your more experienced climbing companions. If you are a quick study and a mature individual, you might be ready to test the lead-climbing waters with a few months' experience. However, many folks spend a year or more toproping and bouldering before they tie into the sharp end. Ultimately, you must take 100 percent responsibility in making the move to lead climbing. As the name implies, you are the leader.

When you do decide to begin lead climbing, you will need to develop several technical and risk-management skills that are not needed in toproping. Learning to efficiently clip into the quickdraws that hang from the lead-climbing anchor bolts is essential. Furthermore, you'll need to become familiar with the potential hazards unique to lead climbing and learn how to mitigate each. Upcoming are the nitty-gritty details on these skills and much more.

Clipping Quickdraws

Unlike toproping, your safety in lead climbing requires clipping the rope into a series of anchor bolts along the path of the route. Most climbing gyms affix a permanent quickdraw to each anchor bolt so that you only need to clip the rope into a carabiner as you pass each bolt placement. Sounds simple, right? Well, if your forearms are pumped or if you are quaking in your boots, this simple task can be frustrating and stressful. Therefore, it's important that you gain lots of practice clipping quickdraws on moderate lead climbs and initially resist the urge to attempt climbs at your toprope

Clipping

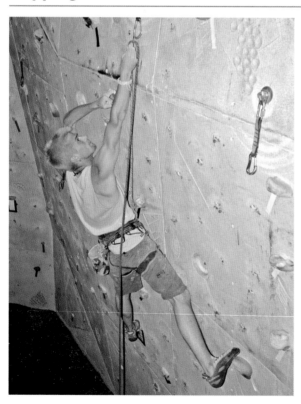

Poor clipping position with the bolt far above head level and a bent, straining arm.

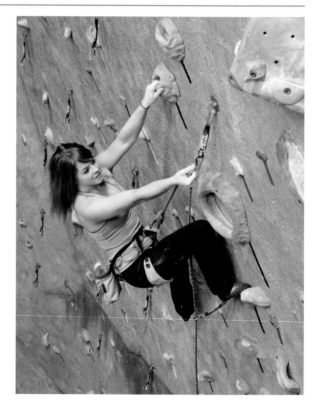

A better position for clipping with a straight arm and the quickdraw near head level.

limit. After a few weeks of ticking easy lead climbs, you'll find that clipping quickdraws becomes an automatic event, instead of the trembling I-can't-get-the-darn-rope-into-the-carabiner epic likely common to your formative efforts.

FIND THE OPTIMAL CLIPPING POSITION

Efficiently clipping each anchor bolt starts with a stable body position from which to act. Good forerunners typical set a specific clipping position—that is, a combination of hand- and footholds that provide a steady stance to pause and clip the rope. A common mistake of novice leaders is attempting to clip too soon. Often you'll see such a climber struggling to clip the rope into a quickdraw at arm's length above his head. This is usually a bad idea, for a couple of reasons. First, such reachy clips tend to be strenuous, since you'll need to pull with one arm in order to reach high with the other. Worse yet, you'll need to pull a greater length of rope to make the clip, meaning a longer fall should you fall while attempting the clip.

A better strategy is to climb high enough so that the anchor bolt is near the level of your head or, better yet, your chest. Usually you will be able to find a high handhold from which to hang straight-armed while the free hand makes the clip. Furthermore, you'll need to pull up less rope in order to complete the clip, making for a faster clip and a reduced fall distance should you come off in the process.

Make a game out of trying to find the perfect body position for each clip. Assume the role of a "clipping position detective" searching to find the least strenuous, most stable position for every clip. Sometimes a large hand- and foothold will greet you upon arriving at a bolt, thus making the task a no-brainer. As the difficulty of the route increases, however, you'll need to be more creative and insightful in order to discover the clip position the forerunner created. Rule nothing out—consider the possible benefits of a twist lock, stem, heel hook, or

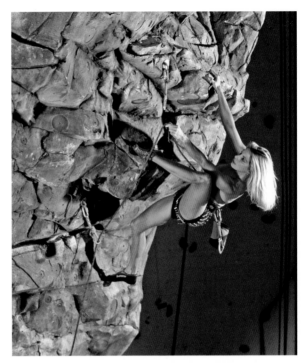

A heel hook provides an excellent clipping position on steep rock.
COURTESY OF NICROS.COM

flag in facilitating a casual clip. Ultimately, it's the experience you accumulate over dozens and hundreds of leads that will make you an ace at gleaning the optimal position and making a quick, efficient clip.

CLIPPING TECHNIQUE

Clipping the rope into the free carabiner of a quickdraw is a one-handed task that many beginners fumble through. To avoid this affliction, you must practice clipping quickdraws just as you practice any other important skill. There are two different techniques that you must learn, since both will be called upon depending on the direction of the carabiner gate in relation to the clipping hand. Practice both techniques with both hands until clipping becomes second nature and automatic.

Finger-Grab Clip

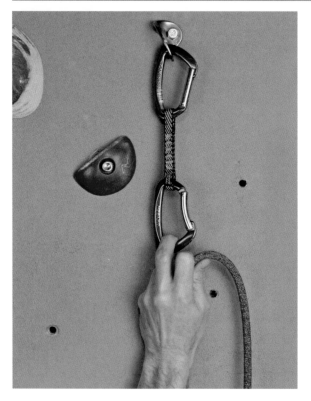

Pinch the rope between the tip of your index finger and thumb, then hook the carabiner with the middle finger to hold it steady.

Push the rope through the gate with your thumb.

Let's first consider the situation where the carabiner gate is facing the opposite direction of your free hand. Reach down and grab the rope by pinching it between the tip of your index finger and thumb. Grab the rope as far as possible below its tie-in spot with your harness, so as to maximize the length of rope available to pull upward toward the quickdraw. Now pull the rope up and hook the carabiner with your middle finger to hold it steady while you push the rope through the gate with your thumb.

The above technique will not work if the carabiner gate is facing to the same side as your free clipping hand. In this case you'll need to reach down

and grab the rope between the tips of your index and middle fingers. Now pull the rope up and place your thumb against the spine of the carabiner while your fingers push the rope through the gate. Strive to hold the carabiner still by thinking about squeezing it between your thumb and forefingers.

If the anchor is above eye level, you may not have enough slack to clip the rope with a single pull. Here you'll need to pull the rope up and hold it in your teeth while you reach down to pull up more rope. Holding the rope in your teeth may seem like a dicey proposition—what if you fall?—but it's actually a very common technique that hasn't caused anyone

Pinch Clip

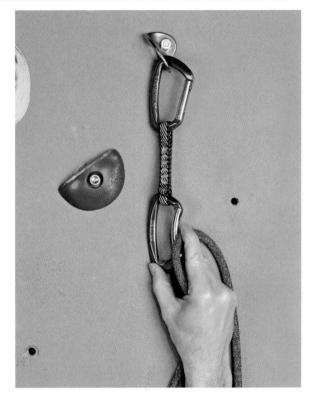

Grab the rope between the tips of your index and middle fingers.

Pull the rope up and place your thumb against the spine of the carabiner while your fingers push the rope through the gate.

serious injury (to the best of my knowledge). Of course, climbing a move or two higher so that the bolt is at chest level eliminates the need for a double pull. When in doubt as to the optimal clipping position, explore climbing a move or two higher in an attempt to avoid a reachy clip that requires a double pull and bite on the rope. Most often you'll be rewarded with a shorter, more casual clip.

The bottom line on clipping: practice these techniques and by all means modify them and make them your own. After a few months of lead climbing the process of clipping the rope into quickdraws will become almost subconscious.

PROPER ROPE PLACEMENT THROUGH A CARABINER

One subtle but important nuance of clipping the lead rope into a quickdraw is that the sharp end of the rope (the end tied to your harness) should exit the outer side of the carabiner. If the lead end of the rope exits on the biner's wall side, the rope may pull across the gate as you climb past the bolt. Though extremely rare, the rope could unclip itself as you climb above—or, in the worst case, unclip as you fall past the anchor bolt. Don't take chances—learn to clip it right every time!

Running the Rope Through a Carabiner

Right: Proper rope path through the carabiner, with the lead end of the rope exiting outside the carabiner.

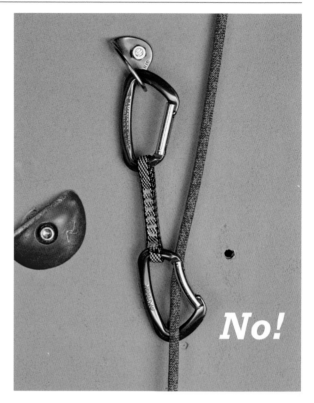

Wrong: Improper clip with the rope exiting on the wall side of the carabiner.

To make a correct clip, observe how the carabiner naturally hangs along the wall surface and estimate how the quickdraw is likely to move as you climb past it. By visualizing this, you will be able to determine the proper way to clip the rope so that the lead end exits the outside of the carabiner. A good belayer will keep a keen eye and quickly notify you if she observes a backward clip. If possible, try to correct the clip before climbing higher.

PRECLIPPING THE FIRST BOLT

On high-end climbs with difficult starting moves, some climbers choose to preclip the first anchor bolt.

In doing so, they essentially gain a toprope for the first section of the climb—not perfect lead-climbing style, but widely viewed as acceptable. Getting the rope preclipped into the first bolt can be achieved three ways. First, you could climb the starting moves to the first bolt, clip the rope, and then downclimb or jump off. Another option is to have a friend or your belayer preclip the rope for you. If you promise to return the favor (or pay cash), you should have no problem finding a volunteer. Finally, you could use a specially made **stick clip** that enables you to extend a loop of rope up through the quickdraw (this is a popular technique among outdoor sport climbers).

Unless the route is at your limit, I suggest you pass on the preclip and send the route in ground-up style, making all the clips yourself. Ask your belayer to give a spot until you clip the first bolt and, if available, place a crash pad at the base of the climb. Think of it as a boulder problem to the first bolt, and then assume a lead-climbing mentality upon making the clip.

Trusting the System and Learning to Take Lead Falls

Excelling as a lead climber demands that you trust the belay system completely and focus your attention on the act of climbing. Should your mind wander to whether the rope, bolt, or belay might fail—ridiculous thoughts, but common among beginning leaders—you will become paralyzed with fear and make lead climbing far more stressful than it need be. The fact is, proper use of the safety systems described in this book make climbing statistically safer than driving a car or riding a bicycle. In chapter 3 you learned the fundamentals of belaying, and now in this section you will learn to evaluate the potential weaknesses in the system as well as the proper way to fall. Yes, falling is an unavoidable part of lead climbing, and there are a few things to keep in mind as you come to take air on lead.

Communicate clearly to your belayer. In a noisy gym environment, it's unfortunately all too easy for a belay request to be misheard or confused with other nearby climbers' comments. When requesting a "take" or "watch me," it's prudent to look your belayer in the eye to confirm that he's heard you.
ROBERT SCOVERSKI

The belay system itself—the belay device, the rope, the anchor bolts and quickdraws, the knot, and the harness—is essentially bulletproof given there is no human error. As covered in chapter 3, there can be no error in tying the rope to your harness; similarly, the belayer must be vigilant in his duties. Given all this, there are just a few remaining weaknesses or hazards that you need to be aware of and thus manage as you engage in lead climbing.

The first such hazard is the unprotected climbing up to the first bolt. As mentioned earlier, you can mitigate the risk of injury by obtaining a spotter or preclipping the rope. The next potential hazard comes when you pull the rope to clip the second bolt. In the case of a high second bolt (or unnecessarily loose belay), the slack in the system as you pull the rope to clip the second bolt may be sufficient that a fall before completing the clip would drop you dangerously close to the ground. The best strategy here is to find an absolutely secure clipping position—one that you couldn't possibly fall from—and have a belayer who doesn't pay out any more rope than necessary. Fortunately, falling

Running the Rope by Your Feet

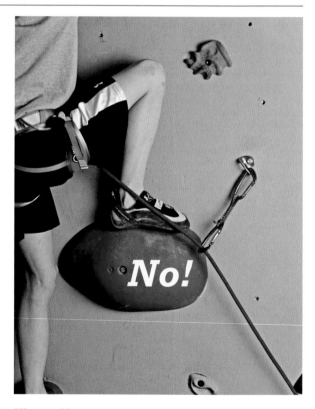

Right: When stepping on a hold near the rope path, always step on the outside of the rope.

Wrong: Never step over the rope to engage a foothold.

while clipping is extremely rare, but in recognizing the hazard you can take actions that will prevent you from getting hurt should it happen.

Another concern is getting your leg looped over the rope while falling—not an uncommon occurrence, and one that often yields a nice rope burn on your leg to remember it by. To avoid this affliction, it's vital to note exactly where the rope is located each time you advance a foot. Your foot (and leg) should never pass between the wall and the rope; instead step up in a way that positions the leg outside the rope. Sequences that take a diagonal or sideways path are most problematic, so sharpen your awareness in these situations.

The final hazard in lead climbing is the slight chance that you might strike a protruding hold or wall feature while falling. Fortunately, most lead climbs that are hard enough to cause you to fall are void of large, protruding holds or steep enough that you mainly fall through air with little or no wall contact (especially if you have a good belayer who knows how to give a soft catch). Still, it's best to climb with an eye out for high-profile holds and recognize when they might be in your fall line. For example, in entering the crux section of a climb— a sequence from which you might fall—visualize the likely distance and trajectory of the fall and assess whether any objects present a risk. Consider whether the fall would be straight down or swinging, and feetfirst or otherwise. Should you envision a potential risk, you will need to decide whether you want to retreat from the climb or push on and assume the risk. If you decide to climb on, continue with prudence and consider downclimbing out of a hard move rather than risking the fall.

It's important to recognize that the large holds and vertical wall angles common to beginner-level climbs often present the greatest hazard to a lead climber. Consequently, such routes are rarely set (as lead climbs) at most commercial gyms, since forerunners are mindful of the risks. Still, should you find yourself struggling on such a route, always attempt to downclimb out of a hard move rather than risk a lead fall that could result in striking a protruding hold.

LEARNING TO FALL

Early ventures at lead climbing will likely have you in the midst of a crux pondering whether to retreat from the difficulties or push yourself to the point of falling (or possibly a success without falling!). No doubt, there will be many mental battles waged as your desire to do a route conflicts with a primal instinct to avoid falling. The result will be a high

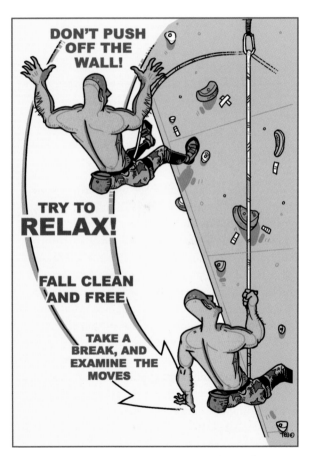

Overcome the fear of falling by taking a few practice falls on a safe, overhanging route.
ILLUSTRATION BY MIKE TEA

once they do fall—experiencing the uneventfulness of the typical lead fall dispels the illusion of danger.

If you can't bring yourself to fall trying, you will need to stage some intentional falls in order to beat the fear. Select an overhanging route void of high-profile holds, and climb up to the fourth or fifth bolt. Confirm that your belayer is ready, and then take your first fall with the last bolt you clipped just a foot or two below your harness. In this case letting go will turn out to be rather anticlimactic: You'll drop only a few feet before the rope arrests the fall—perhaps a bit more if your belayer takes a step forward (or hops up) to soften the fall. Upon taking the fall, analyze how well the belay system worked. It is trustworthy after all! Now climb back up a foot or two higher than before and take another intentional fall. Repeat this process one or two more times, with the goal of taking your final practice fall with the bolt at or just below your feet.

At first, this falling drill will seem like a bitter medicine. Do it a few times per week for several weeks, however, and you'll gradually become accustomed to the feeling of falling. Then, as you begin to pursue on-sight and redpoint ascents, you'll notice a decreasing fear of falling and a new instinctual desire to risk and embrace falling in the attempt of a worthy goal. Recognize this new disposition as a major breakthrough, and pat yourself on the back!

level of anxiety that feeds back and disrupts your ability to climb smoothly and confidently. Recognize, however, that this is a battle all would-be lead climbers must persevere through. Given a committed, disciplined effort, you will eventually conquer the fear of falling and reveal a whole new level of ability. What's more, winning over fear is a process of self-development that will enhance your capabilities in other challenging areas of your life.

To become accustomed to falling, however, happens only via real-life experience at taking lead falls. Therefore, you must force yourself to fall despite what your instincts dictate. Such practice at falling is something that might occur simply by pushing yourself to the limit on a difficult lead climb. Many novice leaders find this to be an impossible task, because it's just too scary to push upward on a hard climb not knowing if they will fall or what the fall will be like. Interestingly, most of the fear evaporates

Learning to Read Boulder Problems and Routes

Climbing strategy isn't confined to the things you do while actually climbing; in fact, a big part of effective strategy involves the things you do in preparing for the ascent. In this section you will learn how to analyze and mentally climb a route without ever leaving the ground. You will learn how to preprogram the ascent with visualization, as well as discover how you can leverage yesterday's successes in helping you climb better today.

Anticipating Moves and Developing a Strategy

The best performers in sport are usually masters at anticipating upcoming difficulties (or the opponent) and developing novel strategies for winning. Climbing is no different. To just climb a route as it comes at you is akin to playing chess one move at a time. You can play chess that way—you can even win—but the best chess players think many moves ahead, anticipate the challenger's actions, and constantly visualize a successful outcome. In this way, you must learn to think like a chess player in the vertical extreme.

The first step is to gather information about the route relating to the location of holds, anchor bolts, and rest positions. View the route from three different perspectives—straight on, from the left, and from the right—and scan for hidden holds in corners, around arêtes, above and below bulges, or anywhere else they might hide. Next, identify the location of each bolt you will need to clip and try to surmise the body position you will assume to make each clip. Finally, locate rest stances and try to figure out the ideal position in each case. Consider the possibility of a heel hook, knee lock, stem, or any other trick position that the forerunner might have slyly built into the route. While none of these moves or rests is guaranteed to be correct, the act of mentally assessing the situation empowers you to climb with more confidence and a greater sense of "knowing" what's likely ahead.

Most important, it's your goal to be able to identify the crux portion of the route and then determine the ideal sequence of moves. As you decipher the best-looking sequence, keep an open mind for alternative possibilities. You may even want to memorize two sequences through the apparent crux section, and then make the choice of which to use when you get there. Finally, don't get stuck in the bottom-up paradigm when figuring sequences. Often you can unlock a puzzling sequence by mentally downclimbing from an obviously good hold or rest.

This skill of reading a route is one part visual intelligence and one part climbing experience. Over time you will develop the ability to see the correct sequence of moves up most, if not all, of the climb. Commit to reading every route, regardless of grade, and you will eventually become a chess master on the rock!

Visualization

The route-reading strategies covered above are but simple mental rehearsal. You can compound the positive effects of such preprogramming by taking a few minutes to engage in detailed visualization of the upcoming ascent.

In previewing the route, you likely pictured yourself on the wall in different body positions and, possibly, testing moves and rest positions. This dissociated, on-TV perspective of envisioning yourself on the route does little to program your nervous system and subconscious for peak performance. To be maximally effective, you must be associated, or get in your body, as you mentally climb the route. You need to see the holds and feel the moves as if you were actually on the wall. Such vivid, realistic visualization programs your nervous system as if you were actually climbing the route and thus increases the odds you'll succeed on the route when you get on it for real.

Using visualization in a noisy gym environment can be difficult—ideally you'd like to find a quiet spot where you can close your eyes and relax for a few minutes while engaging in associated visualization. More likely, you'll be standing with closed eyes at the base of the climb trying to create an associated state. Take a few deep breaths and allow any tension to drain from your body. Now begin climbing the route in your mind's eye. Feel your arms and legs performing the sequence exactly as you read the route a few minutes earlier. See each hand- and foothold as you use it, and feel yourself moving with precision up the route. Finally, feel yourself successfully completing the route. Now open your eyes and return your focus to the present moment. Begin climbing with the same flow as your previous mental ascent.

As a final note, it's important to avoid any negative imagery or thoughts of falling during your visualization. Feeling yourself struggle or fall, while in the associated state, will equally program these outcomes. This explains why worry and fear are often self-fulfilling—such thoughts are usually accompanied by associated visualization of negative outcomes and thus increase the likelihood they will come to fruition.

Leverage Past Experience

Another powerful strategy is to compare the climb you are about to attempt to a similar route you've succeeded on in the past. For example, suppose the desired climb features a large overhang with what appears to be a difficult stand-up past the lip. Close your eyes and think back to a successful past ascent through a large roof—how did you attack the route, what techniques or specific moves were required, and, most important, how did you feel upon sending the route? This process of vividly visualizing all the details and feelings of a past success will

recycle these resources for use in the present. This strategy only takes a minute or two to execute, but it's exceedingly powerful in helping program your mind for peak performance.

Working a Route

Projecting, or working a route, is a common mode among gym climbers. Whether it's an impossible-looking boulder problem or an inspiring lead climb, working to solve the rock puzzle engages the mind and body in a way unlike other life tasks. Projects that take hours or days to complete are often the most gratifying, as you progressively realize tangible improvement from session to session and eventually experience the rapture of success. While there are no trophies or medals to be won, projecting provides the priceless payoff of self-exploration and self-improvement.

Following are several powerful strategies for efficient projecting. You will learn how to chunk down a difficult route into manageable parts and then reassemble the chunks into a successful redpoint ascent. Next, you will learn several crux-busting strategies that you can leverage in solving

---

Mental Preparation Tips for Lead Climbing

1. Scope the route from three different angles to locate holds, determine clipping positions, anticipate moves, identify rest positions, and develop a climbing strategy.

2. Scan the route for potential risks—high-profile protruding holds, the chance of taking a diagonal fall, ground fall potential, and such—then determine how to best mitigate these risks.

3. Mentally rehearse the climb. Consider taking a few minutes to close your eyes and engage in associated visualization of the ascent.

4. Elicit a peak performance state via slow, deep breathing, a narrowing of focus, and an intense knowing of your true ability. Visualize a past successful ascent of a similar route to fortify confidence and foster positive emotions.

the hardest moves of a boulder problem or route. You will then learn how to rehearse the climb for a stylish, ESPY-deserving redpoint ascent!

Chunking Down a Route

The benefits of chunking down a difficult climb into parts are both mental and physical. Psychologically, it reduces the burden of a long, hard route by allowing you to consider its parts as several shorter, doable climbs. Physically, chunking lets you dedicate full energy to solving the hardest chunk first, as if it were a route of its own. Only when this is sent do you begin working on other easier parts of the climb.

Before you can chunk down the route, it helps to have some firsthand knowledge. Take a quick reconnaissance run up as much of the climb as possible to determine its logical parts. On a project with multiple cruxes, you might chunk down the route into four or five sections defined by the obvious stopping points (rest positions or bolt clips). A boulder problem, however, might be broken into three chunks: the section up to the crux, the crux itself, and the final section to the top. After your first run on the route, classify each part according to apparent difficulty. For example, the third and fourth chunks might be the hardest, the first chunk the next hardest, and the second and final chunks the easiest. Solving the hardest part(s) is top priority, so get to work on solving the chunk you deem most difficult. Once it's sent, move on to the second most difficult chunk, and so forth.

Upon solving each chunk, it's time to begin work on linking the chunks into a complete redpoint ascent. While the natural approach would be to simply begin attempting the redpoint from the ground up, it's actually more effective to practice climbing ever-increasing lengths of the route beginning with the top section. In the above example of a route broken into five chunks, you would lower from the top anchors and attempt to link the fourth and fifth chunks. If successful, you'd again lower

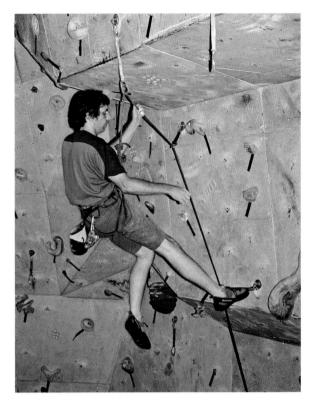

Hangdogging is the common practice of working a hard route section by section with liberal hanging on the rope between attempts.

from the anchors and attempt to link on toprope the third, fourth, and fifth chunks. Continue adding chunks until your starting point is the ground.

This process of linking chunks might seem superfluous, but it is often the most effective strategy for completing a project that's stretching your capabilities. Linking from top down makes you extremely familiar and confident with the final chunks of the route. On redpoint, it's here that you will want to be super dialed in due to increasing mental and physical fatigue. Conversely, the straight-from-the-ground approach may leave you thrashing to rediscover the sequence through the final chunks as aching muscles and anxiety compromise your technique and cloud your memory.

Deciphering a Crux Sequence

It's inevitable that you will occasionally reach a point on a climb where all hope seems to be lost. Suppose there's a blatant lack of good holds, you don't have a clue what to do, and your confidence is tanking. What will you do in such a frustrating situation? Fish or cut bait—or, in climbers' lingo, climb or take dirt?

Hopefully you'll decide to give it a proud effort, realizing that even if you don't succeed in winning, you will still succeed in learning. Climbing is a never-ending cycle of success and failure, and the down phase of the cycle is as important as the up phase for self-development and absolute improvement. The following section details several problem-solving techniques for use on projects that are resisting your best efforts.

EMBRACE THE ROUTE'S FEEDBACK

Many climbers fail on routes they are physically capable of doing because they ignore the feedback the route is providing. Avoid this mind-set by embracing the feedback of failed attempts as clues toward your inevitable success. For instance, if you are tending to barndoor off the crux move, recognize that a flagging leg will increase stability. Or if you can't reach the next critical hold, look for an undercling and hip turn to extend your reach. If you still can't solve the move, the route may be hinting that there is a hidden hold or specific body position you have yet to discover.

No matter what, believe that the route wants you to succeed regardless of your current struggles or the apparent impossible feel of the climb. In this way, view each failed attempt as a signpost directing you toward a better course of action instead of becoming obsessed with a single way the route must be done. A creative, thinking-out-of-the-box approach is most valuable.

THINK OUT OF THE BOX

To break through a sticking point on a climb, you must get outside your current mind-set. The first key strategy is to exercise a flexibility of perspective. For a moment, detach yourself from the situation and visualize the problem spot from a perspective outside yourself. View yourself attempting the crux from a disassociated, on-TV perspective. See yourself trying a wide range of possible solutions, and in particular sequences that you have yet to test out in reality. It can also help to visualize how some great climber you know would attack the route—what tricks and tactics do you see him employing? Maybe a dyno past a long reach, a sequence of small foothold upgrades, or possibly a clever rest position that would provide a more rested attempt on the crux?

Another good strategy is to try a series of ridiculous, improbable moves. For example, try doing a heel hook, a twist lock, a deadpoint, a mantle, and any other move you can think of. Disregard the fact that a given move doesn't seem to be the solution—give it a try without prejudice. In attempting a variety of different techniques, you may very well stumble onto a workable sequence that you would have never surmised while climbing with the blinders on. Be creative and have fun, and above all maintain a belief that the route is possible. You might not send the climb that day, but you will make an important stride toward future success.

FOCUS ON THE FEET

When struggling on a difficult move, it's a natural tendency to obsess on finding the next good handhold that will enable you to pull through. Ironically, the solution is usually a matter of better footwork and body position. Thus it's vital that you assume an intense foot focus and resist the temptation to search for a handhold solution to your difficulties.

Stellar footwork and never-ending foot focus are hallmarks of all top climbers. This is one area where you can, and should, model the actions of these elites. Observe how the best climbers in the gym use their feet in prevailing through heinous cruxes, and then strive to let your feet similarly run the show. You will also benefit by reviewing the fundamentals of effective technique (see chapters 5 and 6) and by performing a few of the foot-oriented drills (such the Downclimbing, Tennis Ball, High-Step, and Tracking drills).

Condition yourself to look down and "think feet" every time you begin to strain or tremble on a route. Make *Focus on the feet* your climbing mantra, and you will be surprised by the ease with which you surmount many so-called cruxes!

Rehearsing a Project

In rehearsing for your redpoint send, it would be wise to consider these common performance-limiting factors (and their cause): poor economy of movement (bad technique and physical tension), overgripping of handholds (anxiety and fear), missed holds and rests (climbing with blinders on), and shaken confidence (negative thoughts). Each of these factors accelerates energy drain, and failure is all but certain if you suffer from two or more of these handicaps.

While we have already covered all these influencing factors in one way or another, it's important that you review every aspect of efficient performance in practicing for a redpoint. Any overlooked detail or minor inefficiency might be enough to sink your ship. So, like cutting fat from a piece of steak, refine your sequence by cutting out any unnecessary movements or time spent hanging out in strenuous positions. Your goal is to move briskly from one rest position to the next, with the highest possible fuel economy. Make a game out of elevating the quality of your ascent with every practice lap, and soon the redpoint will be in the bag.

Redpointing a Project

The nature of projecting is to climb a route at your limit or to break new ground with a hardest-ever ascent. A successful redpoint, therefore, requires near-perfect execution as well as an anxiety-free and well-rested body. In the case of a route that you quickly solved and rehearsed, it may be possible to achieve the redpoint in the same session. But first take an extended break to recover from your practice efforts. Take off your climbing shoes, get

Tips for Working a Route

1. Chunk down the route into workable parts. Hangdog (climb bolt-to-bolt with liberal hanging on the rope) up the entire route to identify the hardest chunk. Then work on solving this section first.

2. Analyze the route's feedback after each failed attempt. Are you missing a hold? Is there a better sequence or body position to be found? Do you need to climb faster or locate another rest?

3. Resist the tendency to lead with your hands and instead focus on your feet. The key to unlocking most crux sequences lies in discovering the optimal use of footholds and the requisite body positions.

4. Upon solving all the chunks, begin linking sections from the top down. Your goal is to rehearse and wire the top portion of the route, which is where you will be most fatigued when attempting your redpoint.

5. Take a long rest (ten to thirty minutes) before going for the send. If needed, take a couple of days off and return to redpoint the climb in a completely fresh state.

a drink, and walk off any existing tension so as to feel completely fresh and relaxed for your redpoint attempt. Depending on your degree of fatigue, you may want to rest anywhere from ten to thirty minutes before going for the send.

As you begin climbing, take the route one chunk at a time, whether it's bolt-to-bolt or rest-to-rest. The burden of looking up and considering the route as a whole can be too great and may plant the seeds of failure in the form of jitters and doubts. Mentally tick off each chunk as you complete it—this will build confidence and help propel you upward. Before you know it you will be clipping the anchors, and the route will be ticked!

An especially severe project may require that you return another day with a full gas tank in order to redpoint the route. Take two full rest days and then return to the gym with the intention of completing the project. Perform an extended warm-up and redpoint a few easier routes to get into a groove. Now take a ten- to twenty-minute rest and send the project.

Going for the redpoint!

CHAPTER EIGHT

Mental Training and Fear Management

A common adage among rock jocks is that *climbing is mostly mental.* This saying is born from the fact that even the strongest, most technically sound climber can be sunk by fearful, anxious, or doubtful thoughts.

Whereas I believe climbing performance is actually about one-third mental—with technique and fitness making up the other two-thirds—most climbers' skill levels in these three areas develop disproportionately. After a year or so of climbing, for example, your fitness and technical attributes will likely be more developed than your mental abilities. Consequently, your mental game may become the greatest constraint to your future growth and your ultimate degree of success in the sport.

The goal of this chapter is to help you turn this common weakness into a strength. For starters, you will learn the importance of self-awareness and how you can make regular self-assessments and course corrections. Next, you will learn how to control anxiety and fear, because you simply cannot climb well (or enjoy climbing) if you are weighed down by negative thoughts or the fear of falling. Lastly, you'll discover the keys to creating a peak performance state from which your best ascents will be born.

But let's begin with a look at getting your head into the game by developing a higher level of self-awareness.

Developing Self-Awareness

Name a top athlete in any sport—Tom Brady, Shaun "Flying Tomato" White, Albert Pujols, and the like—and you are naming a person with an uncommon sense of self-awareness. Similarly, the most talented amateur athletes and weekend warriors possess a level of self-awareness that enables them to maximize their ability, even though their sport is but an avocation. In climbing, self-awareness empowers you to manage stress and fatigue, redirect unproductive thinking, identify weaknesses, and refine your practice and training to be most effective. Let's dig deeper and take a look at a couple of techniques for increasing self-awareness.

Self-Assessing Your Performance

Self-assessment is a process of identifying both your strengths and weaknesses, yet it's the weaknesses on which you must shine the light if you want to climb better. While your real-life experiences with failure will seem to point to a lack of strength, such a conclusion is myopic and often dead wrong. Here's why.

When you get pumped and fall off a climb, there are almost always underlying causes that produced premature fatigue and failure. For example, poor footwork or a missed foothold, improper body positioning, overgripping of holds, fearful

Table 8.1 *Self-Assessment Checklist*

TECHNIQUE	Good	Okay	Poor
Precise, quiet foot placements that carry your weight			
Grip handholds lightly and let arms play a secondary role			
Use of the Left–Right Rule for stable movement			
Economy of movement (rhythm, pace, poise)			
Use of rest positions			
Use of nonpositive handholds (side pulls, underclings, slopers)			
Optimal use of feet and climbing shoes (inside/outside edges, toe, sole, heel)			
Use of flagging to aid stability and prevent barndooring			
Mantling through long reaches; hand–foot matching			
Twist lock and backstep on steep terrain			
Dynamic moves (deadpoints and lunges)			
Clipping quickdraws			

MENTAL	Good	Okay	Poor
Trusting the belay system (and spotter)			
Reading sequences, clip positions, and rest locations			
Anticipating moves and developing a strategy			
Visualizing sequences and a successful ascent			
Deciphering cruxes			
Redpointing projects			
Controlling tension and anxiety			
Managing fear (failure and falling)			
Getting focused and tuning out distractions			
Detachment from climbing outcome			

PHYSICAL	Good	Okay	Poor
Body composition (compared with ideal for climbing)			
Flexibility			
Pull-muscle strength (general pull-up ability)			
Core/abdominal strength			
Antagonist pull-muscle conditioning			
Lock-off strength			
Grip strength			
Anaerobic (climbing) endurance			
Speed of recovery (between climbs and workouts)			
Quality of diet			
Quantity of rest between workouts			

thoughts, climbing too slowly, lack of concentration, a botched sequence, or a missed rest will all lead to accelerated energy drain. Therefore, a meaningful self-assessment must go beyond the superficial issue of "lacking strength" and examine the mental and technical weaknesses that are robbing you blind. I estimate that average climbers unknowingly waste 50 percent (or more) of their energy resources due to lackluster technique and poor mental control. In this case, complaining about a lack of strength is like complaining about the price of gas while driving a heavy gas-guzzling car!

Here are two strategies for effective self-assessment. First, conduct a spot assessment after every fall or failure on a route. Ask yourself a series of probative questions such as *What pressures or fears held me back?* or *What technical or tactical errors did I commit?* or *What physical tension prevented fluid, controlled movement?* Asking questions like these will often reveal your limiting factor on a given route and thus allow you to make an effective course correction on the spot.

Identifying the theme of your weaknesses on a broader macro scale may require a more comprehensive assessment. Use the Self-Assessment Checklist (table 8.1) as a sort of magnifying glass to inspect and assess specific skills and tactics. Of course, it's the low-scoring questions that present major constraints on your performance.

Hire a Coach to Identify Technical and Tactical Flaws

Athletes in pretty much all other sports have coaches, so why shouldn't climbers? Interestingly, most climbers get no formal instruction beyond their first day or two as true novices learning to tie knots and belay. In using this trial-and-error approach to learning, you will inevitably hit some performance roadblocks.

Enlisting a coach to assess your abilities and help direct your training will put you on the fast track to better climbing. All you need is one consultation

per month or quarter, during which time the coach can assess your climbing and then design an appropriate action plan for improvement. Hopefully, this program will include practice drills to improve technique, suggestions for improving your climbing tactics and mental control, and some fitness-training exercises that target critical physical weaknesses. If the coach simply prescribes a strength-training program, then it's time to find another coach.

Tuning into Your Thoughts

On any given day more than 20,000 thoughts surface in your conscious mind. If there is a natural tendency in the direction of thoughts, it's to focus on problems, fears, and frustrations. To some degree, this tendency to focus on the negative and threatening aspects in life is a genetic defense mechanism. However, the tendency to view things compulsively from the cup-is-half-empty perspective or the worst-case scenario is a conditioned habit that will hold you back.

Gaining higher self-awareness, then, must include tuning into your thoughts more often and supplanting negative thinking with positive imagery and productive self-talk. Consider that everything you are and everything you will become is a direct function of your thoughts. Thus, what could be more central to improving your climbing than fostering a curious, positive, goal-motivated way of thinking?

The impact of getting your climbing head on straight can't be understated in terms of both immediate results and long-term improvement. For example, just as finding a hidden hold on a desperate crux can make it feel way easier, the effects of eliminating fearful, doubtful self-talk can feel like taking a 10-pound weight off your back. So if you want to climb better today, lose the mental baggage! The long-term aggregate effects of higher-quality thinking day-to-day could be the difference between you climbing 5.10 or 5.13 a few years from now.

Becoming aware of the unproductive self-talk and negative imagery is the first and hardest step to turning it around. Tune into your self-talk throughout the day, at home, at work, and at the gym. What are you hearing? Ultimately the goal is to modify your thinking in ways that will help you solve problems (instead of wallowing in them), challenge fears (instead of avoiding them), and compel intelligent action toward your goals (instead of backpedaling at the first sign of adversity). Learn to redirect your thoughts onto your goals, replace negative self-talk with can-do language, and focus your energy on current actions that will propel you forward.

Controlling Tension and Anxiety

As the saying goes, *Thoughts are things*. If you possess fearful thoughts, these thoughts will result in anxiety and physical tension. Similarly, if you direct calming, positive thinking, you will naturally shift into a more relaxed, centered state. Given this intimate connection of the mind and body, you can consciously determine how you feel simply by redirecting your thoughts. This is a powerful concept that's vital for climbers to understand and

leverage—such thought control is the essence of mental toughness.

In this section you will learn how to create an optimal, centered state for climbing via proactive thought control. Being centered encompasses the feelings of relaxation, balance, and confidence. You will always climb your best if you begin from this centered state. As you ascend a difficult or scary route, however, your mind and body can rapidly shift into a tense, inefficient state. Thus you must also learn how to regain control—or return to center—while on the climb.

Getting Centered

Whether you're climbing a five-move boulder problem or a 50-foot route, unchecked tension and anxiety will hold you back like gravity on steroids. Physical tension kills motor skills and technique, while mental tension (anxiety and fear) quells creativity, focus, and the opportunity to achieve flow. Interestingly, average climbers are so used to climbing with undue tension that they don't even realize its negative effects. Upon gaining awareness and learning to release the tension, however, they are amazed at their newfound freedom to move smoothly and more efficiently.

You, too, can learn to take control over tension and create a relaxed, balanced, centered state from which to climb your best. The six-step ANSWER Sequence is a highly effective process for identifying and eliminating tension. It's easy to learn and put to work, as evidenced by the thousands of climbers around the world who now use my ANSWER Sequence as their antidote to anxiety and physical tension.

Initial use of the ANSWER Sequence may require a quiet room and five minutes to perform. With a little practice, however, you will be able to incorporate it into your preclimb routine and create a centered state in just a minute or two. I invite you to make a copy of the ANSWER Sequence, and begin using it throughout the day, both in and outside of the climbing gym.

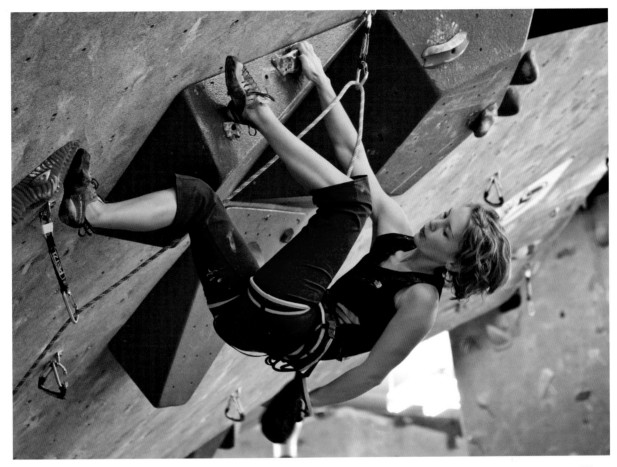

Lead climbing is a heady game, and it's only through experience and conscious effort that you will develop the poise and mental toughness you need to excel.

WADE DAVID

Regaining Control

Climbing near your limit can be stressful. Desperate moves, risk of falling, and the uncertainty of what's next can foster unproductive thoughts and physical tension that snowballs at a rapid rate. Left unchecked, such rising tension will cause you to pump out and quite likely fall. While every climber has been through this type of experience, it should be but a brief phase that you work through. Increasing confidence and experience will go a long way toward mitigating this natural fight-or-flight response. Still, even expert climbers occasionally experience tension when attempting severe routes. They are masters at controlling tension on the fly, however, so that it never grows to a level that hampers performance.

Similarly, your goal should be to develop such awareness and control over rising tension. You can then use rest stances and clipping positions as an opportunity to release the tension and return to center. Here are two strategies for regaining control in the midst of a difficult route.

FOCUS ON BREATH CONTROL

Deep, steady breathing is the number one antidote to tension. Not surprisingly, then, the common tendency to hold your breath on a difficult sequence is a prime cause of tension. While it's okay (and often beneficial) to hold your breath for a single challenging move that requires you to bear down hard, it is common to continue to hold your breath, or breathe unevenly, throughout a series of difficult moves. By being aware of this tendency, however, you can take conscious control of your breathing during stressful times on a route. Strive for slow, deep belly breaths during the moves leading up to a crux, and try to regain steady breathing as you move out of the most difficult moves. This strategy alone will go a long way toward controlling tension as you climb.

Before you start up a route, try to predetermine the location of all rest stances and clipping positions. These spots should offer you the opportunity to take a moment to steady your breathing. Upon reaching one of these spots, close your eyes for a moment and turn your thoughts inward to feel air filling your lungs with each slow breath. As you exhale, visualize the tension exiting your body and feel a renewed sense of being centered. This entire process might only take five to fifteen seconds, but it's invaluable for regaining an optimal state for attacking the next section of the climb. Make it a habit to steady your breathing at every rest; you might even consider using the ANSWER Sequence at good rest positions that allow you a minute or two to hang out.

KEEP YOUR THOUGHTS PRODUCTIVE AND GOAL-ORIENTED

Doubtful, fearful thinking is an on-sight or redpoint terminator. You simply can't climb well with the weight of these negative thoughts in tow. Once again, you need to seize every stopping point on a route as an opportunity to tune into your thinking. Is it productive or unproductive in nature? Quickly evaluate any fears to determine if they are legitimate or just phantom fears trying to scare you off the route. In gym climbing, most fears are fraudulent, and if this is indeed the case, you must write them off as illusions and then redirect your attention onto your goal—sending the route!

The popular sports metaphor *Keep your eye on the ball* is appropriate here. Resist the tendency to doubt your abilities or ponder the fall potential, and simply narrow your focus onto the next section of the climb. As explained in chapter 7, it's best to attack a route one chunk at a time. Concentrate on the moves up to the next rest and forget about what's below you as well as what's yet to come above the next chunk. If your only goal is climbing the 6 feet (or whatever) to the next rest position, the burden is greatly reduced and a big cause of tension is erased.

View Failures as Part of the Success Process

An important part of emotional control is the ability to deal with failure in a productive way. The natural tendency for many folks is to react to failures with emotional outbursts and a torrent of negative, critical thinking. Of course, such reactive behavior will make future attempts on a climb even more difficult. Not only does this create physical tension, but it also creates an emotional anchor to the climb that will plague future efforts. Even if you return to the route with a clear mind on another day, your subconscious can recall the angst and potentially sabotage your efforts.

While no one likes to fail, it's important to embrace your failures as opportunities for growth and learning. Every time a route rejects you, it is also offering you a valuable lesson for becoming a better climber. If you simply write off the failure as "not being strong enough," you miss out on the lesson. Strive to dig deeper and identify the true cause of each failure—is it poor technique, poor strategy, bad sequencing, fear and doubt, or maybe just a lack of "go for it"?

The Answer Sequence

Step 1: **A**wareness of anxiety, tension, or negative thoughts. Tuning into your inner world is the first step in creating a peak performance state. Use the following steps to counter the problem areas you diagnose.

Step 2: **N**ormalize breathing. Irregular breathing multiplies tension, so strive for smooth, even breathing when the pressure is on. Take several slow, deep belly breaths and feel the tension release from your core.

Step 3: **S**can for areas of muscular tension. To reduce tension, contract the affected muscles for a few seconds, then relax them and visualize the tension draining out like air from a balloon.

Step 4: **W**ave of relaxation. Take a final slow, deep breath and feel the wave of relaxation wash from your head to your toes.

Step 5: **E**rase thoughts of the past—engage the present moment with all your attention. Vividly visualize the ideal outcome and believe in it, but then redirect your thoughts with a laserlike focus onto the present moment.

Step 6: **R**eset posture and flash a smile. Trust your abilities, let the outcome take care of itself, and have fun regardless of the results.

The very best climbers, or peak performers in any field, tend to be uncommonly curious individuals. They are always on the outlook for new information, distinctions, or ideas that will help elevate their game, and they possess an intense curiosity as to why they sometimes fail. By training yourself to respond to failure in a similar way, you will gain some of the personal power of these elite performers. The bottom line: Don't curse your falls, embrace them! They are guideposts and stepping-stones to the higher grades.

Managing Fear

Climbing is a great proving ground to develop mental skills for the rest of your life. Given the safe environment of a gym, there's no reason to not challenge your doubts, your beliefs of what is possible, and, most of all, your fears.

Most common to climbing are the fears of failure and falling. In this section you will learn how to manage or even eliminate these fears, although you will do so with two very different strategies. Defeating fear of failure is an internal battle you'll need to win over your ego, whereas fear of falling can only be dissipated through experience at falling.

Defeating Fear of Falling

It's completely natural to fear falling, just as it is normal to feel fearful in your first-ever attempt to snowboard a black-diamond slope or jump off the high dive. Interestingly, it's not the activity that you actually fear, but instead the unknown of what it will be like. For this reason the fear of black-diamond slopes or the high dive abates with each additional exposure to the situation, because the unknown gradually becomes known. The same is true for the fear of falling—as you become aware of the real risks and log some air time, your fear will slowly dissolve.

Thankfully, an element of this fear remains and will kick in at times when it's truly needed to save your neck. Based on your experience you'll recognize a situation that presents a potentially dangerous fall, and you'll be able to heed the warning of this legitimate fear.

Now let's take a look at two strategies for lessening your fear of falling: risk management and the act of taking practice falls.

ANALYZE AND MANAGE REAL RISKS

This first step in dealing with fear is to identify and mitigate legitimate fears while you dispel the illusionary ones. For example, fear of taking a ground fall before clipping the first bolt on a lead climb is a legitimate fear. Recognizing this, you can take action to reduce the risk (say, by preclipping the first bolt or getting a spotter) and thus nix the fear completely. Same goes for a fear of taking a swinging lead fall toward a large protruding hold or wall feature. By analyzing the fall potential and approximating the angle and length of the fall, you can make an intelligent decision as to whether to climb on (and risk the fall) or downclimb to avoid the risk.

Of course, many fears are simply illusions created in the mind of an inexperienced climber. Fear of the belayer not catching your fall and fear of equipment failure are two common phantom fears that haunt many novices. In these cases you must challenge the fearful thoughts and win over them with reason—you know the gear is bombproof and you know you can trust your belayer (assuming he's a mature, experienced belayer). Silence the voice of such phantom fears by redirecting your thoughts to the moves at hand, and repeat a mantra such as *Climb on, Relax,* or *Do it, do it!*

PRACTICE FALLING

The second strategy for beating the fear of falling requires that you embrace falling in the form of occasional practice falls. As described on page 97, taking a series of controlled lead falls is an effective way to stretch your boundaries on the sharp end. A once-and-done practice fall will do little to erase the fear, however; instead you need to take several falls each session over a period of several weeks. The fear of falling is strong, so it takes a committed effort over time to decondition this emotion. Assume a work-through-it mentality and expect the process to take a few months, if not longer, to yield the desired results. Trust that in taking this bitter medicine, you will eventually develop an indomitable go-for-it mentality that continually prevails over unreasonable fears of falling.

Crushing the Fear of Failure

Fear of failure wields tremendous power over climbers who possess an unbending need for success. Not surprisingly, the fear of failure tends to produce failure as you climb timidly in an attempt to not blow it. Consider how often a football team gives up the winning score when they shift into prevent defense.

In climbing, a try-not-to-fail "prevent defense" results in tentative movement and an apprehension over making tenuous or dynamic moves. Furthermore, it leads you into second-guessing sequences, doubting your ability, and focusing on the

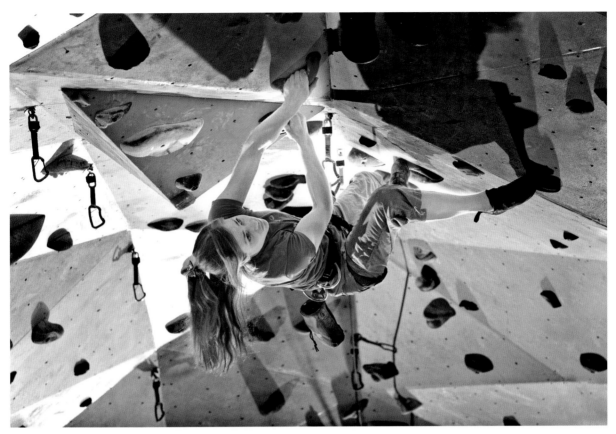

In the relative safety of a climbing gym, you can best quell the fear of falling by focusing completely on the matter of reaching the next hold and attaining the next clip.
NATHAN WELTON

possibility of failure. This mental tension manifests itself as shallow breathing, overgripping of holds, jitters, and tense, inefficient movement. Before long, the very thing you are trying to avoid catches up with you.

Interestingly, this fear is completely self-imposed, and thus eliminating it is completely in your hands. Following are two strategies for killing this fear at its roots.

FOCUS ON THE PROCESS, NOT THE OUTCOME

Fear of failure results from an outcome-oriented mind-set that constantly ponders the odds and

consequences of success versus failure. Therefore, you can defeat this fear by focusing single-mindedly on the process of climbing and never letting your mind wander to the possible outcomes. Concentrate on the things immediate to your performance, such as precise foot placements, relaxing your grip, moving quickly to the next rest position, and such. You can accentuate this laserlike focus by sharpening your visual awareness of the holds and wall features before you. Notice the slight variations and imperfections that make each hold unique, and strive for optimal placement of every hand and foot. If you capture your attention in this way, there will be little opportunity to think about success or failure. Climb in the present!

Anytime your thoughts begin to shift away from this process orientation, immediately respond by redirecting them to your breathing. If possible, pause and take a deep breath or two—feel the air rushing in and out of your chest, and your focus will immediately return to the present moment. Once accomplished, return your focus to climbing with a quick study of your current hand- and footholds. This will get you back into the process of climbing with an optimal mind-set.

PREDETERMINE THAT YOU WILL ACCEPT FAILURE SHOULD IT HAPPEN

A more global approach to permanently deleting the fear of failure is to simply adopt the attitude that it's okay to fail. By willingly accepting this fate (if it should even happen), you totally eliminate the fear and hence liberate yourself to climb to win! Embracing the potential of a negative outcome doesn't mean you aren't going to try your best or that you want to fail. Instead this position simply places you in a frame of mind from which you can try your best to win without reservation.

Of course, gracefully accepting failure is easier said than done for some people. You can only assume this mind-set by consciously detaching your self-image from your performance. This can be difficult in a climbing gym setting, since strangers tend to make first judgments on others based on what they see on the outside—appearance and performance. Your goal, then, must be to recognize that your true friends will like you regardless of your climbing ability, and the opinions of strangers are trivial. Whether or not you can completely embrace this mind-set is a measure of maturity and self-confidence, but striving to possess it is a great mental exercise for developing these traits. Given a long-term effort at assimilating this way of thinking, you will gain mental prowess and free yourself from the chains of needing to perform for others.

Tips for Managing Fear

1. Analyze your fears to determine if they are real or imagined. Take action to mitigate the risk(s) associated with your legitimate fears.

2. Overcome imagined fears with reason—know that these phantom fears are bogus. Redirect your thinking in productive ways and resolve to dismiss all other illusionary fears that might surface.

3. Practice falling (in a safe setting) to develop confidence and trust in the belay system. Your long-term goal is to be able to fall while leading without fear or reservation (if indeed it's a safe climb).

4. Focus on the process of climbing, and detach from the possible outcomes. Let the climb unfold one move at a time.

5. Predetermine that you will accept failure should it happen. Recognize that you are not defined by your successes or failures—however, you are defined by the way you react to success and failure.

Ultimately, it's in climbing for yourself—win, lose, or hanging from a quickdraw—that you will feel most happy and indeed climb your very best.

Creating a Peak Performance State

This final section provides a more holistic look at creating a peak performance state from which you can climb your best. The key is being able to dial in your mind, body, and emotions so they work together in perfect harmony and powerful synergy. In sports this optimal state is often referred to as "the zone."

First, you'll learn four key elements to getting into the zone. The most consistent climbers can create and maintain a highly distinct mental climate that transports them into the zone. You, too, will learn how to tap into this powerful state. Following this we'll look at the importance of preclimb rituals for modulating your mind and body for peak performance. Learning to use these mental techniques will surely elevate your performance, regardless of your absolute level of ability.

Getting into the Zone

The zone is a state where everything comes together for the perfect ascent that seems almost effortless and automatic. Unfortunately, the zone is a state that eludes many athletes. The trick is learning to create this state on demand as opposed to just waiting for it to appear.

Think of the zone as a stable platform from which peak performance occurs. Like a table, this platform has four supporting elements or "legs": a relaxed body, confident emotions, a focused mind, and smooth unforced actions. If one or more of these legs are missing, the table will tip and the zone will be unattainable. This, of course, is the typical situation for many climbers who fail to quash tension, doubts, distractions, and apprehension. The end result is a performance roller coaster where the quality of climbing varies from route to route and day to day.

Following are strategies for solidifying the four supporting elements and getting into the zone more often!

RELAXING YOUR BODY

We've already discussed that you climb most efficiently when you are physically loose and experiencing no excess muscular tension. This is especially important in attempting to climb near your limit, when even the slightest muscular tension will erode fine motor control, drain energy reserves, and most likely lead to failure. Peak performance requires that your muscles feel warm, loose, and free of tension.

The best way to achieve this state is to climb a few submaximal warm-up routes that get your blood flowing, yet don't pump you out. Routes two to four number grades below your redpoint level are ideal. After completing these routes, take off your climbing shoes and perform several minutes of gentle stretching. This combination of warm-up climbs and stretching will prime your body to enter the zone.

Any remaining tension can be eliminated with the ANSWER Sequence described on page 113. After you've put your climbing shoes back on and tied into the rope, spend a minute or two on the ANSWER Sequence and you'll be able to optimize your physical state before starting the route.

BUILDING CONFIDENT EMOTIONS

Self-confidence is a positive mental attitude and anticipation of a successful outcome. Climbing up to your abilities and, for that matter, pushing your limits cannot happen without sufficient self-confidence. On the other hand, an overconfident I'll-try-anything disposition will eventually lead to frustration and failure. Let's sort things out.

You develop self-confidence in proportion to your experience, training, and past successes. Therefore, building self-confidence begins with logging many hours on the rock as well as a steady string of successes on routes of increasing difficulty. Similarly, engaging in a consistent, intelligent training program that improves upon known weaknesses will also build confidence.

Finally, there's positive self-talk and imagery to further fortify confidence. Statements such as *I'm well prepared*, *I'll do great* and *This will be fun* will foster positive emotions. Likewise, visualization can be a powerful confidence builder. Close your eyes and spend a minute or two reliving a past great ascent. By feeling the emotions of that past success, you tap into this powerful resource to empower you in the present moment.

FOSTERING FOCUS

Entering the zone demands a steady, laserlike focus. Precise motor skills and synchronized movements require a tight focus; even a brief break in concentration can result in a botched sequence or fall. Narrowing your focus requires a combination of positive energy and a still mind. Any anxiety or distractions will shatter your focus and make getting into the zone impossible.

A detailed preclimb ritual (to be discussed in the next section) is one of the best strategies for fostering focus. Engaging in a series of preparatory activities—such as scoping the route, tying into the rope, and visualizing a successful ascent—conditions the mind to block out distractions and zero in on the task at hand. Similarly, going through the six-step ANSWER Sequence can further sharpen focus.

In order to understand how to maintain focus, you must understand that distractions are the enemy of focus. Therefore, anything you can do to eliminate distractions before beginning a climb will help foster focus. While climbing, the ultimate goal is to let the rest of the world disappear from your consciousness. Narrowing your world to just you and the climb is the essence of focus.

TRYING SOFTER AND LETTING IT FLOW

Elite athletes often tell of how their best performances somehow seemed effortless or automatic. These experiences describe what is known as "the flow state." You can best access this state by detaching yourself from the past and future, and engaging the route without apprehension. It's also vital that you avoid pressing or trying too hard and instead let your natural climbing skills surface.

Anytime you begin to struggle with a sequence, ease up on the accelerator and assume a "try-softer" approach. If possible, downclimb a few moves to regain a stance so that you can gather yourself. Take a few deep belly breaths and try to return to a relaxed, confident state before you resume climbing. Sometimes you may not be able to downclimb, so you will need to make a few try-softer adjustments on the fly. Begin with a single deep breath, and then focus on improving your foot placements and softening your grip on the handholds. This entire process should take just ten to fifteen seconds, but it's vital for regaining control and fostering flow. Now continue climbing briskly, with confidence and style.

The Power of Preclimb Rituals

The things you think and do in the minutes leading up to a climb largely predetermine the quality of your performance. Rushed preparations and scattered thoughts usually give birth to a shaky performance, whereas detailed, careful preparation and targeted thinking tend to yield a solid, if not exceptional, performance. This exemplifies the power of preclimb rituals.

There are two parts to an effective preclimb ritual: proceeding through a preparatory checklist and the triggering of emotional anchors. The checklist covers all must-do physical tasks in the minutes leading up to the climb, while the leveraging of emotional anchors is a final mental step before launching up the route.

Whether you are lead climbing or highball bouldering, you will be able to relax and climb your best if you can trust the safety system completely. Before lead climbing, check your knot and belayer; prior to starting up a boulder problem, be sure that a crash pad or spotter is in position. COURTESY OF NICROS, INC.

Tips for Creating a Peak Performance State

1. Trust your abilities and don't anticipate the outcome.

2. Develop and use a preclimb routine before every ascent. Scope the route, analyze and mitigate potential risks, identify the keys to the route, and visualize the ascent.

3. Leverage past ascents to create positive energy and fortify confidence in the present moment. Reliving past successes in your mind's eye taps this valuable resource for use in the present.

4. Double-check your harness buckle, knot, and the belayer's device, and then trust the system implicitly.

5. Relax, crack a smile, and have fun climbing!

PRECLIMB CHECKLIST

Like a pilot's preflight checklist, a climber's preclimb ritual should consist of every single activity, big or small, that is necessary to ensure a safe, successful journey. For example, my typical preclimb ritual begins with scoping the route to determine the best path and, hopefully, figure out the key moves and rest positions. Next, I perform a couple of minutes of mental rehearsal and visualization as I try to feel the moves and preprogram in the sequence. Upon gaining a sense of comfort and knowledge about the route, I put on my shoes and tie into the rope. I complete my preclimb ritual by taking a few slow, deep breaths, straightening my posture, and cracking a smile in anticipation of a great climb. This entire ritual typically takes between three and ten minutes (depending on the difficulty and length of the climb), and it leaves me in an ideal state to make my best effort.

Develop your own unique rituals based on what makes you feel most prepared and psyched for a route. Think back to some of your best past performances to gain some clues as to what to include. What did you think and do in preparing for that climb? What did you eat or drink, how did you warm up, and how long did you rest between climbs? Awareness of all the factors—little and big—that lead up to your best performances is a key to being able to reproduce similar results in the future.

Experiment with different rituals and analyze what seems to work best. An effective preclimb ritual doesn't need to be extravagant or long. In fact, a short, concise ritual that quickly gets you prepared and focused to climb is best. Upon developing a ritual that works, stick to it!

EMOTIONAL ANCHORS

Emotional anchors are powerful triggers for peak performance. Have you ever experienced the relaxed pleasure that washes over your mind and body when you hear an old song that instantly connects you to some great past event? This experience exemplifies the power of anchors at transporting past emotions into the present. Your brain associates the song with the emotional state of a distinct period earlier in your life; upon hearing that tune, these emotions are relived in the present. Knowledge of this process empowers you to recall the positive emotions of a previous ascent to aid your performance in the present.

If you've been climbing awhile, you should have a few "perfect" ascents that you can leverage in this way. If not, then tap into some other great life event where you felt exceedingly confident, positive, and successful. Either way, your goal now is to relive this event by creating a brief mental movie that brings as many senses as possible into play. Most people find that bright, crisp visualization is the most effective way to trigger past emotions; however, listening to a particular song can be a powerful anchor, too. Experiment a little in order to discover what works best for you. Be creative and overlook no details in reliving the past event, and you'll learn to consistently release powerful emotions that yield great performances.

CHAPTER NINE

Getting into Climbing Shape

Climbing provides an excellent physical workout that will definitely pump you up. Thus the first step to getting into climbing shape is simply to climb on a regular basis. An hour or two at the climbing gym, three or four days per week, will increase your general level of fitness as well as produce rapid gains in climbing-specific strength. Cancel your health club membership and make indoor climbing your workout of choice!

While climbing offers the most specific training for climbing, there are several good reasons to also engage in supplemental training. First, a modest amount of aerobic training will benefit your climbing measurably by improving stamina and lowering percent body fat (more on this in a moment). Similarly, it would be advantageous for a novice who lacks the base strength needed to learn fundamental climbing moves (can you do ten pull-ups?) to perform some climbing-specific training of the pull muscles. Finally, some basic push-muscle training will help to prevent the muscular imbalances (and reduce the injury risk) that can result from regularly pulling plastic at the gym.

As you progress into the realm of being an intermediate and advanced climber, you will also need to begin some highly targeted training beyond the aforementioned general conditioning. Success at the lofty grades of 5.11 and above often demands specialized strength skills such as the ability to lock off on one arm, hang on a two-finger pocket, or throw a long lunge. Such physical attributes are best developed with a blend of climbing and intelligent training for climbing.

Given the many physical constraints to climbing performance outlined above, you may wonder: Why has it taken until chapter 9 to dig into the subject of fitness training? My answer comes in two parts that I hope you will take to heart and hold as fundamental principles during your formative days as a climber. First, during your initial months learning to climb, you will get enough of a muscular workout simply by climbing a few days per week; premature use of highly stressful exercises, such as the fingerboard, may lead to injury. Second, the steep learning curve of climbing technique means you will make the fastest gains in absolute ability by investing your available workout time into actual climbing versus taking away from climbing time to engage in strength training. The bottom line: For a beginner, climbing is the best training for climbing. Therefore, vow to make paramount the learning of climbing techniques, tactics, and strategy (the subjects of chapters 1 through 8), and you will be on the fast track to become a skilled, successful, and strong climber!

ROBERT SCOVERSKI

General Conditioning

Can you pinch an inch around your waist? Is it a major struggle to touch your toes while keeping your legs straight? Does it take a Herculean effort—or miracle!—to do ten consecutive pull-ups? If you answered yes to one or more of these questions, then you are in need of some general conditioning.

General conditioning focuses on developing the physical foundation needed to learn the fundamental climbing skills described throughout this book. The goal is to optimize body composition, increase flexibility, and build a base level of muscular strength. Let's take a look at effective training for each.

Optimizing Body Composition

If you've ever hiked with a heavy pack or carried someone on your back, you've experienced the negative effects of increased weight on physical performance. Conversely, a reduction in percent body fat or excessive nonfunctional muscle mass can have a positive effect on performance, especially in a sport such as climbing where a high strength-to-weight ratio is fundamental.

The optimal body fat percentage is 6 to 12 percent for men and 8 to 16 percent for women. If you're not sure how you measure up, consider having your body fat tested. Or you can use the economic pinch-an-inch method on your waistline (actually a good gauge). If you can pinch an inch (or more), you are not in the optimal range.

Similarly, excessive muscular weight is about as bad as excessive fat. In fact, since muscle weighs more than fat per unit volume, large muscles in the wrong place are worse than fat. Inappropriate training is the usual cause of unwanted muscle. For instance, the leg exercises performed by bodybuilders or bike racers are a waste of time for climbers since lack of leg strength is rarely a limiting factor on the rock. Biceps curls and heavy bench-press exercises will likewise have a negative impact on climbing performance. Sure, they will pump you up nicely for the beach, but they will also weigh you down on the rock. Fortunately, you can strip away unwanted fat and excessively bulky muscles with disciplined diet and aerobic exercise.

The dietary strategy is to reduce empty calories from junk foods and high-fat fast foods, while maintaining a steady consumption of protein and carbohydrate. The ideal macronutrient caloric breakdown for an athlete is 65 percent carbohydrate, 15 percent protein, and only 20 percent fat. Consequently, you can toss out the high-fat fad diets such as the Zone or Atkins—these are absolutely the wrong diet strategies for a serious athlete!

An active male desirous of some weight loss might restrict his total dietary intake to around 2,000 calories per day (up to 50 percent more on extremely active days). This would break down to about 320 grams of carbohydrate, 80 grams of protein, and 45 grams of fat. Similarly, an active female wanting to drop a few pounds should limit total daily food consumption to about 1,500 calories (up to 30 percent more on extremely active days), striving for a macronutrient breakdown of around 240 grams of carbohydrate, 60 grams of protein, and 35 grams of fat. Upon achieving desired climbing weight, gradually increase caloric intake to determine the appropriate consumption to maintain a stable body weight.

Regarding aerobic exercise, running is by far the most effective method of incinerating fat and shrinking unwanted muscle. Don't worry about losing your climbing muscles, however; they will be preserved as long as you continue to climb regularly and consume at least 1 gram of protein per kilogram of body weight per day. Other popular aerobic activities such as steep mountain biking and the StairMaster will yield mixed results: They do eat up body fat, but they also tend to maintain (or build) undesirable leg muscle. Swimming, rowing, or fast hiking are good alternatives, if you can't run.

Frequency of aerobic training should be proportional to the magnitude of your weight loss goal. For example, if you are significantly overweight, then daily twenty- to forty-minute runs are an important part of your training-for-climbing program. As you near ideal weight, two or three twenty-minute runs per week are sufficient. Upon reaching your optimal weight, very little aerobic training is necessary since indoor climbing requires only modest aerobic fitness. At this point, your training time is better invested on actual climbing and supplemental sport-specific exercises.

Improving Flexibility

While extraordinary flexibility is not needed in climbing, a modest degree of suppleness is necessary for fundamental techniques such as high-stepping, stemming, and heel hooking. Fortunately, just climbing a few days per week provides active stretching that will gradually increase lower-body flexibility. You can expedite the gains in flexibility with supplemental stretching exercises performed as part of your warm-up and cool-down activities. In fact, it's beneficial for all climbers, regardless of their natural level of flexibility, to engage in a few minutes of stretching to prepare the body for the stresses of climbing and help reduce injury risk.

It's important to understand that warm-up stretching should always be gentle and nonpainful, since forceful or ballistic stretching can injure muscles, tendons, and joints. Similarly, intense stretching of a cold muscle can be disastrous, so it's ideal to perform a few minutes of light exercise before stretching. For example, a few minutes of jogging, fifty jumping jacks, or a couple of fast-paced, up-and-down laps on a very easy route will increase your heart rate and warm the muscles for effective stretching.

Following are ten stretches to employ as part of your warm-up routine. Spend thirty seconds to one minute on each stretch, and you'll be ready to begin your climbing workout. It may be beneficial to perform some additional stretching on rest days if you feel that lack of flexibility is a constraint in your climbing.

1. **Buttocks and lower back.** This stretch will improve hip flexion and help facilitate high-stepping. Lie flat on your back with both legs straight. Bend one leg and grasp it behind the thigh or around the shin and pull it toward your chest. Hold the stretch for ten seconds and then release it for a few seconds. Pull the bent leg toward your chest again for a secondary stretch of about twenty seconds. Repeat with the other leg.

Buttocks and lower back

2. **Hamstring.** The muscles along the back of the thigh are chronically tight in many climbers, thus restricting stem and high-step movements. Lie flat on your back with one leg straight and the other bent with the sole of the foot flat on the floor next to the straight leg's knee. Lift the straight leg upward, grab it behind the thigh or calf, and pull gently forward until you feel

Hamstring

the stretch down the back of the leg. Hold this stretch for ten seconds and then release it slightly for a few seconds. Pull the leg once again for another twenty- to thirty-second stretch. Be sure to maintain a straight leg throughout the sequence. Repeat with the other leg.

3. **Adductor and hip.** Begin in a wide straddle with your feet about three shoulder-widths apart. Bend and weight one leg while keeping the other leg straight, until you feel a stretch develop in your groin and along the inside of the straight leg. Keep your lower back as straight as possible; touch the floor in front of you as needed for balance. Gently press on the inner thigh of the bent leg to increase the stretch and hold for twenty seconds. Repeat this stretch twice on both sides.

Adductor and hip

4. **Groin and hip.** This is an excellent stretch for improving hip turnout. Flexibility gains from this stretch will allow you to move your center of gravity closer to the wall—more over the feet—on near-vertical climbs. Sit upright with legs flexed and knees out to the sides so that you can bring the soles of the feet together. Grasp your ankles and rest your elbows on the inside of the thighs. Press down with your elbows to apply light pressure on the thighs until you feel mild tension in the groin and inner thighs. Hold the stretch for ten seconds and then release it for a few seconds. Reapply pressure for a secondary stretch of twenty to thirty seconds. Next, lie down flat on your back while still keeping the soles of the feet together. Relax and allow gravity to pull the knees toward the floor for another thirty seconds to one minute.

Groin and hip

5. **Biceps and shoulders.** Sit on the floor with feet flat and knees bent about 90 degrees. Position your arms just behind your hips with the elbows straight, palms flat on the floor, and fingers pointing back. Slowly walk your hands away from your hips until you feel mild tension in the biceps. Hold this position for twenty seconds. Walk your fingers back a few inches farther to increase the tension a bit more. You may also feel some mild stretching in your shoulders and chest. Hold this position for

Biceps and shoulders

twenty to thirty seconds before releasing the stretch.

6. **Shoulders and upper back.** While in a standing position, bring one arm across your chest until the hand rests on the opposite shoulder. Maintain the bent elbow at chest level so that the arm is parallel to the floor. With the other hand, grasp behind the bent elbow from below. Pull on the bent elbow until you feel tension in the shoulder and upper back. Hold the stretch for ten seconds. Release the stretch for a few seconds before repeating for twenty seconds more. You can stretch the shoulder muscles more completely by slowly working the bent elbow up and down a few inches from the horizontal position. Repeat the stretch with the other arm.

7. **Triceps, shoulders, and back.** Stand erect with arms overhead and bent at the elbows. Grab one elbow and gently pull it toward the back of your head until you feel a stretch in the back of the upper arm. Hold the stretch for ten seconds. Release the stretch for a few seconds and then perform a secondary stretch for about twenty seconds. You can extend this stretch down through the shoulder and the side of your torso by leaning slightly sideways in the direction of the pull. Repeat the stretch with the other arm.

Shoulders and upper back

Triceps, shoulders, and back

8. **Finger flexors.** While in a standing position, bring your hands together in front of your waist. Straighten the arm to be stretched and lay the fingertips into the palm of the other hand. Position the hand of the stretching arm so the palm is facing down with the thumb pointing inward. Pull back on the fingers of the straight arm until a mild stretch begins in the forearm muscles. Hold the stretch for about twenty seconds. Release the stretch and turn the hand 180 degrees so that the stretching arm is now positioned with the palm facing upward and the thumb pointing out to the side. Again, using your other hand, pull your fingers back until a stretch begins in the forearm muscles. Hold for ten seconds. Repeat the stretch, in both positions, with the other arm.

Finger flexors

9. **Finger extensors.** With nearly straight arms, cross your hands in front of your body and interlace your fingers, palms together. While maintaining mild tension throughout the length of both arms, pull with one hand to flex the wrist of the other hand until you feel the stretch develop in the finger/wrist extensors along the outside of the forearm. Hold the stretch for about twenty seconds and then pull with the other hand to create a stretch along the other arm. Perform the stretch twice on each arm.

Finger extensors

10. **Finger stretch.** This isolation stretch, along with massage of the fingers and hands, is very effective for warming up your precious digits. Work through this sequence one finger at a time. Either sitting or standing, position one

hand palm-up at chest level and curl the fingers into a loose fist. Place the index finger of the other hand across the tip segment of the finger being stretched, and position the thumb under the finger near the base (hand) knuckle. Bracing with the thumb below, gradually apply pressure with the index finger to further close the bent finger and push it away from the palm. Stop when you feel mild tension in the joints. Hold the stretch for ten seconds. Release the finger for a few seconds, then repeat the stretch for another ten seconds. Repeat the stretching sequence with all eight fingers.

Finger stretch

Basic Pull-Muscle Strength Training

Learning to climb requires a modest level of base strength in order to move up the wall and learn climbing technique. Assess your level of base strength with the following fitness tests. Can you do five to ten pull-ups, fifteen hanging (from a pull-up bar) knee lifts, and twenty abdominal crunches? A no answer to any of these questions indicates a need for some supplemental strength training. Such basic training is also beneficial if you cannot climb at least three days per week.

What kind of general strength-training program is best for a novice climber? You might engage in a standard health-club-style circuit-training program for a few months, although this is not the type of training-for-climbing program you'd want to engage in long-term. Understand that your workout needs to be more tailored to climbing, and, of course, the motions of a typical weight-lifting or bodybuilding workout have little in common with climbing. So while you may initially utilize a health club workout to get in shape, you should gradually transition into a more sport-specific training routine as your general fitness improves.

The pull muscles of the arms and back are typically the first muscles to pump out while climbing, so they are the focus of your strength training. As explained earlier, poor climbing technique and mental anxiety lead to excessive use of these muscle groups and premature failure. Therefore, you can rapidly increase your apparent strength in these areas by working to improve climbing technique. Still, some supplemental pull-muscle training is quite useful, especially if you can't make it to the climbing gym as often as you'd like.

In formulating an effective pull-muscle workout for climbing, it helps to consider what exercises are most specific to the motions of our sport. For example, pull-ups are far more similar to climbing movements than are biceps curls. Similarly, fingerboard exercises are extremely specific to the way you grip the rock in climbing, whereas the various handheld squeezers are not. Thus fingerboard training will translate to better climbing performance, while squeezing one of the handheld toys will primarily make you better at, well, squeezing that toy!

Following are five excellent exercises for strengthening the pull muscles as well as the supporting core muscles of the torso. Perform these exercises three days per week, either at the end of a climbing session or as a replacement for climbing when it's not possible to get to the gym.

PULL-UPS

Perform your training on a pull-up bar, the bucket holds of a fingerboard, or a set of free-hanging Pump Rocks. Train only in the palms-away position (the way you usually grip the rock) and with your hands initially at shoulder-width. Perform three to five sets to failure with a three-minute rest between sets. As your pull-up strength improves, begin to vary the distance between your hands to better simulate the wide range of hand positions you'll encounter in climbing.

AIDED PULL-UPS

If you are unable to do five consecutive pull-ups, employ one of these two powerful strategies. Place a chair below the pull-up bar and step up into a lock-off position with the bar just below your chin. Remove your feet from the chair and hold the lock-off for five seconds before slowly lowering yourself toward the straight-armed position. Immediately step back up on the chair to the top lock-off position and repeat the process exactly. Do five total repetitions, and then rest for three minutes. Perform two to three sets.

The second strategy is simply to have a spotter hold around your waist and lift a portion of your body weight so that you can do eight to ten less-than-body-weight pull-ups. Do three sets in this manner with a three-minute rest in between. Use these training strategies three days per week, and you'll be surprised how fast your pull-up strength improves.

LAT PULL-DOWNS

Do this in place of, not in addition to, pull-ups. This is the one weight-training exercise in which you can load on weight without limit. Select a weight

Aided pull-ups. Spotter helps lift a portion of body weight on upward phase only.

Lat pull-down machine. Vary hand spacing and pull the bar down to your chest.

that allows you just six to twelve high-intensity repetitions. Perform three to five sets to failure with a three-minute rest between sets. Vary the distance between your hands with every set.

HANGING KNEE LIFTS

This is a strenuous exercise that works the lower abdominals, hip flexors, and many of the core muscles of the torso. Hanging from a pull-up bar, the bucket holds of a fingerboard, or a set of Pump Rocks, lift your knees up to your chest, allowing your legs to bend naturally with the motion. Now lower your legs slowly until they return to a slightly bent position (not straight) and immediately begin the next upward repetition. Continue this knee-lift motion until failure. You goal should be two sets of twenty-five repetitions. It's important to maintain some tension in your shoulders and concentrate on the feeling of a stiff upper body while your abs are contracting and lifting the knees to the chest.

Hanging Knee Lift

Begin with a slight bend at hips and knees.

Lift the knees to chest level.

ABDOMINAL CRUNCHES

Perform this floor exercise with your feet hovering in the air and knees bent at about 90 degrees. Cross your arms over your upper chest or place your hands behind your head (harder), but do not

Abdominal Crunch

Cross arms over upper chest or place hands behind your head (harder), but do not interlace your fingers behind your neck.

Lift shoulders off the floor and exhale as you "crunch" upward.

interlace your fingers behind your neck. Now lift your shoulders off the ground and exhale as you "crunch" upward. The range of motion for this exercise is small—the goal is to lift your shoulders and upper back off the floor, but not to ascend the whole way as in doing an old-school sit-up. Continue at a modest pace for twenty-five to fifty repetitions, then rest for approximately two minutes before doing a second set.

Antagonist-Muscle Training to Prevent Injury

While climbing provides a rigorous workout for the pull muscles, it demands much less of the antagonist push muscles of the chest, shoulders, and upper arms. In the long term this could lead to tendinitis or other injuries, as these stabilizing push muscles may fall out of balance with their opposing pull muscles. The two most common problem spots are the elbows and shoulders. Let's take a quick look at each.

First, consider how climbing ceaselessly works the finger-flexor muscles of the forearms, yet does little to strengthen the extensor muscles on the outside of your forearms. As a result, climbers tend to develop a significant muscular imbalance and a susceptibility to lateral epicondylitis—a painful tendinitis on the outside portion of the elbow (also known as tennis elbow). As many as one in four climbers will eventually suffer from this affliction, although you can greatly reduce your chances by performing a simple preventive exercise. Reverse wrist curls (see page 134) with a light dumbbell will strengthen the extensor muscles on the back of the forearm. Perform this exercise, along with stretching of the forearm muscles, before and after every climbing workout; chances are you'll dodge the elbow tendinitis bullet.

The shoulders are another common site of injury, especially among climbers with a preference for overhanging walls and steep, severe boulder problems. Climbs of this nature place great strain on the shoulder joint, and it's the push muscles of the chest and shoulder area that help maintain stability. Of course, climbing does a poor job at strengthening these vital muscles. The upshot, for some unfortunate climbers, is that shoulder instability can lead to tendinitis, subluxation (partial or complete dislocation), or rotator cuff injury. Again, the use of a few basic exercises will help maintain balance and, hopefully, keep you injury-free. Push-ups, dips, dumbbell shoulder presses, and internal and external rotation (of the shoulder) are five exercises I advocate for this purpose. One or two sets of each, two or three days per week, is usually enough to keep the push muscles in condition to do their job. (Should you possess an existing shoulder injury, however, please consult a physical therapist for more appropriate rehabilitation exercises.)

LIGHT SHOULDER PRESS

Using two dumbbells or a health club machine, perform one set of twenty to twenty-five repetitions, twice per week. Total resistance should be limited to between 20 and 40 percent of your body weight. If you plan to purchase dumbbells, I'd suggest women purchase two 10- or 15-pounders and

men purchase two 20- or 30-pounders—there is no need to go much heavier.

PUSH-UPS OR LIGHT BENCH PRESS

Perform one or two sets of standard push-ups, two or three days per week. The goal is twenty to twenty-five push-ups per set. If you can do more than twenty-five repetitions, increase the difficulty by moving your hands closer together. If you have access to a bench-press machine, follow the same guidelines as in doing the shoulder press. Keep the total weight less than 50 percent of your total body weight—go much heavier and you risk adding unnecessary muscle mass that will only weigh you down while climbing.

Push-ups. Move hands closer together to increase difficulty.

DIPS

Dips are an excellent exercise for strengthening the many muscles of the upper arms, shoulders, chest, and back. Of course, the dip motion is similar to that of pressing out a mantle on the rock, so you have double the reason to perform this exercise twice per week. Many health clubs and climbing gyms have either a pair of gymnastics rings or a parallel-bar-like apparatus for performing dips. Similarly, you may be able to position two heavy chairs or even use an incut 90-corner of a kitchen counter to perform your dips.

Shoulder press. Press the dumbbells up to the straight-armed position.

Ring Dips

Top position with straight arms.

Bottom position with 90-degree bend at elbows (go no lower!).

If you haven't done dips before, you will discover that they are surprisingly difficult, especially if you do them on the rings. Initially, shoot for two sets of six to ten repetitions, but strive for the eventual goal of fifteen to twenty reps. In the meantime, employ a spotter to help lift around the waist (reduce body weight) so that you can achieve at least six dips per set.

REVERSE WRIST CURLS

This exercise is mandatory for all climbers, in order to maintain forearm muscle balance and prevent injury. Using a 5- to 20-pound dumbbell (start light), perform these wrist curls palm-down and with your forearm resting on your knee, a bench, or table. Do approximately twenty half-repetitions; that is, begin with your hand in the neutral position (straight), then curl it upward until it's fully extended. Perform one set as part of your warm-up and two more sets at the end of your workout.

Reverse wrist curl. From the straight (neutral) wrist position, curl the dumbbell up and lower back down to the neutral position (no lower).

EXTERNAL ROTATION

External and internal rotation are two important yet generally overlooked, exercises, as they target the small muscles that stabilize the rotator cuff of the shoulder. To train external rotation, lie on your side with your bottom arm in front of your waist; place a rolled-up towel under your head to support the neck. Alternatively, you can bend your bottom arm up and use it as a headrest. Hold a 2- to 5-pound dumbbell in the hand of your top arm. Rest the upper arm and elbow on the top side of your torso, then bend at the elbow so that the forearm hangs down over your belly and the weight rests on the floor. Now raise the weight upward until the forearm just passes a parallel position with the floor. Pause at this top position for a moment and then lower the weight back to the floor. Your upper arm should remain in contact with the side of your torso and act only as a hinge that allows the forearm to swing up and down. Continue in a slow but steady motion for a total of twenty repetitions. Do one set on each side. As you progress, increase weight in 1- or 2-pound increments, but do not exceed 10 pounds. Use of heavy resistance is not necessary or desirable.

External Rotation

Begin with your elbow on your side and arm hanging straight down over your belly.

Lift the weight upward—keep your elbow and upper arm in place throughout the motion.

Lie on your side with your bottom arm in front of your waist; place a rolled-up towel under your head to support the neck. Rest your other arm along your hip and upper thigh. Hold a 5- to 10-pound dumbbell in the hand of your bottom arm, positioning the forearm perpendicular to your body. Lift the weight up to your body and hold for a moment before lowering it back to the floor. The upper portion of the arm should remain in contact with the floor throughout the range of motion—think of the upper arm and shoulder as a door hinge that allows your forearm to swing "open and closed." Continue in a slow but steady motion for a total of twenty repetitions. Do one set on each side. As you progress, increase weight in 1- or 2-pound increments, but do not exceed 15 pounds. Using heavy weight is not necessary and may even result in injury.

Climbing-Specific Training

The previous section on general conditioning presented a wide range of basic exercises ideal for developing a solid physical foundation for entry-level climbing. Such basic training is appropriate for all climbers from novice up to one year of experience. Beyond a certain ability level, however, more advanced training is required to build the very specific strength needed to break into the higher grades. To this end, the following section on climbing-specific training is all about developing the lock-off strength, power, anaerobic endurance, and contact (finger) strength that are essential for success at climbs rated 5.11 and above.

By definition, climbing-specific training must stress the muscles in ways that are extremely similar to their use in climbing. Furthermore, this advanced

Internal Rotation

Begin with your bottom arm bent at 90 degrees and the elbow tucked in against your belly.

Lift up the dumbbell to touch your top arm—keep the elbow stationary throughout.

Guidelines for General Fitness Conditioning

1. Climb two to four days per week to develop climbing strength. For the time being, resist the urge to engage in the high-intensity, targeted exercises used by advanced climbers at the gym.

2. Concentrate on improving body composition and general all-around fitness. Moderate aerobic training (such as running) and basic conditioning exercises will effectively build base fitness.

3. Favor body-weight exercises such as pull-ups, push-ups, dips, and abdominal crunches over machines or free weights. Skip any strength training for the legs—your legs are generally strong enough for climbing if you can ascend a stairway two steps at a time!

4. Engage in regular stretching to improve flexibility and reduce injury risk.

5. Perform some modest training of the rotator cuff, push muscles, and forearm extensors to maintain muscular balance with the pulling and gripping muscles that naturally grow stronger as a result of climbing.

6. Begin a transition to climbing-specific exercises (see below) when your climbing ability exceeds the 5.10 benchmark (you can regularly climb 5.10 without falling).

---

protocol must work the muscles at a sufficiently high intensity to trigger neuromuscular adaptations that may not be gained through regular climbing activities. This is a vital distinction—advanced strength training will not be effective unless it targets the climbing muscles at a higher intensity level than they are regularly exposed to while climbing routes. Upcoming are four different methods of achieving this outcome: bouldering as training, high-intensity pull-muscle training, and fingerboard or Pump Rocks training.

Before we move ahead, it's important to point out that the following exercises are not appropriate for a true beginner. While you may begin incorporating a few of these exercises after six months of regular climbing, it's best to hold off on serious climbing-specific training until you have at least a full year of climbing under your belt. Use the material in this chapter as a primer on the subject of advanced training, but consult *Training for Climbing*

(FalconGuides's How to Climb series) for comprehensive coverage of advanced training theory and instruction.

Bouldering as Training

Bouldering is arguably the best all-around training method for climbers since it can produce improvement in all three areas of the performance triad: physical, technical, and mental. Without the constraints of the rope and clipping bolts, bouldering allows you to narrow your focus onto the mission of climbing the hardest moves you are capable of doing. From a strength-training perspective, you can also select maximal boulder problems of differing lengths to target training of maximum strength and power (problems with less than ten hand movements), or anaerobic endurance (ten to forty hand movements), or endurance (greater than forty hand movements). In doing so, it is best to choose nontechnical routes that will test your physical capabilities, not your technique. Recognize that failure on a boulder problem because of technical limitations, not muscular failure, means that you have also failed to effectively train the muscles for strength gains.

Consider that in bouldering, it's the upper-body pull muscles and the forearms that take the brunt of the workout. With these muscles in mind, pre-determine a purpose for a given session: to train for maximum strength and power, or to train for anaerobic endurance. Following are training guidelines for each type of workout.

TRAINING MAXIMUM STRENGTH AND POWER

Short, steep, high-intensity bouldering problems are the ticket for training maximum strength and power. The ideal problem should be hard enough to require a maximal physical effort, not necessarily a perfect technical effort—remember, the goal here is to train strength. In terms of length, select a route of between six and twelve hand movements that will not allow you to rest and chalk up midroute. Each bouldering problem should be a definitive, continuous muscular effort that quickly zaps your finger strength and upper-body power. Your goal is to do six to twelve boulder problems or an equal total of laps on the same problem. Rest for at least three minutes between sets, so that you feel reasonably fresh and can make a strong effort on each set.

You can increase the efficacy of this program by selecting—or better yet, setting—a boulder problem that targets a specific move or grip position. For example, a steep problem featuring a series of long reaches between holds would train lock-off strength or lunging power. Or a series of six to twelve small crimp holds would be the ultimate for training crimp-grip strength. You could similarly apply this strategy to train pinch grips, pocket grips, Gaston strength, twist-lock strength, and more. Working such isolation problems is simply the best wall-training strategy for building maximum strength and power.

TRAINING ANAEROBIC ENDURANCE

Anaerobic endurance, also sometimes called AE, strength endurance, or power endurance, is the ability to perform long, continuous sequences of strenuous climbing. Your level of anaerobic endurance is tested on boulder problems or roped climbs possessing between ten and forty difficult hand movements without rest. It's this type of steady, near-maximal climbing that produces the "pump" and burning feeling in the forearm muscles.

Interval training is the gold standard for training AE. A staple of serious runners, or any athlete desiring more speed and stamina, interval training should also be a part of any serious climber's training program. Consider how a runner alternates a near-full-speed lap with a slow lap or rest interval; a climber's interval training must similarly cycle near-maximal climbing with brief rest periods. Here's how to do it.

First, forget about working specific boulder problems—your focus here is to engage in effective interval training, not sending routes. Your interval-training goal is to complete five to ten "burns" with only a two-minute rest in between. Each interval, or burn, should be a continuously strenuous sequence that allows between twenty and forty moves before you approach muscular failure. The key here is to stop a few moves short of the forearm muscles reaching complete failure, so that you don't completely wreck yourself. Take exactly a two-minute rest, and then begin your next climbing interval. Consider using a stopwatch to time your rest breaks, or enlist a training partner to join in on the fun! No doubt you will soon discover the physical and mental pain inherent to interval training. In this case, however, the old saying is true: *No pain, no gain.* Engage in interval training once or twice per week, and you will develop remarkable anaerobic endurance.

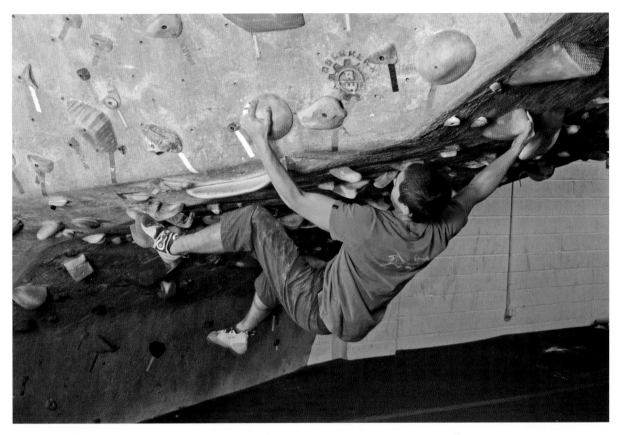

Short, steep, high-intensity boulder problems are ideal for training maximum strength and power.

High-Intensity Pull-Muscle Training

The standard pull-up has long been a staple exercise for climbers. Several sets of pull-ups performed a few days per week will provide most climbers with a base level of pull-muscle strength needed to learn all the basic climbing techniques. Beyond a certain intermediate level of difficulty, however, climbing requires more specific forms of strength such as the ability to lock off a handhold (to make a long reach) or make a quick, powerful upward movement. Consider the benchmark of being able to do fifteen solid pull-ups and solidly climb 5.10 as the point at which you should

graduate to more targeted training of the pull muscles.

Before we dive into the details of three excellent pull-muscle exercises, it is important to reconsider what exactly is the ultimate constraint on your climbing performance. Sure, more pull-up power and lock-off strength is a good thing, but many climbers still fail due to lackluster technique, poor mental control, or simply because they climb too slow. If any of this sounds familiar, it would be wise to invest more training time on your true weaknesses rather than on acquiring more pull-muscle strength.

This may be the best exercise for developing one-armed strength and lock-off ability. The technique here is to execute the pull-up motion with one hand on the bar and the other holding on to a towel looped over the bar (or with two or three fingers through a loop of webbing). Alternatively, you can use a set of free-floating Pump Rocks hanging in an offset position. Both hands pull, but the upper hand will do a disproportionate amount of the work depending on the vertical separation between hands. Initially, perform uneven-grip

Uneven-Grip Pull-Ups

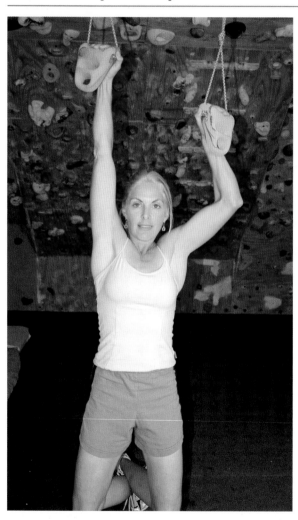

To start, grasp the Pump Rocks with a 1-foot vertical separation between your hands.

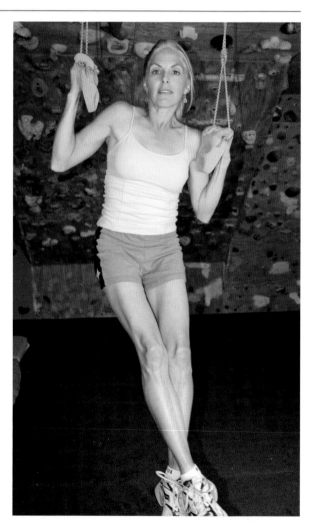

Pull up, allowing the upper hand to do most of the work. Over time, increase the distance between hands to increase the difficulty.

pull-ups with one hand about 1 foot below the other, but progress incrementally toward the goal of a 2-foot separation. Do a set to failure, then rest for two minutes and switch sides. Repeat twice. Increase the vertical distance between hands if you can do eight or more reps.

FRENCHIES

Frenchies rule for building anaerobic endurance in the pull muscles—but they're also extremely strenuous and fatiguing. The upside of this training technique is the marked improvement in pull-up and lock-off ability that you will undoubtedly notice after just a few weeks of training. Here are the details on these uniquely effective modified pull-ups.

Begin with a single pull-up (palms away, hands shoulder-width apart) and lock off in the top position for a five-second count. Now lower to the bottom and pull up to the top again; this time, however, immediately lower halfway down to an arm angle of 90 degrees. Hold a solid lock-off here for a five-count, then lower to the bottom. Immediately crank another pull-up, but this time lower to a lock-off with an arm angle of about 120 degrees. Again, hold this steady for a true five-second count before lowering to the bottom position. This sequence of three lock-offs constitutes a single cycle, but you should continue on with another cycle (or more) until you reach complete failure. Take a well-deserved five-minute rest between performing a second and third set.

Frenchies

Lock off the top.

Lock off the middle with an arm angle near 90 degrees.

Lock off low with an arm angle near 120 degrees.

WEIGHTED PULL-UPS

The quickest way to develop maximum strength is by means of my hypergravity training techniques, detailed in *Training for Climbing*. In a nutshell, this technique simulates hypergravity (greater than gravity's natural pull) by means of adding training weight to your body in the form of a 10- or 20-pound weight belt. Your neuromuscular system will gradually adapt its maximal pull-up and lock-off capabilities in proportion to your higher apparent body weight. Then, when you return to climbing at normal body weight, you will feel noticeably lighter and climb stronger given this überstrength.

As with the previous exercises, execute weighted pull-ups only on your normal training-for-climbing days, ideally toward the end of the session when your muscles are well warmed. Using a pull-up bar or the bucket holds on a fingerboard, perform three to five sets of pull-ups with a 10-pound weight belt (available on the Internet) around your waist. Rest

Grip training on Pump Rocks.

for at least three minutes between sets, and increase the weight to 20 pounds when you are able to do fifteen repetitions with the 10-pound belt.

Fingerboard Training

The fingerboard, also known as a hangboard, is a staple training tool for use in commercial and home gyms alike. Its popularity should be obvious, given that it addresses the common weakest link to the rock: the fingers. Unfortunately, this simple training tool can be misused (or overused), which can lead to finger-tendon and elbow injuries. You can best avoid this outcome by employing a fingerboard as just one part of a good training program, not the cornerstone. Furthermore, it's important to reiterate that fingerboard training is inappropriate for novice climbers or anyone with recent incidence of finger, elbow, or shoulder injury.

While the large holds of a fingerboard offer an ideal platform for many of the pull-up exercises presented in this chapter, the focus of this section is use of the board to train grip strength. The genius of a good fingerboard (see photo on page 144) is the multitude of finger positions and grips that it enables you to train. This is especially useful if you are unable to regularly boulder or climb at a commercial gym. Why not install a fingerboard or set of Pump Rocks at home for some substitute training?

Regardless of where you work out, however, it's imperative that you perform a complete warm-up before commencing with finger training. Begin with a few minutes of light exercise such as jogging around the block or doing fifty jumping jacks. This might seem like a funny way to begin a finger workout, yet it's absolutely vital for elevating your heart rate and core temperature. Warm muscles are less likely to be injured. Next, perform a few submaximal sets of pull-ups as well as the arm and upper-body stretches described on page 128. Complete the warm-up with some self-massage of the finger and forearm muscles to further loosen the muscles and enhance blood flow for a great

Three firm turns of tape around the base of the fingers provides some additional support of the commonly injured tendon pulleys of the middle and ring fingers.

workout. Finally, consider reinforcing the tendons at the base of your fingers with a few tight turns of tape (see photo). Following are two excellent fingerboard-training strategies.

TRAINING CONTACT STRENGTH WITH REPEATERS

Repeaters may be the single best fingerboard regimen because they will build your contact strength—your initial grip strength upon engaging a handhold. One set of repeaters involves a series of ten maximum-intensity hangs on the same pair of holds. Each hang should last just three to ten seconds, so you may need to wear a 10-pound weight belt (or use smaller holds) to make this a more difficult task. Rest just five seconds (or less) between each of the ten hangs. The complete set of repeaters should take less than two minutes and, of course, lead to a growing forearm pump.

Take a two-minute rest before launching into your next set of ten repeaters. Use a different pair

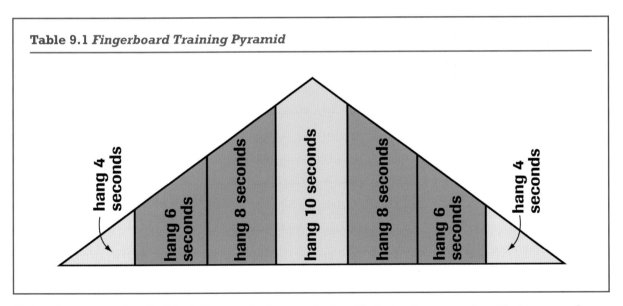

Table 9.1 *Fingerboard Training Pyramid*

hang 4 seconds

hang 6 seconds

hang 8 seconds

hang 10 seconds

hang 8 seconds

hang 6 seconds

hang 4 seconds

Using the same pair of holds, follow each step precisely with just a five-second rest between each step. That is, hang four seconds, rest five seconds, hang six seconds, rest five seconds, hang eight seconds, and so on.

Though not for beginners, the fingerboard is an excellent tool for supplemental pull-up and grip training.

of holds for each set of ten repeaters, beginning with your most problematic grips, and then gradually progress to larger holds as you tire. It's also good to vary the grip positions trained to spread out the neuromuscular stimulus. For instance, you might begin with shallow two-finger pockets, then progress to small crimps, narrow pinches, small slopers, shallow three-finger pockets, medium crimps, deep two-finger pockets, medium slopers, medium crimps, and large slopers. Performing one set of repeaters (ten repetitions) for each of these ten grip positions would result in a total of one hundred near-maximal contractions—a pretty good finger workout!

TRAINING ANAEROBIC ENDURANCE WITH PYRAMIDS

Pyramid training simulates the way your forearm muscles might work in climbing a medium-length gym route. In this way, it tends to train forearm endurance over pure strength. As shown in table 9.1, one run through the Fingerboard Training Pyramid involves seven hangs on the same pair of holds. The rest interval between each hang is only five seconds, so a complete cycle will take just under one and a half minutes. Take a one-minute rest before performing another pyramid cycle on a different set of holds. Your goal is seven to fifteen total sets.

As you progress through the sets, strive to hit all the primary grip positions, including full and half crimps, all the two-finger pocket teams, pinch grips, and open-hand slopers. It's good to vary the size of the holds used for a given set based on your level of fatigue, but be sure to stay on schedule in terms of the timing of your hangs and rest intervals.

Campus Laddering

Campus training is a climbing-specific exercise that develops upper-body power and grip strength. Performed on a specialized campus board (see photo), this unique explosive exercise works the entire chain of climbing muscles, including the fingers and forearms, biceps, shoulders, back, and core. There are a few different ways to train on the campus board, but only "campus laddering" is appropriate until you reach a high level of climbing skill and conditioning. As a guideline, you should not attempt campus laddering during your first few months as a climber. As you gain experience and conditioning (say, after six to twelve months of regular climbing), you can begin to add a small amount of laddering to your training. I strongly discourage you from attempting the other, more stressful types of campus training used by advanced climbers!

As the name implies, campus laddering involves climbing in a hand-over-hand, ladderlike motion up the campus board with no aid from your feet.

Beginning from the lowest rung on the campus board, ladder upward, hand-over-hand. Match hands on the top rung and then descend hand-over-hand to regain the starting rung.

Guidelines for Climbing-Specific Training

1. Make bouldering the foundation of your climbing-specific training. It's hard to beat steep-wall bouldering for developing lock-off strength and power.

2. Frequently dedicate entire sessions to training endurance. Climbing laps on submaximal routes and performing long, moderate traverses will build climbing stamina. Employ interval training on a bouldering wall to develop high-intensity anaerobic endurance.

3. Commit to regular training of your antagonist muscles. As little as fifteen minutes of push-muscle training, two days per week, will help maintain muscle balance and reduce injury risk.

4. Perform reverse wrist curls as part of every climbing session. The health of your elbows depends on it.

5. Err on the side of over-resting, instead of over-training. Limit yourself to three or four days of climbing and climbing-specific training (in aggregate) per week.

Laddering on small rungs tends to train finger strength, whereas longer reaches on larger rungs better isolate one-arm power and lock-off strength. Here's how to do them.

Begin by hanging with nearly straight arms from the bottom rung of the campus board with your hands about shoulder–width or slightly less apart. Striving for brisk, fluid motion, begin laddering hand-over-hand up the campus board using alternating rungs for your left and right hands. Your goal is to ascend the board as quickly as possible. Match hands on the top rung and then descend carefully by dropping hand by hand down alternating rungs to the bottom position. To increase difficulty, skip rungs as you hand–over–hand up the board. Limit yourself to a single set during your formative workouts; you can do two to four sets as your conditioning improves. Rest for a minimum of three minutes between each set.

Nutrition and Rest

A chapter on getting into climbing shape would be incomplete without a look at performance nutrition and rest habits. This often overlooked subject is especially important for serious, hard-training climbers. Proper nutrition and adequate rest are as important a part of the training-for-climbing equation as the workout itself, because training adaptations—getting stronger!—occur predominantly during rest days and while sleeping. Therefore, if you deny your body the time it needs to fully recover, your body will deny you the gains in strength you had hoped to achieve; you might even slip into the overtraining syndrome (more on this in a bit). Let's first take a look at rest and nutritional requirements for a serious climber.

Rest and Recovery

Complete recovery from a workout typically takes anywhere from twenty-four to seventy-two hours, depending on the intensity and volume of the training and climbing. For example, it might only take one day to recover from a session of easy toprope climbing that failed to produce a major muscular pump. Likewise, recovery from moderate aerobic activities such as running and biking usually takes but twenty-four hours. On the other hand, an evening of high-intensity bouldering, pushing your limit on toprope or lead, or advanced training of the pull muscles can take two or three days (sometimes more) to recover from completely.

Consider that the body repairs itself and new growth occurs primarily while you are asleep. Therefore, the amount of sleep you get the night of a hard workout is as important as your use of proper training exercises and consumption of sufficient nutrients. The bare minimum amount of sleep per night is seven to eight hours, with nine hours being optimal after an especially hard day of climbing. If you're like most people, that kind of free time is hard to come by, but you might be able to pull it off by giving up some nighttime activities (TV and such) in favor of going to bed earlier. Remind yourself that sleep is an essential part of your training. What are your priorities?

Nutrition

While your muscles can do little rebuilding until you go to sleep, they can begin restocking glycogen (sugar fuel in the muscle) immediately following a workout. You can shorten recovery time by kick-starting this repletion process with a sports drink and some liquid protein. Postworkout is the one time it's good to consume a sugar-based sports drink such as Gatorade. Chase the sports drink with a glass of high-quality protein like Designer Whey (available at all health food stores), and you'll be on the way to accelerating your recovery by as much as 50 percent. Research has shown, however, that you must consume the sports drink and protein within two hours of ending your workout (the sooner, the better) in order to accelerate recovery in this way.

Outside the postworkout period you benefit by eating well-balanced meals comprising low-fat proteins such chicken, fish, or skim milk, along with healthy portions of fruits, vegetables, and whole-grain carbohydrates. Forget everything you've heard about the value of high-fat, low-carbohydrate diets. Such fad diets may help overweight businessmen, desperate housewives, and Aunt Jemima lose some weight, but they are inappropriate and counterproductive for a serious athlete. Carbohydrate is, in fact, the primary source of energy for your training and climbing, so use of a low-carbohydrate diet will leave your muscles flaccid and weak on the rock.

A good nutritional strategy is to consume six smaller meals or snacks spaced evenly throughout the day as opposed to the typical three large meals per day. At least three of your meals should contain a significant portion of protein. For instance, breakfast could include a couple of eggs, skim milk, or whey protein; lunch might include some yogurt, skim milk, or a can of tuna; and for dinner it might be good to eat a piece of lean red meat, chicken, or fish. Each of these meals should also include some carbohydrate in striving to meet the 65/15/20 (carbohydrate/protein/fat) macronutrient profile detailed earlier in the chapter. The other three meals—actually snacks—are vital for maintaining steady blood glucose and continuing the recovery process 24/7. A piece of fruit, a balanced-type energy bar, or a glass of protein drink each makes an excellent choice.

Another important but often overlooked part of the performance nutrition equation is drinking lots of water. Proper cellular function—and peak mental and physical performance—requires full hydration. Make it a goal to drink a minimum of eight glasses of water (two quarts) per day, and more when working or climbing in hot conditions. At the gym, make it a habit to sip water throughout your session at the rate of at least one pint per hour. (If you aren't going to the bathroom regularly, you aren't drinking enough water for optimal performance.)

So what foods should you avoid? Anything highly processed (which will unfavorably spike blood sugar), as well as foods containing a high amount of added sugar or any hydrogenated oils (check labels for "trans fats") whatsoever. Similarly, high-fat fast foods and anything fried should be left out of a serious climber's diet. Save these junk foods as a rare reward after a personal-best send or upon reaching a major training or climbing milestone. As a regular part of your diet, they will hold you back. Again, it's a matter of personal values and priorities—you set the rules!

Finally, in this age of pre-prepared foods, it's quite difficult to consume the vitamins and minerals that you need as an athlete striving for optimal recovery and peak performance. Taking a daily multivitamin each morning is a good first step, though you might further benefit by consuming an extra 500 to 1,000 milligrams of vitamin C and 200 to 400 IUs of vitamin E. Research has shown that both of these vitamins can enhance recovery and overall health in a hard-training athlete.

Avoiding Overtraining Syndrome

The antithesis of getting into climbing shape is the downward spiral of overtraining syndrome. Far too many enthusiastic and good-intentioned climbers have been drawn into the black hole of overtraining. In actuality, overtraining syndrome is often the result of a combination of under-resting and

Nutrition and Recovery Tips

1. Plan your workouts and rest days on a calendar, and then stick to the schedule. Any less than three days per week of rest (from climbing and climbing-specific training) tempts injury and reduces workout effectiveness.

2. Eat three well-rounded meals per day with a portion of quality protein and carbohydrate in each feeding. Avoid most fast foods, anything that's fried or contains trans fats, as well as any calorie-dense junk foods (except as an occasional reward!).

3. Snack on fruit and balanced-style energy bars between meals and during workouts.

4. Drink at least eight glasses of water per day, and twice this amount in hot conditions. Sip water throughout your climbing session at a rate of one pint per hour.

5. Consider taking a daily vitamin, as well as small supplemental doses of antioxidants such as vitamins C and E.

Table 9.2 *Two Sample Workout Schedules*

Three Days of Climbing

Mon	Tue	Wed	Thur	Fri	Sat	Sun
CL	A/GC	CL	A/GC	Rest	CL	Rest

Four Days of Climbing

Mon	Tue	Wed	Thur	Fri	Sat	Sun
A/GC	CL	A/GC	CL	Rest	CL	CL

CL – climbing day and/or climbing-specific training

GC – general conditioning (aerobics, stretching, and so on)

A – antagonist-muscle training

Rest – rest day (no training of any kind)

undereating. The bottom line: Climb too often, train too hard, rest too little, eat a poor diet, and you will eventually slip into overtraining. You'll know that you have crossed to the dark side because you'll begin to feel weaker (not stronger), your climbing ability will plateau (or sink), and you might eventually get injured or sick. If any of this ever begins to sound familiar, view it as a red flag and immediately take a couple of weeks off from all training and climbing.

Of course, it's your goal to avoid this affliction altogether. Here are a few tips to help keep the grim reaper of overtraining at bay. First, keep your training and climbing sessions reasonable in length so as to not dig yourself too deep a hole from which to recover. Two to four hours of bouldering at the gym should be more than enough to get a good workout. Surely more than half of this time will be spent resting as you belay or spot other climbers, so your actual aggregate amount of climbing time should be more along the lines of sixty to ninety minutes.

On a more macro scale, it's important that you never climb (or train for climbing) more than four days per week. Unlike activities such as bicycle riding or playing golf, which you can engage in daily, subjecting yourself to the stresses of climbing day

in and day out will eventually lead to an overuse injury. Three or four days per week at the gym provides plenty of muscular stimulus and motor learning to advance you toward your climbing goals—climbing more than this may actually prevent you from reaching them! Get on a regular training schedule and stick to it. One popular gym climbing schedule is Monday, Wednesday, and Saturday. Another popular schedule is Tuesday, Thursday, Saturday, and Sunday. There are many other possibilities. Either way, don't even think about going to the gym on your designated rest days. The only acceptable training on these days of rest from climbing would be aerobic activity, flexibility training, or training of the antagonist push muscles.

You also need to foster an uncommon sense of self-awareness and self-discipline. When you wake up in the morning with sore muscles (known as delayed-onset muscle soreness), it's a sign of microtraumas that will require at least another twenty-four hours for repair and complete recovery. You have two choices in this situation: Go climbing (or work out) for a second straight day, despite the soreness, with reduced performance and increased injury risk. Or take a day or two off and allow your neuromuscular system to recuperate to a level of capability higher than before the initial workout. The latter choice is clearly the more intelligent approach—one that will make you a better, stronger climber in the long run. Sure, you'll probably be okay climbing sore every once in a while, but if it becomes a regular practice, you risk the pitfalls of overtraining. Remind yourself constantly that the goal is to perform an optimal amount of training and climbing, not the maximal amount you can pack into your schedule.

CHAPTER TEN

Training for Youth Climbers

What do you get when you combine video-game-like cognitive engagement with the physical rigors and thrill of ascending a rock wall? Surely, you get one of the very best recreational and character-building activities available to youths of the twenty-first century.

The safe and convenient setting of an indoor climbing gym makes for an ideal recreational activity in which youths can challenge themselves in an individual manner while still being able to develop interpersonal skills with their peers. The captivating nature of climbing has led to rapid growth of youth climbing as a competitive sport, now formalized with a sanctioning body (USA Climbing) and national championship event. Many climbing gyms have burgeoning climbing teams, some of which train for and participate in both bouldering and roped climbing competitive seasons. In fact, it has been proposed that—given the tantalizing nature of indoor climbing, combined with the rapid worldwide growth of youth climbing competitions—it's an ideal sport to be added to the Olympic Games!

Given the emergence of youth climbing as a competitive sport, it's not surprising that many young climbers (and their parents) are looking for personalized training and formalized coaching. While many gyms are fortunate to have a qualified coach on staff, some budding youth climbers are left with the daunting task of self-coaching or parent-directed coaching. Little has been published on the subject of training for youth climbers, and so without proper guidance some youths end up copying the training practices of adult climbers they observe at the gym.

All kids have a climber inside of them ready to reap the many developmental benefits of indoor climbing.

Five-time US climbing champion and now leading youth climbing coach Robyn Raboutou stresses that youth climbers need proper coaching and age-appropriate training. She states that "all kids have a climber inside of them ready to reap the many developmental benefits of climbing, and it can start with kids as young as age three."

When it comes to safe, effective training for climbing, however, youths cannot simply be treated as "little adults" who are given a proportionally smaller serving of an adult training program. Youth climbers have unique strengths and limitations, and they are vastly different from adults both physiologically and psychologically. A growing body of research and real-life coaching experiences will hopefully soon lead to a full book on the subject of training for youth climbers. In the meanwhile, here's a primer on this important subject—written for coaches and parents—including guidelines for training skill and strategy, cognitive development, physical fitness training, and injury prevention.

Skill Development

Climbing is first and foremost a skill sport, and it should always be treated as such, especially when dealing with youth climbers. Much like golf, climbing requires proficient use of a wide range of skills, while strength and power are secondary. Consequently, skill development is paramount for novice climbers (of all ages), while extensive strength training is unnecessary and inappropriate early on. Interestingly, preteen brains are predisposed to prolific learning of motor skills, and so they have a time-limited gift to develop and refine climbing skills at a much higher rate and with greater ease than adults.

While climbing in general is extremely intuitive—and many youngsters might seem to be able to successfully teach themselves—there are in fact many complex techniques and skills that novices are unlikely to discover on their own. This is where knowledgeable climbing coaches are indispensable,

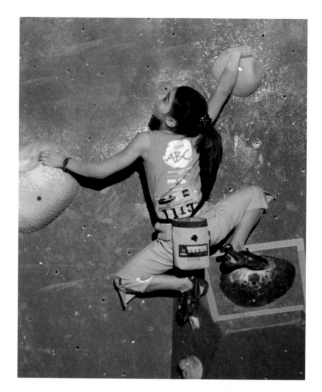

Naturally high grip-strength-to-weight ratio, flexibility, and a carefree mind allow some well-coached kids to climb at an extraordinarily high level.
ROBYN RABOUTOU

since they can present new skills to be learned with proper form and in a logical progression, all the while keeping the climbing activities safe and fun.

A good coach will have a lesson plan of sorts that begins with a warm-up period and then progresses through several periods focused on learning new skills, practicing previously learned skills, engaging in some form of "performance climbing" (attempting to climb entire roped routes or "limit" boulder problems), and concluding with some basic conditioning exercises and cool-down stretching. All the while the coach will engage the students, actively correcting lackluster form and inefficient movement patterns.

Feedback is essential to the learning process—the coach must help direct effective practice that will encode fundamentally correct movement skills into the brain and foster a high level of climbing efficiency, rather than allowing youth climbers to muscle through a move with poor technique and call it "okay." As in learning any physical skill, it's paramount that young climbers avoid encoding sloppy, inefficient ways of moving that will be more difficult to correct once they are firmly wired in the brain. (Again, golf is a good analogy: Many adult golfers futilely struggle to overcoming technical flaws that were deeply encoded during their formative days.)

In the long-term, youth climbers should be encouraged to explore unfamiliar terrain. An early focus on slab climbing should expand to the more challenging terrain of overhanging walls and bouldering caves. When they've achieved a high level of proficiency at face climbing, youths should be exposed to cracks and corners, which demand acquisition of new skill sets. An early focus on bouldering and toprope climbing should eventually progress to an introduction to lead climbing, although this is obviously a risky, headier form of climbing that is not to be rushed into prematurely. Some strong, talented youth climbers will develop the skill and confidence to begin lead climbing by age eight or

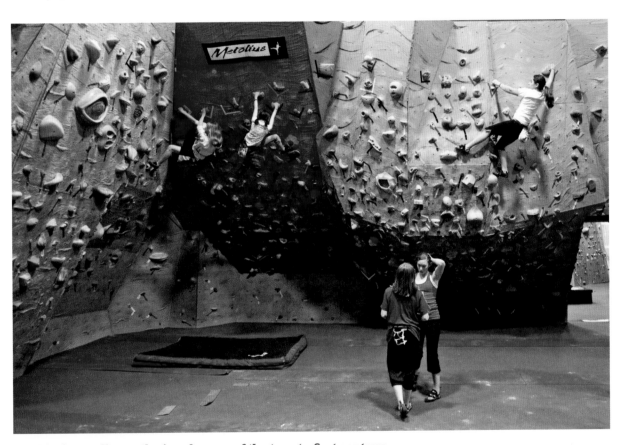

Bouldering walls are the jungle gym of the twenty-first century.
ROBERT SCOVERSKI

Training for Youth Climbers **153**

nine, while others may take years longer. There are no rules (no specific age) for when a climber is ready to lead—obviously this is a critical decision for the coach and parent to make together, and not something the youth climber should unilaterally decide.

A final and most important coaching matter involves climbing frequency and degree of dedication to the sport. Understandably, many youths fall in love with climbing—to the point that they would like to make it their one and only recreational/sporting activity. It's my opinion, however, that single-sport specialization should be discouraged before the age of thirteen. Research has identified a finite "golden period" of accelerated acquisition of motor abilities that lasts only through the early teenage years. This period of heightened neurodevelopment should be used to learn a wide range of sports skills that include running, jumping, flipping, throwing and/or shooting a ball, swinging a club or racquet, swimming in a pool, and many other wonderful and pleasurable ways to engage in skilled movement. A youth's brief opportunity to learn at hyperspeed should be invested in learning more than just how to dance and pull up a rock wall. It's my experience that young athletes can come to climb at a national-class level while at the same participating in—and perhaps excelling at—one or two other sports and school, as well!

Cognitive Development

My advice on cognitive training for youth climbers parallels almost everything I've outlined above on training technical skills. Start with the most basic mental challenges—developing confidence and poise in climbing hand-over-hand up juggy vertical routes—and gradually introduce more challenging terrain that requires visualization of sequences and the vertical chess match of reading several moves ahead while on a climb. For some kid climbers the process is a natural and apparently simple one to learn, as they quickly solve climbing wall puzzles on the fly. Other kids will require more coaching input to help them solve the puzzle and "see" the moves to be performed. (A laser pointer is a must-have coaching tool for helping a young climber see and mentally rehearse a tricky sequence.)

For younger climbers—say, under age nine—it's important to treat a climbing session as more a playground experience than a training session. A good coach will present climbing games that keep the focus on having fun, with learning of climbing skills and strategies a by-product.

Climbers between the ages of nine and thirteen can be presented with more complex instruction on critical cognitive skills such as mental rehearsal, visualization, arousal and fear control, risk management, and such. With good instruction, it's within this age range that many youth climbers, usually those with several years of experience, come to put together the complex technical-and-mental puzzle that is hard climbing and suddenly break into the lofty grades of bouldering V8 and/or lead climbing 5.12 (or harder).

Given a growing mastery of the fundamental technical and mental skills, some youth climbers between eight and twelve are ready to be introduced to the challenges and joys of outdoor climbing. As with the introduction to lead climbing indoors, however, taking youths outside is a big step that should not be rushed. The earliest transitioners to outdoor climbing will be those youths whose parents are experienced climbers themselves—this way the parent can be responsible for making the tough calls on what climbs are safe or unsafe for a youth to attempt. For those kids without a climbing parent, it's best to wait until at least twelve or thirteen to venture outdoors—and even then, to do so only in the presence of a mature, qualified climbing coach and/or instructor.

No matter if the outdoor climbing adventure is bouldering, toproping, or lead climbing, the game is pretty much the same as it is indoors, although the technical and mental demands are far greater on the

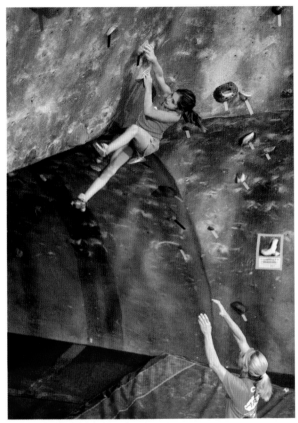

The individual nature of indoor climbing competitions offers kids a great supplement or alternative to team-oriented field sports.
KEITH NORTH

infinite playing field of Mother Nature's rock walls. Given a good coach or experienced parent, however, climbing outdoors offers an extraordinarily rich environment for learning and experiencing the wonders of nature. The bottom line: Outdoor climbing can be nearly as safe as indoor, but there is certainly far greater potential for climber error, belayer error, objective dangers, and more to come into play. Proceed with caution.

Just as outdoor climbing will stretch a youth climber's cognition in new and exciting ways, so will competition climbing—which for many

youths whose parents don't climb offers an excellent way to add a more difficult cognitive aspect to the game. Many climbing gyms hold local youth competitions, which offer a great introduction to the unique challenges and pressures of competition climbing. More formalized regional competitions for both bouldering and roped climbing are professionally organized and sanctioned by the governing body USA Climbing. Youths between the ages of eight and eighteen compete in five different age divisions for medals and to qualify for a national championship event. Learn more at USAClimbing. org.

Age-Appropriate Strength Training

With the growing popularity of youth climbing competitions and the recent press of preteen climbers sending V10 and 5.13 routes, many parents—and some coaches as well—jump to the conclusion that these elite youth climbers must be involved in some secret, arduous strength-training program. No doubt this speculation has led some to direct aspiring youngsters to perform unnecessary and potentially dangerous exercises. The truth is, however, that youth climbers reach elite levels as a result of consistent practice, high-quality instruction, the featherweight prepubescent physique, and to some degree the genetic blessings of uncommon flexibility, grip strength, and power. By simply climbing three or four days per week for several years, many youth climbers develop the ability to pull through steep terrain on tiny holds with an efficiency and ease that can make a grown man weep!

Given this, there is no harm—and indeed some benefit—in having youth climbers do a limited amount of strength training. Disregard any old wives' tales you've heard that "strength training is not for kids" or that "strength training will stunt a youth's growth." The American Academy of Pediatrics and the American College of Sports Medicine both support basic strength training for kids, as long as the exercises are age-appropriate and not overly dynamic or stressful, and youths are coached to exercise with proper form. So what are the age-appropriate exercises for youth climbers? Let's take a look at three general classifications: ages six through nine, ten through fifteen, and sixteen through eighteen.

Ages Six Through Nine

Prior to the adolescent growth spurt, most apparent gains in strength come from motor learning, not hypertrophy (muscle growth), and so any manner of extensive strength training is unnecessary and largely a waste of time at this age. Motor learning comes when adaptations of the nervous system—specifically, improved coordination and synchronization of muscular motor units (groups of muscle fibers that fire together)—lead to a greater expression of strength and power. Therefore, movement-oriented training should be the backbone of every workout. Developing climbing-specific strength, then, is simply a matter of following through with a consistent schedule of climbing (which will yield measurable gains in strength despite little or no change in muscle size).

Use of a few supplemental climbing-like exercises is fine, as long as it doesn't take away from movement training and climbing-for-fun time. Body weight exercises such as pull-ups, push-ups, abdominal crunches, and other similar gymnastic movements are the only strength-training exercises needed at this age.

Ages Ten Through Fifteen

Given a year or more of climbing experience and assuming a solid command of technical skills, it is not inappropriate to introduce a moderate amount of strength training for climbers ages ten to fifteen. These are the years of the adolescent growth spurt, with peak height velocity occurring at age 11.5 for girls and age 13.5 for boys. Changing hormone levels will lead to a noticeable growth of the muscles as weight velocity peaks between twelve and fifteen.

It's during this period that some fast-growing youths perceive a disturbing decrease in strength-to-weight ratio as their weight gain outpaces their strength gains. Once again, quality coaching is critical so that concerned youth climbers understand why they are apparently getting weaker despite a consistent climbing schedule. Some misguided youths will react by beginning a strict diet or extensive strength- or power-training program (or both) in an attempt to regain their physical capabilities. This response is unfortunate and in fact unhealthy, and it often ends in injury, anorexia, or burnout.

A good coach will explain the changes that all youth climbers face during puberty, and how the end result will undoubtedly be a physique that is stronger, taller, more powerful, and supremely capable of climbing at a very high level. The coach should direct a gradual introduction of general and sport-specific strength-training exercises that will train the newly gained muscle to be more efficient and effective for performing in the vertical plane, as well as reduce injury risk as the growing youths attempt harder climbs.

With the overriding training emphasis remaining on the development of outstanding climbing technique and mental fortitude, youth climbers can engage in twenty to forty minutes of strength training three days per week. Climbing-specific exercises such as pull-ups, lock-offs, fingerboard pull-ups and hangs (in small doses), slow, controlled campus laddering (never double dynoing!), and various core-strengthening routines should be executed on climbing days, not rest days. Most important, the youth should forgo most advanced and stressful exercises (as used by older elite climbers), such as double-dyno campus training and high-resistance hypergravity isolation training (HIT)—these can lead to growth plate fractures in the fingers and a necessary withdrawal from climbing for an extended period.

Perhaps the most important addition to a youth's training program is a small number of exercises to target the muscles that oppose the prime movers in climbing. A regular schedule of climbing (even without use of climbing-specific strength exercises) will lead to significant gains in strength of the pull muscles that are the prime movers for the vertical athlete. Maintaining stable joints and proper posture, reducing injury risk, and pursuing peak performance in climbing demands a small commitment to training the antagonist push muscles of the upper body. Specifically, the training should target the extension-producing muscles of the chest, shoulders, and arms, and the small muscles of the rotator cuff. A modest investment—fifteen to twenty minutes, two or three days per week—will strengthen these important yet often overlooked muscles, and vastly lower the risk of the elbow and shoulder injuries common among avid and expert climbers alike.

Most of the necessary climbing-specific and antagonist-muscle-training exercises are described earlier in this book (consult *Conditioning for Climbers* for other options). For the antagonist muscles I suggest beginning with two sets of push-ups, one or two sets of dumbbell shoulder presses, two sets of dips (with assistance, if needed), and one set each of external and internal rotations of the shoulder. Each exercise should be performed with a relatively light weight that allows twenty to twenty-five repetitions. These exercises can be performed at the end of a climbing workout or on rest days from climbing.

A final facet of effective training for youth climbers is flexibility training. While most climbing moves do not require extraordinary flexibility, quickly growing bones and muscles can lead to an increasing sense of tightness that may somewhat limit movement on the rock. A moderate amount of daily stretching can go a long way toward maintaining smooth, flexible movement. Gentle stretching of the arms, torso, and legs should be performed

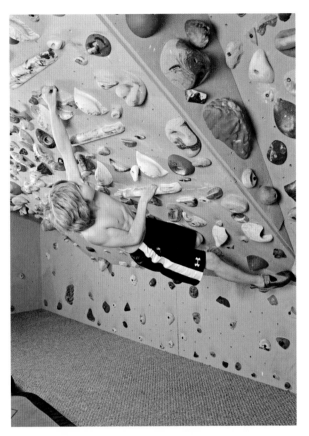

Indoor climbing is one of the best sports for building both a fit, healthy body and a strong, confident mind.

as part of a more comprehensive warm-up before engaging in maximal climbing. Furthermore, engaging in ten to fifteen minutes of stretching each evening (while watching TV or during quiet time before bed) is highly effective in helping relax and lengthen the tired, growing muscles of a hard-training youth climber.

Ages Sixteen Through Eighteen

As youth climbers approach their adult height, they can begin a gradual transition into a more intensive climbing-specific training program. Still, growth

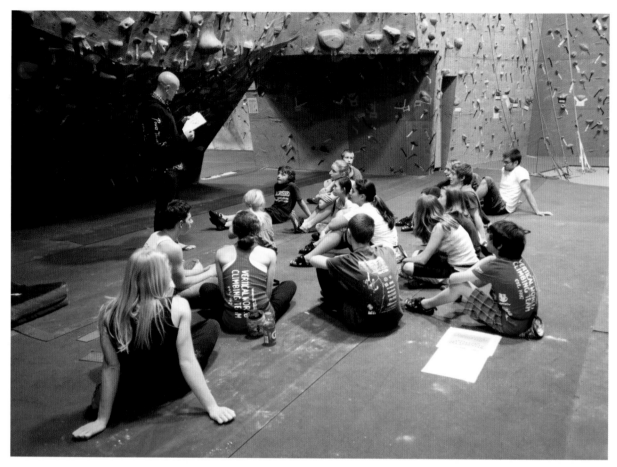

Many climbing gyms have professional coaches to direct effective, age-appropriate training sessions for youth climbers.
ROBERT SCOVERSKI

plates remain vulnerable to injury; they may not fully fuse until around age twenty. What's more, increases in training volume and magnitude can lead to overuse and acute injuries of the fingers, elbows, and shoulders. For these reasons, among others, a fully engaged coach or climbing parent is highly beneficial during this transition into becoming astute, self-directed adult climbers.

Many of these late-teen climbers will already be highly accomplished, and a few will be proven to possess world-class capabilities. Elite-level training

techniques, such as one-armed pull-ups, campus laddering, and weighted bouldering (say, with a 10-pound belt), can be added incrementally during this multiyear ramp-up period. However, hold off on fully dynamic double-dyno campus training and advanced hypergravity-training protocols until after the eighteenth birthday (and even later in the case of a late bloomer). Strengthening the antagonist muscle groups remains an essential for muscle balance, proper posture, and reducing the risk of elbow and shoulder injuries—all potential issues for hard-training late-teen and twenty-something climbers.

All the while, it's imperative that the training program remain focused on improving the complete climber—including mental and technical training—rather than a narrow, impulsive quest for greater strength and power as the sole pathway to improvement. Maturing youth climbers should be reminded frequently that sharp advances in ability often result from mental breakthroughs, and that becoming a true master of rock comes only by way of gaining vast experience on a wide range of climbing walls and rock types. Toward this end, a good coach will constantly dovetail physical training with ongoing instruction on advanced climbing techniques, tactics, and the many facets of the mental game. The most thoughtful and introspective teenagers will be ready to begin a study of the book *Maximum Climbing: Mental Training for Peak Performance and Optimal Experience*—a challenging text that explores powerful metacognitive skills that will enhance performance in climbing as well as many other life endeavors.

Beyond the above tips, the complex details of an advanced youth training program are outside the scope of this book—hire an experienced climbing coach, or consult *Training for Climbing* to develop an intelligent, self-directed program.

Injuries in Youth Climbers

The most common non-impact injuries among teenage climbers come from overuse and involve the tendons, joints, and bones of the fingers, including stress fractures and damage to the growth plates. Juniors experiencing chronic pain in the fingers (or elsewhere) should cease climbing for a few weeks and consult a doctor if the pain continues. As a hard-and-fast rule, climbing and climbing-specific training must be limited to an aggregate of four days per week. The guidance of an adult climber or coach is extremely beneficial both in helping structure workouts and in monitoring rest and nutritional habits. Let's delve deeper into the subject, including important strategies for preventing overuse injuries in youth climbers.

Injuries to the Growth Plates of the Fingers

The most disturbing injury trend among youth climbers is the increase in fractures to the epiphyseal plate, or growth plate, of a bone. Though most often observed in the hardest-training, hardest-climbing youths, all youth climbers should be monitored for the onset of joint pain in the fingers. Growth plate injury often develops over time, first revealing as minor joint swelling and pain while crimping and, if not treated with rest, progressing to acute pain, increased swelling, reduced range of motion, and in the worst cases disfigurement that can become permanent.

Adolescent climbers are most at risk for growth plate fractures during their growth spurt years (ages eleven through fourteen in girls, and twelve through sixteen in boys), although they can occur up to the age of eighteen or nineteen, prior to complete fusing of the growth plates. European research and anecdotal evidence here in the States reveal that double-dyno campus training is a leading cause of growth plate injuries. However, epiphyseal fractures can also develop in youths who engage in extensive severe bouldering—the kind involving copious dynamic movements and extreme crimping.

Regardless of how the injury develops, complete withdrawal from climbing is essential until pain and swelling subside (in minor cases, just a month or two). Resumption of climbing should be gradual, with a primary focus on large-hold bouldering and roped climbing, rather than a quick return to the same program that produced the injury in the first place. Recurrence of finger pain and swelling will require a longer break from climbing—perhaps a full season or year. Consulting a doctor would be likewise prudent.

Preventing Growth Plate and Other Injuries

First and foremost, climbers ages eleven through sixteen should do absolutely no double-dyno campus training. A small amount (one or two sets, once or twice per week) of the less dynamic campus laddering may be permitted in climbers strong and mature enough to do it with smooth, controlled movements. Also of high importance is a conscious favoring of the open-handed grip over the crimp grip on all but the smallest holds (which require use of the crimp grip). Finally, youth climbers should do little, if any, hypergravity training—that

is, climbing with weight added to the body in the form of a weight vest or belt.

Given the immense popularity of bouldering today, many youth climbers come to prefer it over roped climbing. Unfortunately, year-round specialization in bouldering places them in a high-risk group for growth plate fractures, as well as other maladies such as finger-tendon injury, elbow tendinosis, and shoulder injury. A far better approach is for a coach to direct a near-equal focus on roped climbing and bouldering. Roped routes generally have less severe cruxes and fewer dynamic moves, and instead test a climber's endurance, serial movement skills, and mental abilities. By alternating

---

Table 10.1 *Summary of Training for Youth Climbers*

Training Strategy or Exercise	Ages 6–9	Ages 10–15	Ages 16–18
Warm-up activities and stretching before climbing	✓	✓	✓
Climb 1–3 days per week	✓		
Climb 2–4 days per week		✓	✓
Climbing games (rather than performance climbing)	✓		
Drills to train climbing technique	✓	✓	
Basic mental rehearsal (with laser pointer guidance)	✓	✓	
Visualization and advanced mental training		✓	✓
Flexibility training		✓	✓
Body weight exercises (pull-ups, push-ups, crunches)	✓	✓	
Fingerboard training (no weight added)		✓	✓
Campus laddering (only if slow and controlled)		✓	✓
Campus double dynos (when adult height is reached)			✓
Hypergravity training (bouldering and training with weight added)			✓
Antagonist-muscle training (rotator cuff exercises, etc.)		✓	✓
Sensible nutrition (no dieting and infrequent junk food)	✓	✓	✓
Lots of sleep (8–10 hours per night)	✓	✓	✓

between roped climbing and bouldering every few weeks or months, injury risk is reduced, while at the same time climbing skills are expanded thanks to the exposure to a wider range of climbing situations. In terms of climbing frequency, three or four days per week is ideal—anything more increases injury risk in hard-climbing youths.

Earlier I covered the importance of warm-up exercises and stretching, antagonist-muscle training, and end-of-session or nighttime flexibility training. Disciplined follow-through in all of these areas will both reduce climbers' injury risk and enhance on-the-rock performance.

Proper nutrition and adequate sleep are the other side of the training-for-climbing coin. Calorie restriction is inappropriate in almost all situations for adolescents, although some restriction in the consumption of unhealthy junk and fast foods can be beneficial and is certainly wise. Youth athletes should be encouraged to eat "three squares" a day, including lots of fruits, vegetables, lean meats, and low-fat dairy products. Healthy snacks, such as energy bars, bagels, and sports drinks, are excellent as between-meal and climb-time snacks. In terms of sleep, nine to ten hours per night is best, with eight hours being the bare minimum.

In closing, perhaps the best way to prevent the various injuries mentioned above, including mental burnout, is for youth climbers to participate in activities and sports outside the climbing world. While an overbearing coach or parent may preach otherwise, young climbers absolutely can come to perform at a national- or even world-class level while at the same time participating in other extracurricular activities. With proper planning, guidance, and encouragement, they can become excellent in several life areas and come to enjoy the rich experiences available in both the horizontal and the vertical world. Need proof? Consider nineteen-year-old superstar, Sasha DiGuilian. In high school Sasha ran cross-country and track, climbed a few evenings per week at the gym, and aced her classes at school—and, oh yeah, she also climbed 5.13a at age eleven and 5.14a at age sixteen!

CHAPTER ELEVEN

The Secrets to Climbing Your Best

Your initial days and months of climbing will yield rapid improvement and a corresponding sense of tremendous accomplishment. For this I say, "Kudos to you!"—for challenging your fears, pushing your physical boundaries, and resolving to extend your reach beyond your current grasp.

As a climber of more than thirty years, I continue to find the experience rewarding and self-revealing. I trust you will, too, as long as you find ways to keep climbing fresh and avoid falling into a rut. If climbing ever becomes just a workout, then you will surely begin to lose interest and eventually look to some other activity for a new challenge. However, this need never be the case with climbing. There are hundreds of different indoor climbing gyms at which to test your mettle as well as myriad outdoor crags to explore for a challenge should you decide to climb beyond the confines of human-made walls.

In closing this text on learning to climb, I'll reveal a few of the secrets to sustaining your excitement about climbing and maintaining a sense of steady growth. First, we'll examine the keys to staying motivated and upwardly mobile in ability. Next up is a look at the many benefits of building a home training wall. Lastly, we'll take a peek into the unique techniques, risks, and rewards of climbing outdoors. If you love indoor climbing, then you may someday venture outside and discover that real rock climbing is even more gratifying and addictive than pulling plastic indoors.

Create Long-Lasting Motivation

As with any sport or activity, if you engage in climbing long enough, you will experience occasional lapses in motivation. Sometimes this drop in desire is the result of a hard, stressful day at school or work. Such temporary motivational troughs affect us all from time to time, and they are something that you just need to resolve to push through. If you can prod yourself to the gym and climb a first route, chances are you will snap out of the funk into a more energetic, positive state. Interestingly, it may be this very state-changing power of climbing that makes it so addictive.

More long-lasting motivational doldrums are often related to a growing dissatisfaction with your climbing. For example, a plateau in performance, a rise in frustration and failures, or a feeling of persistent fatigue or mental stress can all lead to diminished motivation. In some cases these symptoms result from overtraining, as your mind and body begin to run aground. As discussed in chapter 9, excessive climbing and training beyond your body's ability to recover will lead to an unavoidable drop in performance—and possibly to injury. More commonly, however, the reduced motivation is simply the result of a stagnant climbing routine. If you do any activity in the same way, with the same people, at the same time, week after week, it will become monotonous and unexciting. Following are three prescriptions for pumping up your motivation and keeping your climbing sessions fresh, fun, and interesting.

Set Performance Goals

Goals are the ultimate motivator. As a new climber, you have a very clear, specific goal: "to learn to climb." Once you master all the basic techniques and develop a degree of success at climbing, however, you need to set new goals that will maintain a high level of motivation. Performance-related benchmarks are ideal, as they provide an open-ended structure to goal setting. Let's set some performance goals.

The most common type of performance goal is a desired climbing grade to achieve. This month it may be "to climb 5.10"; next month it may be "to boulder V4"; next year it may be "to redpoint 5.12." Similarly, you can set training goals that will pique motivation to achieve the physiological changes you desire. For instance, you might set a goal "to do ten pull-ups" or "to lose five pounds." Training goals are most effective if they are concrete and measurable, as opposed to a less specific goal such as "to improve flexibility." Over many weeks of training, you will see tangible progress toward your performance benchmark, and this will elevate your motivation even more.

The beauty of performance goals is that there is always room for more improvement—technically, physically, and mentally—and you can therefore continue to formulate new goals for the length of your climbing career. Here are five tips for setting effective goals.

1. Write down your goals—this makes them more real and far more achievable. Begin keeping a training notebook or climbing diary in which you can record your goals, workout plan, and climbing accomplishments.

2. Define your goals specifically and with as much detail as possible. While measurable goals are best, it doesn't hurt to set a few style or mental goals such as "to improve footwork" or "to climb with more economy." With such subjective goals, ask a partner or coach to observe your climbing and decide when you have, in fact, achieved the desired style goal.

3. Make your goals lofty and challenging, but keep them realistic. Setting unreachable goals—"to lose ten pounds this week" or "to climb 5.14 by year's end"—is counterproductive and a real motivation killer. Instead set incremental goals that will yield a motivation-generating "win" every few weeks.

4. Set a deadline for the accomplishment of each goal. A goal best inspires you into action when a deadline is affixed to the performance benchmark. Goals such as "achieving ten consecutive pull-ups by year's end" or "bouldering a V5 by my birthday" will light a fire for action—a fire that burns stronger as the deadline nears. Conversely, goals without deadlines are more fuzzy and tend to inspire halfhearted action.

5. Write down one thing that you will sacrifice in order to reach this goal. This final step is vital, and, interestingly, it's a step missing from most traditional goal-setting exercises. Considering what one thing you could give up to help attain your goal is a powerful exercise. This will open your eyes to the reality that achievement doesn't just come by doing more of something or trying harder; it also requires that you eliminate or detach from things that are holding you back.

Begin a Focused Training Program

In your first few months or even year or two of climbing, you will realize steady improvement by just climbing a few days per week and using a handful of basic training exercises. As you become a solid intermediate climber possessing sound mental and technical skills, however, your improvement curve may level off as physiological constraints come to light. This is a common and extremely frustrating situation that most climbers face at some point. Fortunately, most physical constraints can be shattered with an intelligent sport-specific training program.

As stressed in chapter 9, high-intensity sport-specific training is not something to jump hastily into—begun too early in the learning curve, it can have a negative effect on learning technique as you obsess on strength as the answer to all climbing woes. Therefore, I propose the following litmus test for beginning a targeted training-for-climbing program: You should be able to climb 80 to 90 percent of 5.10s on-sight and with good, efficient style. Although there is nothing magical about the 5.10 grade, it's my experience that the majority of climbers become competent at this grade strictly through a program of climbing a few days per week supplemented with only basic fitness training.

Passing this test indicates that you are ready for some sport-specific training, as long as it's properly designed and executed. This distinction is critical, since sport-specific training will yield few positive results if it fails to target your physical weaknesses. Chapter 8 touched on the importance of self-awareness as well as the value of enlisting a coach to help assess your weaknesses and design an appropriate training program. Many gyms have a qualified coach on staff, so I encourage you to consider this option.

You may prefer a self-directed training program, and you can no doubt get excellent results given due diligence in researching and designing the program. Chapter 9 provided a primer on sport-specific training, but I encourage you to also consult *Training for Climbing* for comprehensive and cutting-edge instruction.

Regardless of your information source or the program details, it's important to create a written plan of action that will dictate a firm, long-term workout strategy. Irregular or haphazard training programs will produce mediocre results at best and may even lead you down the wrong path of action. You are better off just using climbing as training as opposed to launching into the darkness of trial and error. The bottom line: Do your research, design an appropriate program, and then commit to executing the program long-term. This is the prescription for an uncommonly effective training program.

Tap into the Human Resource

While the social and often crowded nature of a climbing gym can pose many distractions and roadblocks to peak performance, it's important to recognize the tremendous resource that is present in the form of the aggregate experience of the membership. People are the ultimate catalyst for adding new life to your gym climbing sessions. In fact, the simple act of making new acquaintances will elevate your motivation to get to the gym more frequently.

View each person, no matter his ability, as a possible source of the secret you need to break into the next climbing grade. Use this as your incentive to reach out and open up to strangers, even if it's not exactly in your nature to do so. Make it a goal to rope up or boulder with one new person each week, and you'll discover a new kind of excitement and energy for climbing. Enjoy getting to know each person and attempt to gain a glimpse at what drives her. Similarly share your passions, and I guarantee a resultant synergy will develop and empower both you and your new comrade.

Build a Home Wall

For many climbers, time is the primary constraint on performance. Metropolitan traffic and the complexities of work and family life can make it difficult to get to the climbing gym on a regular basis. As I've stressed throughout this text, optimal results come from a firm schedule of climbing three or four days per week, yet for some folks this is just not possible. Given a limited climbing schedule, it's natural to get frustrated and lose motivation—but don't despond, respond, by building a home wall!

Although no match for a full-service commercial gym, a small home wall can provide a convenient, sport-specific workout that's highly effective. What's more, a home training wall saves time and money (how many hours and gallons of gas do you burn driving to and from the gym?), and it allows you to do other things, such as study, read, work, or play with the kids, while resting between burns on the wall.

So what's the investment needed for a modest home wall? A bare-bones, 8-by-10-foot, 45-degree-overhanging wall could cost you as little as $300—the cost of wood and a few dozen handholds. Of course, you could easily spend $1,500 or more if you build a more lavish setup with a few different wall angles and a few hundred handholds. Straight ahead is a primer on building a home wall, followed by an overview of effective home-gym training.

Designing and Building the Wall

Designing a home gym has to begin with an analysis of possible locations for building the wall. While it's possible to construct a small freestanding wall in a dorm room or apartment living room (it's been done many times), the most popular site is a garage or basement. Garages provide the advantage of a higher ceiling, whereas the basement offers a site with more stable temperatures. If you have both options, weigh the pros and cons of each location, recognizing the temperatures you'll face in winter and summer if you build the wall in the garage. I'm fortunate enough to have a basement with a high ceiling (well over 8 feet), so the decision to build my wall inside was an easy one.

As for design, recognize that it will be difficult to train vertical wall technique or endurance on a small home wall, so the primary goal is to train lock-off strength, power, and grip strength. And for this, nothing beats a "45"—an 8-foot-wide, 45-degree wall that begins 16 inches off the floor. This gives you an 8-foot-wide, 16-inch-high "kicker board" along the base of your wall onto which you'll mount some small footholds. Depending on ceiling height, the 45-degree wall will run 8 to 10 feet (the hypotenuse of the right triangle profile) to intersect the existing ceiling beams. The frame should be built with 2-by-8s on a 16-inch center. Make sure the frame is anchored

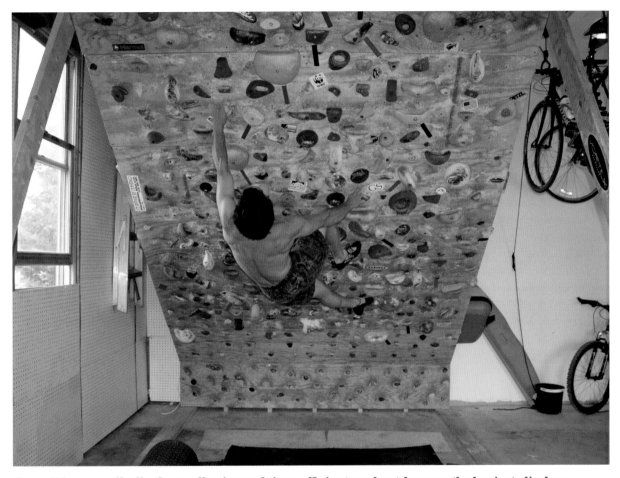

A small home wall affords an effective and time-efficient workout for even the busiest climber.

in a bombproof way to existing wall and ceiling structure via lag bolts, galvanized truss plates, and concrete anchors. The climbing surface is ¾-inch plywood attached to the frame with drywall screws.

The hand- and footholds anchor to the plywood with special T-nuts available from any handhold company as well as most hardware or fastener stores. I suggest you purchase and install a minimum of three T-nuts per square foot of wall surface. The basic 8-by-10-foot wall described here would thus require 240 T-nuts as well as a couple of dozen more for the kickboard. While you may never fill all

the T-nuts with holds at one time, the large number of T-nut holes affords you a wide variety of placements when you're moving holds around the wall to create new problems (important to keep things fresh).

You'll want to purchase the same types of modular holds that you are familiar with from your local commercial gym. Several companies make specialized training holds that are affordable and ideal for a home wall. Expect to pay anywhere from $1 for a tiny foothold up to $10 or even $25 for a large roof hold or mega-jug. Since your wall is steep, favor medium-size shapes, which typically cost about $5 each (commonly sold as sets of ten for around $50). Select holds with what appear to be usable features and avoid any with sharp edges (skin shredders) or abrasive texture. Purchase a variety of holds that will train different grip positions such as crimps, two-finger pockets, pinches, slopers, and such. As a guideline, select hold sizes as follows: 10 percent tiny foot chips, 20 percent small crimp edges, 20 percent pockets, 20 percent medium-size edges, 20 percent slopers and pinches, and 10 percent large buckets or roof holds. Now mount the holds and start climbing!

Many people start small and then add more wall surface as time, resources, and space allow. Consider adding a 4-foot-wide panel that overhangs 20 to 30 degrees past vertical, a super-steep section that overhangs about 60 degrees, and an 8- or 10-foot section of horizontal "roof" surface. Be creative and have fun with your design. Finally, if you have kids between the ages of about two and six, consider building a small section of vertical wall for them to play around on while you are training on the 45-degree wall. This will make for a joyous and rewarding time for Mom, Dad, and kids alike.

Home Training Guidelines

Home-wall training is all about the high-intensity, sport-specific training that is so beneficial for intermediate to advanced climbers. Such targeted training of the climbing muscles is highly stressful and demands adequate rest to realize the full fruits of your labors. As you then might expect, the one downside to home walls is the temptation to climb every day. Don't fall into this injury-producing, overtraining trap!

An effective home-gym workout comprises three parts: a twenty- to thirty-minute warm-up, thirty to sixty minutes of serious climbing, and ten to twenty minutes of supplemental and strength-training exercises.

As described in chapter 9, each workout should commence with a warm-up period. After completing your stretches, begin climbing some easy problems using only the largest handholds. Avoid getting a rapid flash pump, and instead strive to slowly increase the intensity of your bouldering over the course of twenty to thirty minutes.

Now it's on to the core of your workout, thirty to sixty minutes of near-maximal bouldering. The goals of this portion are twofold: to develop efficient movement and to increase sport-specific strength.

If training maximum movements and upper-body power is the goal du jour, then working on difficult four- to ten-move boulder problems is the winning ticket. Exercise your creativity and develop boulder problems that test the movements and body positions you find difficult or most strenuous. Of course, working such movements will in the long run make you stronger and more competent at them. Make it a goal to establish specific boulder problems versus just climbing around on the wall. Rest a few minutes between each problem so that you can give each attempt your best effort. Enlist a training partner to join in on the fun, and take turns setting problems.

Over the course of several sessions, you will come to know and perfect many different boulder problems of varying difficulty. This achievement opens the door to a powerful strategy for training anaerobic endurance—interval training. As the name implies, interval training involves alternating brief, intense bouts of climbing with brief rest intervals. Beginning with some of your hardest established boulder problems, send one at a time with just a two-minute rest in between each burn. The goal isn't necessarily to successfully ascend each problem, although it's ideal if each training interval does last between thirty and sixty seconds. Continue in this interval-training fashion for thirty to forty minutes. If you keep to the proper time structure, this will equate to about fifteen to twenty complete intervals—a heck of a workout that will yield big payoffs when redpoint or on-sight climbing.

Home-Wall Construction Tips

1. Search the Internet and talk to other climbers for home-wall ideas. Enlist a friend with a background in construction if you are uncomfortable with framing and the use of power tools.

2. Sketch out the proposed design and determine all the beam lengths down to the inch based on the wall angles you choose (time to revisit your trigonometry from high school). Make a list of everything you need, then price out the supplies at a couple of building supply stores.

3. Don't skimp on wood. Buy 2-by-8s for framing and use only ¾-inch mid- or high-grade plywood for the climbing surface.

4. When framing, err on the side of overkill in terms of anchoring the support beams to the existing ceiling and walls.

5. Drill the T-nut holes and hammer in the T-nuts before mounting the plywood sheets. Be sure to drill from the "good" side of the plywood, but then flip the panel and hammer in the T-nuts on the splintered backside of the holes. Install about one hundred T-nuts per 4-by-8-foot sheet of plywood. Attach the plywood to the framing with 2½-inch drywall screws placed every 6 inches.

The final stage of the workout takes place off the wall as you execute supplemental exercises such as pull-ups, dips, reverse wrist curls, sit-ups, and such. Most important are the antagonist push-muscle exercises that help maintain muscular balance in the elbows and shoulders. Conclude the session with some light stretching to encourage blood flow and speed recovery.

Begin Climbing Outdoors!

From a more holistic perspective, you will climb your best and tap into the full experience of being a climber only when you step onto rock in the great outdoors. While many of the technical skills and muscles used are the same as in climbing indoors, dancing up a cliff in all the natural elements (sun, wind, and sheer vertical exposure) produces a unique bond with this rock on which we were born.

Everything is amplified in climbing outdoors—the need for efficient technique and use of strength resources, the demand of climbing partners to work together in synergy, and, of course, the level of absolute risk and reward. Clearly, climbing outdoors is not an activity to rush into without proper instruction in the many unique real-rock techniques and safety systems. Following is a primer on taking your climbing out to Mother Nature's domain.

Get Proper Instruction

Competence, or even expertise, at indoor climbing carries little weight when venturing outdoors. Sure, you'll adapt to outdoor climbing more quickly than someone with no prior climbing experience, but all first-time outdoor climbers are novices when it comes to learning the specialized safety systems. Thus it is absolutely mandatory that your journey onto real rock begin with a few climbing lessons with a professional guide.

Many climbing gyms offer group classes on learning to climb outdoors. You can expect to pay $100 or more per day—money well spent, since you will learn the proper safety techniques from the get-go. Remember, it only takes one mistake to bring an ultimate end to the game. Don't be cheap (or foolish) and attempt to teach yourself!

Another option is to search the Internet or ask a local outdoor store for a local guide certified by the American Mountain Guides Association (AMGA). Nothing beats one-on-one instruction for learning

all the subtleties of real-rock technique. If you find climbing in the great outdoors rewarding, your next step would be to join a local climbing club or find an experienced and mature individual to partner up with for regular visits to the crags. Since lead climbing outdoors often requires placing of protection (if no anchors bolts are resident), it's vital that you initially confine your outdoor climbing to toproping and bouldering. Lead climbing outdoors is a very serious undertaking that most climbers don't engage in until after a few years of rock climbing.

Learn to Crack Climb

Though they're rare on indoor walls, vertical fissures, or cracks, are commonplace at many crags. Ascending such fissures demands a novel set of technical skills commonly classified as "crack climbing."

Central to crack-climbing technique is placement of your hands and feet into the crack in order to gain purchase and facilitate upward movement. Therefore, instead of gripping edges or pockets with your fingers as in gym climbing, crack technique involves inserting your fingers, hand, or arm (depending on the size of the fissure) into a crack and jamming them into place. Initially, such jamming techniques will feel insecure, painful, and a bit scary. With practice, however, you will discover that many jams offer a better fix to the rock than gripping a standard down-pull handhold at the gym.

Crack climbing also requires special foot-jamming techniques, although you will sometimes be able to edge or smear on small holds outside the crack as you are accustomed to doing indoors. Let's take a look at the fundamental crack-climbing techniques, but consult John Long's *How to Rock Climb* for a more comprehensive study of outdoor climbing.

HAND TECHNIQUES

Just how your hands engage a crack depends on the size of the fissure. The narrowest cracks—only about ⅜ inch wide—will accept little more than the tips of your fingers. The jamming technique to use here involves inserting the tips of your index and middle fingers as deep as possible into the crack—often your ring and pinkie fingers will be left floating outside the crack, or barely gripping the crack edge. Most often you'll place this jam with your index finger on the bottom and your elbow out to the side. This way, when you pull on that arm the elbow will rotate downward and produce a twisting of the fingers that further anchors them into the crack. Slightly larger cracks ranging from about ½ to 1 inch in width require a similar technique—you simply insert as much of your fingers into the rock as possible. One thing you will notice in large finger cracks (around an inch wide) is that the fingers tend to slide down this oversize crack. In these situations it's vital to look for constrictions or bottlenecks along the crack and attempt to place your jams in or just above these narrow spots.

Cracks ranging from 1 to 3 inches wide are the domain of hand jams. As the name implies, you need to insert as much of your hand as possible and then jam it into place. There are several different ways to perform hand jams, and with practice you'll learn to quickly assess the best technique for a given situation.

First, it's important to point out that you can execute a hand jam in the thumb-up or thumb-down position. Vertical cracks are often better climbed in the thumb-down position, whereas cracks that slant slightly are more easily climbed with the lower hand jamming thumb-up and the high hand jamming

Taking your climbing outside opens the doors to a whole new world of challenge and adventure. Mount Lemmon, Arizona.

Finger- and Hand-Jamming Techniques

Fingertips jam

"Sinker" fingers jam

Thin hand jam

"Bomber" hand jam

Fist jam

ILLUSTRATIONS
BY MIKE TEA

thumb-down. Next, you'll want to scan the hand crack for a constriction or bottleneck that will provide the most bombproof jam imaginable. Cracks with little variance are more challenging, as they require a bit more effort to create a solid jam. The key is to cup your hand inside the crack to generate outward pressure and friction on the inside of the crack. To make the jam most solid—and almost effortless—try to tuck your thumb under your palm and focus on contracting the muscles of your hand while relaxing your forearm muscles.

Fist jamming is the optimal technique for cracks about 4 inches wide. The technique here is simply to insert your hand with the palm facing into the crack and then make a fist. In closing your hand

tightly, the width of your fist increases, making it stick like an oversize cork stuck in the top of a wine bottle. Cracks larger than 4 inches are less frequently encountered, and the techniques required to ascend these wide fissures are beyond the scope of this entry-level book.

FOOT TECHNIQUES

There are two primary foot techniques used in crack climbing: feet inside the crack and feet on the rock face. On many climbs it will be obvious which technique you'll need, because a hand or fist crack will readily accept your feet while most finger cracks will not. Let's break things down.

In climbing thin finger cracks, you have little

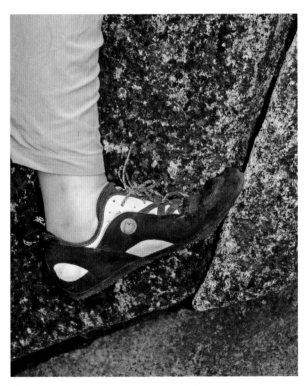

Cracks too small for foot jamming require that you smear on the edge or step on some other feature on the rock face.

KEITH MCCALLISTER

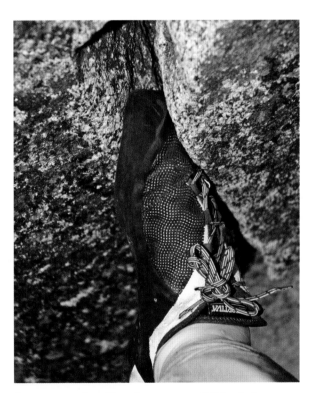

Larger cracks allow for more solid foot placements by jamming part or all of your foot into the crack.

KEITH MCCALLISTER

choice but to search for edges on the rock surface on which you can edge or smear. The exceptions are offset cracks (where one edge of the crack is set out from the opposite edge) and larger finger cracks, which occasionally afford a foot smear on the exposed edge. As a rule, however, small cracks require that you think like a gym climber in terms of footwork. Look for stems, high steps, outside edges, and even backsteps in attempting to use your feet optimally.

Cracks wider than about 1 inch in width provide exceedingly solid foot placements by means of foot jamming. The simple technique involves turning your foot sideways—so that the sole of the shoe is facing inward and your knee is bent outward—and inserting as much of your foot as possible into the crack. Depending on the size of the crack, you may be limited to jamming just the toe portion of the shoe (narrow hand cracks) or its entire front half (fist cracks). Once you're secured in the crack, your knee will naturally rotate back to center as you stand up on the foot. In climbing a continuous hand or fist crack, you will simply need to leapfrog one foot above the other in a series of foot jams about 1 foot apart.

LIEBACK TECHNIQUE

Finally, there's liebacking, a unique method of climbing cracks that are located in the vertex of a dihedral or corner. The lieback technique places your body in a sort of rowing position with your arms pulling and your legs pushing in a powerful opposition. Both feet smear on one wall of the corner while your fingers cling to the edge of the crack and arms remain as straight as possible. Move upward by simply walking your feet up the wall and sliding (or leapfrogging) your hands up the crack.

Most people find liebacking to be more intuitive and easy to learn than other crack climbing techniques—but they also discover that it's extremely strenuous. With practice you'll learn to position your hands and feet in an optimal way that

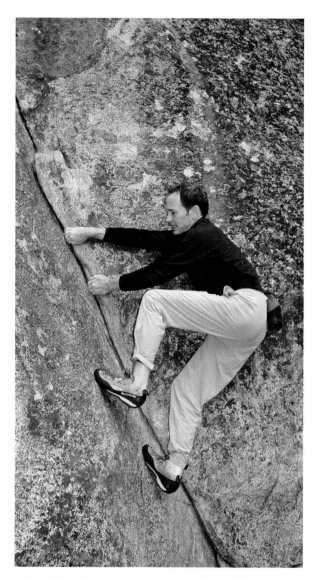

The lieback technique is most useful when climbing a crack in a corner.
KEITH MCCALLISTER

provides the greatest leverage at the lowest possible energy expenditure. Of course, as in all kinds of strenuous climbing, moving quickly is fundamental to maximizing your performance.

CRACK-CLIMBING STRATEGY

Effective crack-climbing strategy is virtually identical to the optimal indoor climbing strategy you know so well—climb briskly and efficiently, utilize the legs as much as possible in generating locomotion, and pause for long periods only at definitive rest stances.

Just as in your clumsy first days at attempting indoor climbing, expect your initial forays at crack climbing to feel awkward and frustratingly difficult. But as in gym climbing, you will rapidly learn the many unique motor skills. Jamming cracks will quickly become less strenuous and a heck of a lot of fun.

Use the security of a toprope to experiment with different techniques and subtle variations on the basic jamming skills described above. Don't be satisfied with just thrashing up a crack to the top; instead strive to learn the best way to do each move with the goal of climbing each crack in good style and with minimal use of strength. To this end, it's a great practice strategy to climb a few laps on each crack in an attempt to achieve a smooth, proficient use of crack-climbing technique.

Climb at Many Areas

There is a world of rock climbing wonder awaiting you—go explore it and enjoy it!

In terms of growing your ability, exposing yourself to a wide range of rock types is another of the secrets to climbing your best. Consider that each new area requires distinctly unique skills and techniques you cannot learn elsewhere. Only through a diverse sampling of climbing areas can you achieve true mastery.

As an indoor climber transitioning to the great outdoors, it's ideal to pursue a 50–50 split in days spent climbing indoors and outdoors. The most practical and popular approach is to climb indoors on two weekday evenings, then spend Saturday and Sunday pulling down on the real stuff outdoors. In this way, you obtain quality sport-specific muscular training during the week, but gain in the important technical and mental areas by cragging or bouldering outside on weekends. It's a great schedule from a training perspective, and it's an unbeatable game plan from a motivational and experiential standpoint.

Finally, I want to tell you the biggest secret to climbing your best: Decide to love climbing unconditionally. Embrace the notion that any day spent climbing—indoors or out, and success or failure—is a great day. With this disposition you will climb more confidently and at peace with whatever the results may be. Your mind and body will work in magical unison and most often lead to a superb and transcending outcome.

Guidelines for Beginning to Climb Outdoors

1. Obtain professional instruction! Self-instruction may work in learning most other sports, but applied to outdoor rock climbing it can get you killed. Hire a veteran instructor, ideally one certified by the AMGA.

2. Engage only in bouldering, toproping, or following a leader for your first year (or more) climbing outdoors. Outdoor lead climbing is not something to rush into.

3. Learn to crack climb. The experience and skills gained from your crack-climbing ventures will feed back and enhance your skill at all other types of climbing.

4. Travel to crags near and far to experience all the wonder and joy of outdoor climbing.

Afterword

In my three decades as a climber, perhaps the biggest breakthrough occurred when I realized that almost all the mental skills and strategies I learned through climbing could be applied to other areas in my life.

Detailed below are some of the powerful lessons of the vertical world, as revealed on the pages of *Learning to Climb Indoors*. Learn more success strategies "from the steep" at MentalWings.com.

On achieving success:

To succeed, you must embrace and learn from failure.

On stretching personal boundaries:

Pushing through discomfort and harnessing anxiety into productive energy is the strategy for uncommon experience and personal success.

On the importance of elevating quality of thinking:

Everything you are and will become is a direct function of your thoughts. Self-improvement, then, must begin with a fine-tuning of your internal dialogue or self-talk throughout the day. The goal is to modify your ways of thinking so as to help you solve problems (instead of wallowing in them), challenge fears (instead of avoiding them), and compel intelligent action toward your goals (instead of backpedaling at the first sign of adversity).

On the performance mind-set:

The best mental approach for peak performance is to focus on the process and let the outcome unfold on its own. Enjoy the process regardless of the results, and you'll always be a winner.

On self-induced pressure:

The more pressure you place on yourself, the more difficult it becomes to think and act proficiently. Paradoxically, you will perform better by not needing to!

On fear of the unknown:

In pushing personal boundaries and confronting the unknown, it's common to ponder the benefits of a retreat. Acknowledge such mental battles—between your desire to do new things and your primal instinct to avoid discomfort and failure—as being a normal part of the process. Resolve to persevere, and you'll redefine your abilities and perception of what is possible.

On leveraging past experience:

Another powerful strategy for persevering in times of challenge and self-doubt is to think back to a similar

The author climbing at the Needles, South Dakota.

encounter and subsequent success. Close your eyes and review that successful past event. How did you rise to the challenge, what strategies did you use, and, most important, how did you feel upon achieving success? This process of vividly visualizing all the details and feelings of a past success will recycle these resources for use in the present.

On using feedback and criticism:

View the feedback of failed attempts not as a sign you can't do something, but instead as a dynamic source of clues leading toward your inevitable success. Embrace each failed attempt as a signpost directing you toward a better course of action and the pathway to success.

On problem solving:

Breaking through sticking points and solving problems demands that you must get outside your current mind-set. Exercise flexibility of perspective by detaching from the situation and visualizing the problem from a perspective outside yourself. Imagine a wide range of possible solutions and give them a try without prejudice. Be creative and have fun, and the solution will reveal itself to you.

On developing mental toughness:

Your thoughts are precursors to both failure and success. Fearful thoughts will generate performance-killing anxiety and tension, whereas calming, positive thinking will foster a relaxed, optimal performance state. Knowing this intimate mind–emotion–body connection, you can control how you feel and perform by consciously directing your thoughts in productive ways. Such thought control is the essence of mental toughness.

On developing self-awareness and elevating performance:

Acute self-awareness empowers you to manage stress and fatigue, redirect unproductive thinking, identify weaknesses, and refine your actions and strategy to be most effective. Perform regular "spot assessments" by asking yourself a series of probative questions, such as *What pressures or fears are holding me back?* and *What mental or physical errors am I committing?* Pay close attention to the answers, since they hold the keys to effective course correction and enhancing performance.

On dealing with setbacks and failure:

Top performers in any field possess uncommon resilience to criticism, setbacks, and failure. They are always on the lookout for new information, distinctions, or ideas that will help elevate their game, and they possess an intense curiosity as to why they sometimes fail. Learning to respond to adversity in this way is tantamount to gaining some of the personal power possessed by these elite performers. So don't curse setbacks—view them as guideposts and stepping-stones to eventual success.

On managing fear:

The two steps to managing fear: First, identify and mitigate legitimate fears via risk management; second, dispel illusionary fears born of an inexperienced mind. Such phantom fears are the scourge of novices in any activity or venture. In these cases you must challenge fearful thoughts head-on and conquer them with reason and courage.

On eliminating the fear of failure:

Fear of failure wields tremendous power over those who possess it—ironically, the fear of failure often leads to failure! Consider how a football team often gives up the winning score when they shift into prevent defense. Such a prevent defense in your personal action will result in apprehension, doubt, and, worst of all, thoughts of failure. Fortunately, you can defeat this fear by focusing single-mindedly on the process of effective action and purging any thoughts of possible outcomes. Concentrate on the things immediate to your performance—technique, strategy, and relaxation—and the ideal outcome will likely unfold.

A more global approach to permanently deleting the fear of failure is simply to adopt the attitude, *It's okay to fail*. By willingly accepting this fate (if it should even happen), you totally eliminate the fear and, hence, liberate yourself to play to win!

On building confidence:

Pushing your limits (in anything) demands a healthy self-confidence. You can best elevate self-confidence with positive self-talk and visualization. Statements such as *I'm well prepared*, *I'll do great* and *This will be fun* will foster positive emotions. Likewise, visualization can be a powerful confidence builder. Close your eyes and spend a minute or two reliving a past great ascent. By feeling the emotions of that past success, you tap a powerful resource for use in the present moment.

Eric's powerful five-step, goal-achievement strategy:

1. Write down your goals. This makes them more real and therefore more achievable.

2. Define your goals specifically and with as much detail as possible.

3. Make your goals lofty and challenging, but keep them realistic. Set incremental goals—a goal gradient will yield a motivation-generating win every few weeks.

4. Set a deadline for the accomplishment of each goal. A goal best inspires you into action when a deadline is affixed to the performance benchmark.

5. Write down one thing that you will sacrifice in order to reach this goal. This will open your eyes to the reality that achievement doesn't just come by doing more of something or trying harder; it also requires that you eliminate and detach from things that are holding you back.

On tapping into the human resource:

People are the ultimate catalyst for adding new ideas and life to fledgling projects. View each person, despite background or ability, as a possible source of the secret you need to break through a given obstacle. Reciprocate by sharing your passion and energy. The resultant synergy will empower all parties involved to a new realm of possibility.

On what defines character:

You are not defined by your successes or failures. You are defined by the ways in which you react to success and failure.

On the secret to happiness:

Love the process of living, unconditionally. Embrace every day as a gift, no matter what it brings. With this grateful disposition, you will experience a richer, more joyful and transcending journey.

Glossary

The following is a compilation of some of the technical terms and climbing jargon used throughout this book.

adaptive response—Physiological changes in structure or function particularly related to response to a training overload.

aerobic—Any physical activity deriving energy from the breakdown of glycogen in the presence of oxygen, thus producing little or no lactic acid, enabling an athlete to continue exercise much longer.

anaerobic—Energy production in the muscles involving the breakdown of glycogen in the absence of oxygen; a by-product called lactic acid is formed, resulting in rapid fatigue and cessation of physical activity.

anaerobic endurance—The ability to continue moderate- to high-intensity activity over a period of time; commonly called power endurance or power stamina by climbers, though these terms are scientifically incorrect.

antagonist—A muscle providing an opposing force to the primary (agonist) muscles in action.

arête—The sharp vertical edge of an outside corner, as in the exterior corner of a building.

auto belay—A mechanical device that provides a secure belay, via a toprope cable, thus eliminating the need for a belay partner.

backstepping—Outside edging on a foothold that's behind you while climbing a move with your side to the wall.

barndoor—Sideways swinging or uncontrolled turning of the body resulting from poor balance or body positioning.

belay—A rope-management technique that allows a pair of climbers to protect each other during an ascent.

beta—Any prior information about a route, including sequence, rests, gear, clips, and so on.

bouldering—Ropeless climbing on short, often overhanging, sections of wall or along the base of larger walls.

bucket hold—A large, secure handhold.

campusing—Climbing an overhanging section of rock or artificial wall with no feet, usually in a dynamic left-hand, right-hand, left-hand (et cetera) sequence.

campus training—A sport-specific upper-body exercise performed on a specialized campus board.

carabiner (biner)—A spring-loaded aluminum alloy snap link used to connect ropes to other pieces of gear such as harnesses and anchor bolts.

center of gravity—The theoretical point on which the total effect of gravity acts on the body.

chimney—A crack wide enough to admit a climber; typically ascended by opposing forces of the arms, legs, and back pressing against opposite walls of the crack.

concentric contraction—Any movement involving a shortening of muscles fibers while developing tension, as in the biceps muscle during a pull-up.

contact strength—Initial grip strength upon touching a handhold.

crash pad—A portable gymnastics-like pad, specifically designed to provide cushioning below climbs or boulder problems.

crimp grip—The most natural (and stressful) way to grip a rock hold, characterized by hyperextension of the first joint in the fingers and nearly full flexion of the second joint.

crimp hold—A small, sharp hold requiring a desperate cling by the fingertips.

crux—The hardest move, or sequence of moves, on a route.

deadpoint—The "peak" position in a dynamic movement where, for a moment, all motion stops.

dihedral or open book—A wall feature formed by the intersection of two wall planes, as in the inside corner of a room or building.

dropknee—An exaggerated backstep, commonly used on overhanging rock, where the inside knee is dropped toward the ground, resulting in a stable chimney-like position.

dynamic move—An explosive leap for a hold otherwise out of reach.

dyno—Short for "dynamic."

eccentric contraction—Muscle action in which the muscle resists as it is forced to lengthen, as in the biceps during the lowering phase of a pull-up.

endurance—Ability to perform physical work for an extended period of time. Cardiovascular endurance is directly related to VO_2 max, whereas muscular endurance is influenced by circulation and oxygen available.

epicondylitis—Inflammation of the tendon origins of the forearm flexors (medial) or extensors (lateral) near the elbow.

extension—A movement that takes the two ends of a jointed body part away from each other, as in straightening the arm.

fall—Disengaging the rock wall, intentionally or unintentionally, as in "falling onto the rope" or "falling off a boulder problem."

fingerboard or hangboard—A training apparatus, commonly found in climbing gyms or installed above a doorway at a climber's residence, that facilitates climbing-specific finger and arm training (pull-ups, finger hangs, and such).

flagging—A climbing technique in which one foot is crossed behind the other in order to avoid barndooring and to improve balance.

flash—To climb a route on the first try without ever having touched it, but with the aid of beta.

flash pump—A rapid, often vicious, muscular pump resulting from strenuous training or climbing without first performing a proper (gradual) warm-up.

flexion—A movement that brings the ends of a body part closer together, as in bending the arm.

forerunner—A professional route setter, who establishes the climbs at a climbing gym or competition.

Gaston—A technique for grabbing an inward-facing vertical edge near your face, typified by an elbow-out, bent-armed position and a thumb-down hand orientation.

G-Tox—A technique that uses gravity to help speed recovery from a forearm pump. It involves alternating (about every five seconds) the

SHAKE OUT for 5 Seconds!!!

ALTERNATE

SHAKE OUT for 5 Seconds!!!

Research has shown the G-Tox technique to be effective in speeding forearm recovery at marginal rest positions.

ILLUSTRATION BY MIKE TEA

position of the resting arm between the normal hanging-at-your-side position and a raised-hand position above your shoulder.

hangdogging—Climbing a route, usually bolt-to-bolt, with the aid of the rope to hang and rest while practicing the sequence.

heel hook—Use of the heel on a hold, usually near chest level, to aid in pulling and balance.

highball—An uncommonly high and dangerous boulder problem, typically more than 15 feet in height.

honed—In extremely good shape, with low body fat.

hypergravity training—A highly effective method of training maximum strength, which involves climbing or training with weight added to the body (simulates hypergravity).

hypertrophy—Enlargement in size, as in muscular hypertrophy.

interval training—A method of anaerobic endurance training that involves brief periods of intense training interspaced with periods of rest or low-intensity training.

isometric—Muscular contraction resulting in no shortening of the muscle (no movement).

jamming—The technique used to climb vertical cracks, in which the hands and feet are wedged, or jammed, into the fissure.

lead climbing—The challenging climbing style in which the rope hangs downward from a climber's harness, as opposed to being secured atop the climb via a toprope.

ledge—A flat, horizontal stance on an otherwise steep wall.

lieback—A technique, usually used in crack climbing, in which the hands pull and the feet push in opposition.

lunge—An out-of-control dynamic move; an explosive jump for a far-off hold.

mantle—A movement technique in which a handhold is pressed downward, in a motion similar to pushing yourself out of a swimming pool.

maximum strength—The peak force of a muscular contraction, irrespective of the time element.

modeling—A learning technique where an individual watches, then attempts, a skill as performed properly by another person.

motor learning—The set of internal processes associated with practice or experience leading to a relatively permanent gain in performance capability.

motor skill—A skill where the primary determinant of success is the movement component itself.

muscular endurance—The length of time a given level of power can be maintained.

offwidth—A crack too large for hand jams, yet too small to admit a climber's body.

on-sight—When a route is climbed on the first try and with absolutely no prior information of any kind.

open-hand grip—The less stressful finger grip involving only slight flexion of the finger joints.

overhang—A section of wall that juts out horizontally, parallel to the floor.

overhanging—A wall surface that angles outward beyond vertical, so that the top of the wall overhangs its base.

overtraining—Constant severe training that does not provide adequate time for recovery; symptoms include increased frequency of injury, decreased performance, irritability, and apathy.

overuse—Excessive repeated exertion or shock that results in injuries such as inflammation of the muscles and tendons.

problem or boulder problem—A short climb, typically 7 to 15 feet high, that is ascended without a safety rope.

projecting—The process of working on and rehearsing a difficult route with the goal of eventually climbing the route bottom-to-top in one push.

proprioception—Sensory information from within the body arising from the sensory receptors found in muscles, tendons, joints, and the inner ear that detect the motion or position of the limbs and body. Also known as kinesthesis.

psyched—Raring to go or very happy.

pumped—When the muscles become engorged with blood due to extended physical exertion.

quickdraw—A short webbing sling with a carabiner on each end, used to clip the climbing rope into anchor bolts.

redpoint—Lead climbing a route bottom-to-top in one push.

roof—A large overhang that juts out horizontally more than a body length.

screamer—Slang term used to describe a scary lead fall.

send—Short for "ascend."

sharp end—The lead climber's end of the rope.

skill—A capability to bring about an end result with maximum certainty, minimum energy, and minimum time.

slab—A wall surface with an average angle that is less than vertical.

sport climbing—Usually refers to any indoor or outdoor climbing on bolt-protected routes.

spotter—A person designated to slow the fall of a boulderer and help facilitate a controlled, feetfirst landing.

stabilizer muscle—A muscle that is stimulated to help anchor or stabilize the position of a bone.

stem—The technique of bridging between two widely spaced footholds.

stick-clip—A telescoping pole often used—especially in outdoor climbing—to pre-clip a lead-climber's rope to a high first bolt of a route.

strength—The amount of muscle force that can be exerted; speed and distance are not factors of strength.

supercompensate—The body's recovery process of adaptation and overcompensation to the stress of exercise.

tendinitis—A disorder involving the inflammation of a tendon and synovial membrane at a joint.

tendon—A white fibrous cord of dense connective tissue that attaches muscle to bone.

toproping—Climbing with the belay rope running through a route-top anchor before connecting to the climber's harness—this is the most secure method of roped climbing.

traverse—Climbing sideways across a wall without any gain in height.

tweak—To injure, as in a tweaked finger tendon.

undercling—An inverted, downward-facing handhold.

vert—Short for "vertical," as in a vert climbing wall.

visualization—Controlled and directed imagery that can be used for awareness building, monitoring and self-regulation, healing, and, most important, mental programming for good performances.

V-Scale—An open-ended scale for grading the difficulty of boulder problems.

wired—Known well, as in a wired route.

working—Practicing the moves on a difficult route via toprope or hangdogging.

Yosemite Decimal System (YDS)—The primary rating scale for technical rock climbs.

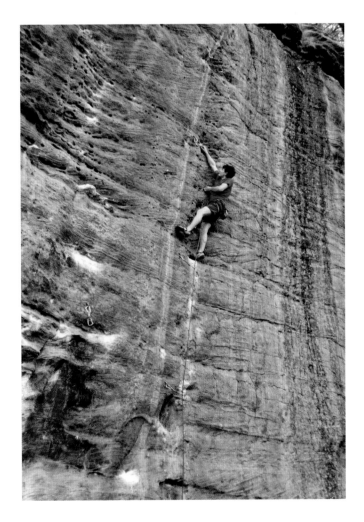

Outdoor sport climbing is pretty much the same game as indoor lead climbing—although the holds are more singular and tricky to find on Mother Nature's infinitely variable rock walls! Red River Gorge, Kentucky.

Suggested Reading

Ament, Pat. *How to Be a Master Climber*. Boulder, CO: Two Lights, 1997.

Gnade, Lisa, and Steve Petro. *Crack Climbing!* Guilford, CT: Globe Pequot Press/FalconGuides, 2009.

Hörst, Eric J. *Conditioning for Climbers*. Guilford, CT: Globe Pequot Press/FalconGuides, 2008.

———. *How to Climb 5.12,* 3rd edition. Guilford, CT: Globe Pequot Press/FalconGuides, 2012.

———. *Training for Climbing*. Guilford, CT: Globe Pequot Press/FalconGuides, 2003.

Hurni, Michelle. *Coaching Climbing*. Guilford, CT: Globe Pequot Press/FalconGuides, 2003.

Long, John. *How to Rock Climb,* 5th edition. Guilford, CT: Globe Pequot Press/FalconGuides, 2010.

Sherman, John. *Better Bouldering,* 2nd edition. Guilford, CT: Globe Pequot Press/FalconGuides, 2012.

Resources

Web Resources

Accessfund.org—The Access Fund is a national, nonprofit organization dedicated to keeping climbing areas open and to conserving the climbing environment. If you plan to venture into outdoor climbing, please support the Access Fund by becoming a member and contributing some time to local grassroots stewardship.

ACMG.ca—Association of Canadian Mountain Guides (ACMG).

AMGA.com—American Mountain Guide Association (AMGA).

LaSportiva.com—Manufacturer of top-shelf climbing shoes for climbers of all ability levels.

MountainProject.com—A comprehensive online resource for outdoor climbing information from across the United States.

Nicros.com—The nation's leading manufacturer of commercial climbing walls and modular handholds.

RockClimbing.com—Launched in 1995, this fantastic site contains information on more than 7,000 climbing areas (in a hundred countries and all fifty states), but it's the large photo database and discussion forums that make RC.com a favorite site of many climbers. For beginners, this site represents an endless treasure trove of information.

SterlingRope.com—Manufacturer of premium ropes for indoor and outdoor climbing, rappelling, and rescue.

Training4Climbing.com—The planet's number one resource for information on training for climbing and climbing performance research. This free website provides new training tips and articles each month.

USAClimbing.org—USA Climbing is the national governing body for multiple disciplines of competition climbing: Difficulty, Bouldering, and Speed. The group's mission is to promote and encourage climbers of all ages in competitive climbing, and to sanction, organize, and promote competitive climbing events in an atmosphere of camaraderie and respect, utilizing the support of climbers, parents, coaches, climbing facilities, and industry. It's run and supported by volunteers.

Magazines

Climbing—Published nine times per year ($14.97/year). Subscribe at Climbing.com.

Deadpoint—This free climbing magazine is published quarterly; the DeadpointMag.com site is updated weekly.

Gripped—Canada's only climbing magazine, published six times per year ($22.95). Subscribe at Gripped.com.

Rock & Ice—Published eight times per year ($25.95/year). Subscribe at RockAndIce.com.

Index

About the Author

An accomplished climber of more than thirty years, Eric J. Hörst (pronounced *hurst*) has climbed extensively across the United States and has established hundreds of first ascents on his home crags in the eastern United States. A student and teacher of climbing performance, Eric has personally helped train hundreds of climbers, and his training books and concepts have spread to climbers in more than fifty countries. He is widely recognized for his innovative practice methods and training techniques, and since 1994 he has served as a training products design consultant and online Training Center editor for Nicros, Inc., a leading manufacturer of climbing walls and handholds.

Eric is author of *Training for Climbing, Rock Climber's Exercise Guide, Maximum Climbing,* and *How to Climb 5.12,* all of which have foreign translations. His articles and photos have been published in many outdoor and fitness magazines including *Climbing, Rock & Ice, Deadpoint, Urban Climber, Outside, National Geographic Adventure, Men's Health, Muscle and Fitness, Experience Life,* and *Men's Journal.* Visit Eric's website, **TrainingForClimbing.com**, for training articles and information on all his

The author and his wife, Lisa, and sons, Jonathan and Cameron
HÖRST COLLECTION

books, or to schedule a training seminar, an editorial interview, or a speaking engagement.

Eric currently lives in Lancaster, Pennsylvania, with his wife, Lisa Ann, and his sons, Cameron and Jonathan.

Other Books by Eric J. Hörst

Rock Climber's Exercise Guide (FalconGuides, 2017) is the ultimate manual for climbers who are looking to improve their physical capabilities. The book follows a logical progression of self-assessment, goal setting, general conditioning and weight loss, core conditioning, and climbing-specific training to develop strength, power, and endurance. Regardless of your age, ability, or sports background, this book will empower you to develop and engage in your own supremely effective conditioning program.

How to Climb 5.12 (FalconGuides, 2012) is a performance guidebook to attaining the most rapid gains in climbing ability possible, and it's written specifically for intermediate climbers looking to break through to the higher grades. It provides streamlined instruction on vital topics such as accelerating learning of skills, training your mind and body, and becoming an effective on-sight and red-point climber.

Training for Climbing (FalconGuides, 2016) is a comprehensive, science-based tome that covers all aspects of climbing performance including strength training, technique development, and mental training, as well as in-depth chapters on nutrition, accelerating recovery, and preventing/treating injuries. *TFC* is the definitive climbers' resource, and it's the training text of choice by climbers in more than fifty countries!

Maximum Climbing (FalconGuides, 2010) presents a climber's guide to the software of the brain, based on the premise that you climb with your mind—your hands and feet are simply extensions of your thoughts and will. Becoming a master climber, then, requires that you first become a master of your mind. In this breakthrough book, Eric Hörst brings unprecedented clarity to the many cognitive and neurophysical aspects of climbing and dovetails this information into a complete mental-training program.

USA Climbing is a 501(c) 3 not-for-profit organization that
sanctions and hosts over 200 climbing competitions a year. As
the National Governing Body in the United States for Competition
Climbing, USA Climbing is recognized by the International
Federation of Sport Climbing, the International Olympic
Committee, and the United States Olympic Committee.

www.usaclimbing.org